The Most
Delightful Country
of the Universe

The Most Delightful Country of the Universe

Promotional Literature of
The Colony of Georgia
1717-1734

INTRODUCTION BY

TREVOR R. REESE

The Beehive Press

SAVANNAH, GEORGIA, 1972

Contents

Introduction

N November 1732 a two-hundred-ton frigate carrying 114 emigrants and, according to a contemporary report, "ten tons of Alderman Parson's 'best beer,'" sailed from England to found the colony of Georgia in the territory of South Carolina lying between the Savannah and Altamaha rivers.[1] The new settlement was to be administered from London by a corporation constituted by royal charter under the name of the Trustees for Establishing the Colony of Georgia in America, which was authorized to receive contributions from the public and legislate for the colony's government over a period of twenty-one years, after which the responsibility would revert to the crown. The motives for establishing the settlement may be classified broadly as strategic, commercial, and social or philanthropic. Strategically, it was expected to strengthen the security of South Carolina against the French and Spaniards; commercially, it was expected to contribute to the trade and resources of the British Empire; and socially or philanthropically, it was expected to give insolvent and unemployed persons in Britain and persecuted Protestants from the continent of Europe the chance to repair their fortunes and freely

1. Martyn to Johnson, Jan. 24th 1732/3 C.O. 5/666 (Colonial Office Series 5, Vol. 666, Public Record Office, London), page 3. *Gentleman's Magazine, II* (1732), 1029, 1079–80.

practice their religion in a new environment whose praises had been sung for many years and which was now the subject of an intensive publicity campaign.

These motives for establishing the colony had been reflected in schemes published earlier in the century which had advocated a new settlement south of the Savannah river and which set the style for the propaganda literature of the Trustees in 1732 and 1733. The British government had long been concerned about the defense of the empire. The French in New France and Louisiana, the Spaniards in Florida and Cuba, and the Indian nations along the back of the English settlements were a constant source of danger to the security of British territory in America. The southern frontier was recognized to be of vital importance, for the loss of South Carolina would endanger the fur traffic and growing rice trade and bring the French and Spaniards close enough to Virginia to imperil the tobacco trade. The southern colonies could not afford to ignore the menace of the Spaniards stationed at St. Augustine on the coast of Florida, a region where boundaries had never been satisfactorily defined and where frontier incidents were common. The Spanish governor of St. Augustine welcomed fugitive Negro slaves from South Carolina and organized them into a regiment with their own officers. The British government was well aware of the dangers to which the colonies were exposed, and by 1721 when the Board of Trade prepared an account of the state of the plantations in America, the need for defense improvements was recognized. The account warned that South Carolina was open to French, Spanish, and Indian incursions and recommended that its boundaries should be clearly defined, forts built, and particular care taken to secure the navigation of all rivers, especially the Altamaha.[2] The British government was obviously already anxious about the safety of the empire in America, but the most ambitious plans for barrier settlements were those conceived by enterprising individuals which foreshadowed the ultimate creation of the colony of Georgia.

The most remarkable of these precursory schemes was that of

2. British Museum Additional MS. 35907, fols. 25–6. British Museum Kings MS. 205, fols. 23–4, 37.

Sir Robert Mountgomery, a Nova Scotian baronet, who in 1717 published *A Discourse concerning the Designed Establishment of a New Colony to the South of Carolina in the Most Delightful Country in the Universe*. The design, its author proclaims, is due not to any sudden whim but to "a strong bent of genius" he has inherited from his ancestors. On 19 June 1717, the lords proprietors of Carolina had granted him all the land between the Savannah and the Altamaha for the express purpose of erecting "a distinct province" under the name of the Margravate of Azilia. The contract was to be operative only if settlement had commenced within three years, so that Mountgomery is obliged to indulge in some fanciful advertizing of the prospects in order to attract immediate support. According to him, a terrestrial paradise lay in the country south of Carolina: "Its gentle hills are full of mines, lead, copper, iron, and even some silver;'tis beautified with odoriferous plants, green all the year." Its fertile soil will render the mother country independent of foreign markets in an immense variety of commodities including coffee, tea, figs, raisins, currants, almonds, olives, silk, wine and cochineal, although in the early stages the shareholders are to derive their profits mainly from potash and rice. More significant is the intention to settle the margravate in symmetrical departments, each separately secured against attack, so that the whole will be "one continued fortress." In other words, it will act as a barrier against the French on the Mississippi, the Spaniards in Florida, and the Indians of the backwoods, though Mountgomery naturally says little about this aspect because he wishes to entice investors. The Carolina proprietors recommended the scheme to the Privy Council,[3] which favored the idea of a barrier province, and Mountgomery indicated that he had almost collected the finance to despatch the first settlers. In fact, investors were not persuaded by Mountgomery's facile optimism, and his appeal was not as successful as he pretended. Moreover, circumstances changed, first with the ending of proprietary rule in South Carolina in 1719 and second

3. *Journal of the Commissioners for Trade and Plantation, 1704–1782* (14 vols., London, 1920–38), February 20, 1717/18; hereafter cited as *Board of Trade Journal.*

with the collapse in January 1720 of the South Sea Company, bringing financial panic and leaving investors skeptical and wary of all overseas schemes. There was little hope, therefore, that further promotional literature in 1720, notably *A Description of the Golden Islands*,[4] would gain an adequate response from the disenchanted public, and by the end of the year the design had fizzled out.

Nevertheless, the British government remained sympathetic to the idea of a barrier province in the south and showed some interest when, in 1721, Jean-Pierre Purry, a native of Neufchâtel in Switzerland, asked permission to found a new settlement in Carolina. Purry had already visited Carolina to collect information, and now claimed that by reason of the latitude it could be productive of the richest plants, fruits, and drugs, provided there were no impediments such as rocks, marshes, or deserts. Like Mountgomery, Purry dilates fondly on the valuable commodities that might be produced, which include wine, oils, cotton, indigo, wax, fruit, coconuts, timber, tar, flax, hemp, rice, and wheat, besides silk as good as that of France, Spain, or Italy. He offers to convey Protestants from Switzerland to the New World and settle them in a part of Carolina he proposes to call Georgia whence their settlement will extend gradually westward until the Mississippi is reached, thereby cutting French communication between Canada and Louisiana. He entered into a contract with the British government to receive a certain amount of land for every hundred men he transported to America, and in 1732 the outpost of Purrysburg was established by Swiss settlers on the north side of the Savannah river.[5]

In the meantime, some measures had been taken to provide for the defense of the southern colonies. In 1720, in order to guard against French encroachments on South Carolina and preserve the

4. See also *Account of the Foundation, and Establishment of a Design, now on foot, for a settlement on the Golden Islands, to the South of Port Royal in Carolina* (London, 1720).

5. *Board of Trade Journal*, June 9–11, July 23, 1724; June 15, 1725; March 25, 1729/30; June 13–16, 1732. V. W. Crane, *The Southern Frontier, 1670–1732* (Durham, N.C., 1928), 283–7.

trade with the Indians, the British government instructed the governor to construct a fort on the Altamaha.[6] The fort, named after King George and built at the confluence of the Oconee and Ocmulgee rivers, sixty miles from the margin of English settlement, had a checkered history. Burnt down in January 1726, possibly with the connivance of its turbulent garrison, who were dissatisfied with living conditions and some of whom seized the opportunity to desert to the Spaniards at St. Augustine, it was quickly rebuilt, but the garrison were morose, mutinous, and so lazy that they could not be prevailed upon to fetch themselves wholesome water, and in the autumn of 1727 they were finally withdrawn.[7] The significance of this and other fortifications was that they were clearly intended to become the nuclei of frontier settlement and indicated that, in spite of the abandonment of the fort on the Altamaha, the British government was anxious lest the river fall under foreign control. Consequently, when it received a petition for lands on which to plant the new colony of Georgia, the possibility of its functioning as a defensive barrier was a strong argument in its favor. It is noticeable that the Trustees stressed the defense value of their design, and for a generation after its foundation the strategic importance of Georgia remained a recommendation in the eyes of the British government.

The British government was also conscious of the economic and commercial advantages which Mountgomery, Purry, and other writers, ever since Tudor times, had described as likely to accrue to the mother country from colonial possessions. Englishmen had romantic impressions of all uninhabited territories in America and believed that almost any tropical product could be raised there. Valuing colonies as sources of raw materials, they liked to imagine that overseas settlements would supply the homeland with the luxury goods that so often had to be sought from foreign lands. This

6. *Board of Trade Journal,* August 16 and 23, 1720.

7. *Collections of the South Carolina Historical Society* (5 vols., Charleston, 1857–97), I, 236. Keene to Walpole, November 3, 1727, Add. MS. 32752, page 316. Nicholson to Board of Trade, C.O. 5/360, fol. 22. E. McCrady, *History of South Carolina under the Royal Government, 1719–76* (New York, 1899), 76–7.

conception was based largely on arguments of geographical latitude. Silk, for instance, could be expected from southern colonies because their latitudes and proximity to the sea were similar to those of the coastal provinces of China, India, Persia, Turkey, Italy, Provence, and Languedoc,[8] and in emphasizing the possibility of cultivating silk the Georgia Trustees were applying an old and widely advertized notion to ingratiate their project with the government. It is not surprising, therefore, that in their promotional literature the Trustees should have referred in optimistic terms to their projected colony's potential export trade to Britain. Informed opinion in the country was on their side and the contribution the enterprise might make towards the realization of the commercial principles of the old colonial system was another important recommendation to the government.[9]

Nevertheless, it was the plight of insolvent debtors and the unemployed in London, and latterly of persecuted Protestants in other countries of Europe, that focused the attention of the philanthropists on the idea of creating a new colony in America. The Trustees were interested primarily in the charitable benefits of a colony, but in order to gain governmental and public support they were obliged to stress also the likely strategic and commercial benefits. In August 1732 the Trustees decided to advertize their scheme in the newspapers and try to prevent the publication of anything detrimental to it.[10] The social, commercial, and strategic arguments were subsequently paraded in a mass of advertizements and propaganda pamphlets published in such relentless succession in 1732 and 1733 that the English people were rapidly, if only temporarily, made Georgia-conscious. All classes of the community were invited to subscribe to the enterprise. In *A New and Accurate Account of the Provinces of South Carolina and Georgia* they are asked to consider the problem of "the multitude of unfortunate

8. K. E. Knorr, *British Colonial Theories, 1570–1850* (Toronto, 1944), 81–2.

9. See T. R. Reese, *Colonial Georgia: A Study in British Imperial Policy in the Eighteenth Century* (Athens, Ga., 1963), 14–16.

10. *Colonial Records of the State of Georgia*, edited by A. D. Candler (26 vols., Atlanta, 1904–16), 3; hereafter cited as *Col. Rec. Ga.*

people in the Kingdom of reputable families and of liberal, or at least, easy, education: some undone by guardians, some by law-suits, some by accidents in commerce, some by stocks and bubbles and some by suretyship." Since these persons are obliged to live on others, their exodus will be no loss to the nation. In *Reasons for Establishing the Colony of Georgia* it is argued that "as every wise government, like the bees, should not suffer any drones in the state," so these unfortunates should be transferred to places where they might be an asset to the commonwealth instead of a burden on the community. The Trustees will not deprive the country of anyone who might be useful at home, but will send over to Georgia only those who are unable to obtain even the most meager subsis-tence in England. They have decided to publish the names of em-igrants at least a fortnight before embarkation so that no debtor will be able to seize the opportunity to leave the country without the consent of his creditors.

The Georgia advocates did not forget to mention that persecuted Protestants of Europe as well as unfortunate debtors of England would benefit. By sending over persecuted German Protestants, Britain would be both strengthening its empire and performing a religious duty. The point is made strongly in *A New and Accurate Account* and in *Some Account of the Designs of the Trustees for Estab-lishing the Colony of Georgia in America*. The Society for the Propa-gation of the Gospel, it is announced, has already resolved to supply the Trustees with enough money to organize the emigration of seven hundred Protestants from Salzburg, where the Roman Catholic archbishop is pursuing a repressive religious policy and, it is ar-gued, "Subjects thus acquired by the impolitic persecutions, by the superstitious barbarities of the neighboring princes, are a noble addition to the capitol stock of the British Empire." In this way, the cause of true Christian religion will be advanced. The good dis-cipline enforced in the colony will improve the characters of the settlers, whose example, in turn, will contribute towards the con-version of the Indians.

The economic benefits which the mother country would get from the new colony are stressed in these pamphlets in conventional terms. British manufacturers will be employed in supplying the settlers with clothes, tools, and other necessities, while in return Georgia will provide silk, wine, oil, dyes, drugs, and other commodities which Britain purchases from foreigners. Silk, in particular, it is predicted, will thrive if proper measures are taken to assist and encourage its cultivation, and its production will give employment to at least twenty thousand colonists for about four months a year, and to another twenty thousand persons in England all the year round working the raw silk and manufacturing the goods sent in exchange. By encouraging the growth of silk, Britain may save over £100,000 a year of what she pays to Italy, and perhaps even be able to undersell its European rivals in silk manufactures. This was heady stuff, and must have created a good impression upon those who took the trouble to read it.

The Georgia propagandists list the social, commercial, and strategic advantages of a colony on the southern frontier in America and affirm their confidence in the success of the venture. For precedents they turn to Virginia and Pennsylvania. Virginia was colonized in spite of enormous difficulties and at first depended wholly on England for provisions, but now it is a mighty province. It is scarcely fifty years since Pennsylvania was as much a forest as Georgia is now, but under William Penn's wise management its population has grown to ninety thousand. Georgia's prospects are better than those of either Virginia or Pennsylvania were, for neighboring South Carolina abounds with provisions, the climate is known, and experienced men are ready to demonstrate how the soil should be cultivated. In the event of an enemy attack, Georgia can be relieved from Port Royal or the Bahamas, and assistance on land can be furnished by the South Carolina militia.[11] Here then, in the Trustees' eyes, is a charity worthy of every patriotic Englishman's support: the risks are slight, the prospects good, and the ultimate rewards dazzling. They ridicule objections that a new settlement will take away workers needed at home, or that if the colonies continue to grow they will become independent. The colonists

11. See also the *London Journal*, no. 684 (Aug. 5, 1732).

will not throw off their dependence, say the propagandists, so long as they are governed by mild and wholesome English laws and their property is guaranteed, and it must be remembered that the majority of colonists invest in British funds or land and send their children to the mother country to be educated. It is very unlikely that they will entertain thoughts of independence until Englishmen in the homeland are themselves oppressed. And assuredly, applying the argument to the particular instance of Georgia, no colony will be more dependent on Britain, both for a market and for its supply of manufactured goods.

Select Tracts relating to Colonies is undated but was probably issued in 1732 as a contribution to the Georgia publicity campaign. The selection is from old, historically respectable, tracts that together present an effective case for colonization and refute some of the objections that were expected to be raised against the proposed new settlement. The other advertizements and publications of these years were the work largely of two persons who, each in his own way, were to play the most influential roles in the development and administration of Georgia during its first decade. *A New and Accurate Account of the Provinces of South Carolina and Georgia*, perhaps the best known of the Georgia pamphlets, is normally attributed to James Edward Oglethorpe, a man of thirty-six when Georgia was founded and in the middle of an active, vigorous life. He came from a family with strong military and parliamentary traditions and Jacobite sympathies. He had been educated at Eton and Oxford and served in eastern Europe in the armies of Prince Eugene of Savoy. In 1722 he had been elected a Tory Member of Parliament, and it was in that capacity that he had acquired his interest in the scheme for the colonization of Georgia. His was the principal inspiration from the start, and the fact that he alone of the Trustees went to Georgia gave his opinions greater weight in their counsels. He commanded the first shipload of emigrants, and as soon as he was across the Atlantic and beyond the Trustees' immediate control he rapidly expanded the authority that they had bestowed upon him. Since there was no governor nominated as such, and since the officials appointed by the Trustees were necessarily sometimes men who had been paupers or failures in England, it was natural for the settlers to look for leadership and guidance from one who was decidedly a member of the upper classes and the personal representative of the Trustees. In the main, Oglethorpe exercised his broad and undefined authority with justice and sense, and there is ample evidence of the respect which most settlers felt for him in the early years. He left Georgia finally in 1743, and in the September of that year acquired financial security and a home at Cranham Hall in Essex by marrying a wealthy heiress.[12] Thereafter his interest in the province diminished. His initial enthusiasm, however, is evident in his *New and Accurate Account*, which is somewhat extravagant in its admiration for the Trustees, and its florid, mannered language, while not uncommon in that period, is not easy to digest nowadays.

In composing *A New and Accurate Account* Oglethorpe probably received assistance from the Trustees' secretary, Benjamin Martyn, and it is conceivable that Martyn was, in fact, the author, for most of the Georgia advertizements and tracts in the 1730s were Martyn's work. A bachelor throughout his life, Martyn was maintaining his mother and sisters on a modest income from government employment when he was recommended to the Trustees, who found him a very eligible candidate for the post of their secretary, especially as he offered his services gratis until they had prospered sufficiently to be able to pay him.[13] He came from what may be conveniently termed the English middle class, was educated at Charterhouse, a famous public school, and became a man of considerable culture and a variety of intellectual interests. He was the first promoter of a scheme to erect a monument to William Shakespeare in Westminster Abbey and wrote a special prologue in 1738 for a

12. The only home Oglethorpe had in Georgia was a modest cottage on St. Simon's Island, the supposed site of which is now marked with a commemorative granite stone.

13. Historical Manuscripts Commission, *Manuscripts of the Earl of Egmont: Diary of the first Earl of Egmont (Viscount Percival) 1730–47*, edited by R. A. Roberts (3 vols., London, 1920–3), I, 286; hereafter cited as *Egmont Diary*. *Col. Rec. Ga.*, II, 3.

performance of Shakespeare's *Julius Caesar* at Drury Lane that brought in the money to put the idea into effect.[14] Martyn, indeed, appears to have been particularly interested in the theatre, and he wrote a tragedy entitled *Timoleon* that he dedicated to the King. The first performance was at Drury Lane in January 1730, and it was said that "the author's friends were so zealous on the first night that not a scene was drawn without a clap, the very candle-snuffers received their share of approbation, and a couch made its entrance with universal applause—it is remarkable that in another new tragedy very soon after, the same couch met with a severe repulse, tho' it had acted its part altogether as well."[15] The play was in blank verse throughout, but it was coarse and obscene, especially the epilogue spoken by a lady, and after a run of fourteen performances it retired into the oblivion where it rightly belonged.

Martyn lacked the creative impulse or inspiration to make a commercial success in the world of drama or literature, and, when all is considered, his most important literary work was done in the service of the Georgia Trustees. In 1732 he published *Some Account of the Designs of the Trustees*, a handsomely produced and well-written invitation to support the new colonial venture. In 1733 his *Reasons for Establishing the Colony of Georgia* confirmed his ability to sustain his case with a powerful combination of sense and enthusiasm. Both tracts were published with the sanction of the Trustees in order to acquaint the public formally of their designs and to attract contributors. Martyn continued to write in the service of the Georgia project after the publicity campaign of the 1730s faded towards the end of the decade, and in 1752, when Georgia passed under royal government, he became the colony's first agent in London. Throughout the Trusteeship period he performed his duties efficiently, punctually, and consistently, and there was never cause for complaint on either side of the Atlantic about the work of the secretary. Martyn's competence accounts in large measure for the orderliness with which the Trustees transacted their business, and

14. *A General Dictionary, Historical and Critical* (1739), IX, 189.
15. J. Genest, *Some Account of the English Stage* (10 vols., Bath, 1832), III, 252.

the volumes of papers in the Colonial Office series relating to Georgia in the Public Record Office in London provide abundant evidence of the secretary's diligence. Letters and instructions were written with a clarity of expression and legibility of hand that are a joy to their reader. He died in 1763 at the age of sixty-four, and was buried in the churchyard at Lewisham near London beneath a pithy epitaph which ignored his loyalty and industry in the cause of the settlement of Georgia and merely described him as "a man of inflexible integrity, and one of the best bred men in England; which, with a happy genius for poetry, procured him the friendship of several noblemen."[16]

The promotional literature of 1732 and 1733 was supplemented by notices in newspapers and periodicals, especially in the *Gentleman's Magazine*, the *Political State of Great Britain*, and the *London Journal*, which reported the early development of the colony and occasionally published somewhat florid poetry in its honor. A regular feature in the publicity was the publication of the anniversary sermon preached every year before the Trustees when they had their annual general meeting. The sermon in February 1734 by Dr. Thomas Rundle in St. George's Church, Hanover Square, is an interesting example of this form of advertizing, not least because of the unusual circumstances in which it was delivered. In 1733 Rundle had been nominated by the lord chancellor, to whom he was chaplain, for promotion from the Prebendary of Durham to Bishop of Gloucester, and the appointment was announced in the press early in 1734.[17] The preferment was hotly opposed, however, by a number of leading churchmen, including the Bishop of London, who doubted his orthodoxy. The affair was an embarrassment to the Trustees because their secretary, Martyn, without consulting them, had already invited Rundle to preach the anniversary sermon and become a Trustee at the next selection meeting. The opposition to Rundle within the episcopacy prevented his succession

16. D. Lysons, *The Environs of London* (4 vols., London, 1792–6), IV, 523, 528. T. R. Reese, "Benjamin Martyn, Secretary to the Trustees of Georgia," *Georgia Historical Quarterly*, 38 (June, 1954), 142–7.

17. *Gentleman's Magazine*, 4 (1734), 52.

to Gloucester, and he was appointed instead to the wealthier see of Derry in Ireland, indicating, so it was commonly suggested in London, "that a person unfit to be a small Bishop in England is good enough for Ireland."[18] Rundle preached his sermon to the Trustees, was elected one of their number in March 1734, and donated twenty pounds with the promise of more to follow.[19]

With the wonders of Georgia thus ventilated in a variety of forms, it was hoped the request for support would have a ready response, but the project suffered from the disadvantage that, unlike former colonizing schemes, it was explicitly a charity. The Trustees could offer no hopes of profit to contributors. They had to rely for success on what *Some Account of the Designs of the Trustees* describes as "the goodness of providence" and "the compassionate disposition of the people of England," but it was soon obvious that something more was required to produce adequate funds. The Trustees campaigned energetically in an attempt to stimulate people's generosity, ridding possible apprehension over the disposal of the money and making emotional appeals for support. In *Reasons for Establishing the Colony of Georgia* it is declared that all money received will be deposited in the Bank of England, each contribution will be registered in a book kept for that purpose by the Trustees, and printed copies of the accounts will be distributed to the principal subscribers. Despite these guarantees and impassioned appeals to patriotism, benevolence, and Christian kindness and pity, contributions came in very slowly. There were several notable benefactors, but generally the public response was disappointing. Gifts of money, books, and other articles, many of them anonymous, were always coming in, but they were not sufficient to meet the needs of the Trustees, who, by the beginning of 1733, were hoping for Parliamentary assistance.[20] By April the Trustees had decided to ask Parliament formally for a financial grant and to distribute *Some Account of the Designs of the Trustees* in both houses to help

18. *Egmont Diary*, II, 23–4, 137, 151.
19. *Ibid.*, 66. *Col. Rec. Ga.*, III, 45.
20. Martyn to Oglethorpe, Jan. 24, 1732/3, C.O. 5/666, page 7.

create a favorable attitude towards the petition.[21] Georgia was to become unique in colonial history as the only colony to depend almost from its very beginning on the financial support of the home government.

The auguries for a grant from Parliament were good. Many of the Trustees were themselves Members of Parliament, and the ministry and general public were well disposed towards the new settlement, partly because of the publicity campaign and partly because of the uncommon amount of vagrancy in London at that time which was weighing heavily on the parishes of the city. Sir Robert Walpole and most of the prominent figures in the House of Commons seem to have been in favor of the project, and there was no serious wish to oppose a motion for financial assistance.[22] In 1733 the Trustees were voted ten thousand pounds "to be applied towards defraying the charges of carrying over and settling foreign and other Protestants" in the new colony.[23] The money was paid out of the exchequer without any deductions, the treasury officers waiving their customary fees as it was for a charitable use and the national benefit.[24] Other government departments did what they could to help the emigrants. The Admiralty instructed all warships on the Atlantic and American stations to assist Oglethorpe and gave him a general requisition on any ships from which he might require aid.[25] The Duke of Newcastle, secretary of state, wrote to all governors in America asking them to help the new colony, and the Privy Council ordered Governor Johnson of South Carolina to give the emigrants a proper welcome.[26] Johnson personally subscribed fifty pounds to the Georgia fund, and when the settlers

21. *Egmont Diary*, I, 367.
22. *Ibid.*, 272–3.
23. 6 Geo. II, c. 25, par. 7.
24. *Political State of Great Britain*, 46 (Sept. 1933), 241.
25. Admiralty 2/465 (Public Record Office, London), page 460. *Egmont Diary*, I, 296.
26. H. M. additional instructions to Johnson, Sept. 30, 1732, C.O. 324/36, pages 376–8. Privy Council Registers, (Public Record Office, London), Series 2, Vol. 92, pages 23, 27, 49–50, 59.

arrived in America he persuaded the South Carolina Assembly to vote them substantial provisions.[27]

Thus, Georgia began with expressions of goodwill on both sides of the Atlantic. In July 1732 the Trustees held their first regular meeting in London.[28] In January 1733 Oglethorpe and the first settlers reached America. After traveling some fifteen miles up the Savannah river, they found a suitable place for settlement on a sandy, pine-crowned bluff, and there built the town of Savannah, the administrative center and chief port of early Georgia. Other towns and villages were quickly started. Protestant exiles from Salzburg established the village of Ebenezer farther up the river from Savannah; some Scottish Highland families erected Darien on the northern bank of the Altamaha; French families settled at Highgate, about five miles southwest of Savannah; Swiss colonists established Purrysburg; and German Swiss settled at Vernonburg. Although these early settlements were necessarily small, primitive, and precarious, they represented the successful founding of the colony whose imagined wonders and advantages had been so embellished and extolled in the literature of the time. The pictures painted by the promoters were now to be viewed in the harsh light of reality.

27. Johnson to Council of Trade, Jan. 8, 1733, C.O. 5/364, fol. 182. *Egmont Diary*, I, 304.
28. *Col. Rec. Ga.*, I, 65–6.

The Most Delightful Country
of the Universe

A
DISCOURSE

Concerning the defign'd

ESTABLISHMENT

Of a New

COLONY

TO THE

South of *Carolina,*

IN THE

Moſt delightful Country of the Univerſe.

By Sir ROBERT MOUNTGOMERY, *Baronet.*

LONDON:
Printed in the Year. 1717.

The Most Delightful Country

of the Universe

I T will perhaps afford some Satisfaction to the Gentlemen of *Carolina*, to know, that my Design arises not from any sudden Motive, but a strong Bent of Genius I inherit from my Ancestors: One of whom was among those Knights of *Nova Scotia* purposely created near a hundred Years ago, for settling a *Scots Colony in* America. But the Conquest of that Country by the *French* prevented his Design, and so it lies on his Posterity to make good his Intentions for the Service of their Country.

The Humour however Descended, and ran down with the Blood: For my Father was so far of this Opinion, that, together with Lord *Cardross* the late Earl of *Buchan*, and some other Gentlemen, he enter'd into Measures for Establishing a Settlement on *Port-Royal River* in *South-Carolina*, and Lord *Cardross* went thither in Person; but the *Spaniards* dislodg'd them, and destroy'd the Plantation: Advantage being taken of some Confusions, which arose through the want of full Powers, and distinct Jurisdiction.

The charming Descriptions, which, on this last Occasion, I met with, of the natural Sweetness, and Beauties, of *Carolina*, inspir'd me with an early Affection to that Place, in particular. But the Wars intervening, and calling for my Sword, in the more immediate Service of my Country, gave me no Opportunity to put in Practice certain Schemes which occur'd, for effectually forming a Settlement there, till just now; when together with some of my Friends, who unite their Endeavours with mine, I am like, by continuance of the *Indian* Disturbances, to enjoy my own Wish, with the Additional Pleasure of being useful to the Province.

Tho' our Design does not altogether depend on the Subscription of Purchasers, herein propos'd, yet our own Stock so encreas'd will be made more effectual, and we shall give at the same Time an Opportunity to many of Sharing in our Benefits, who cou'd not be otherwise concern'd in the Undertaking.

If therefore, the Offer, which we make, shall meet with Encouragement, 'twill, by Dividing our Burthen, somewhat lighten it; If it fails, 'twill no further Disappoint us, than as it leaves us to do That *alone*, which might better, be done with the expected Assistance.

R. M<small>OUNTGOMRY</small>.

Of the Motives, and Foundation of the Undertaking.

PLANTATIONS of new Countries, says the Great Lord *Bacon, are among the Primitive, and most Heroick Works of Man.* They are meritorious in a double Sense; *Religiously*, as they illuminate the Souls of Heathens through the Darkness of their Ignorance, and *Politically*, as they strengthen the Dominion, which sends out the Colony, and wonderfully more than any other Means enrich the Undertakers.

But as such Attempts are *Great*, so also are they *Dangerous*. One early Caution easily secures their future Benefits; one little Error in Foundation overthrows the Building. It is to a Defect *in setting out*, that all our noble Colonies upon the Western Continent have ow'd their Disappointments; *To a want of due Precaution* in *their Forms of settling*, or rather, to their settling without any Form at all: The Planters grasp'd at an undue Extent of Land, exceeding their Capacity to manage, or defend: This scatter'd them to Distances unsafe, and solitary, so that, living in a Wilderness, incapable of mutual Aid, the necessary Artizans found no Encouragement to dwell among them; Their Woods remain'd unclear'd; their Fens undrain'd; The Air by that Means prov'd unhealthy, and the Roads impassable; For want of Towns, and Places of Defence, they suddenly became a Prey to all Invaders; even the unformidable *Indians* took Advantage of the Oversight; and *Carolina*, is, at present, groaning under a most bloody Persecution, from a wild, and despicable Kind of Enemy, who had not dar'd to think of the Attempt, but from an Observation daily made, how open and unguarded they might take the *English*.

From these Examples, and the Neighbourhood of the intended Settlement to *Carolina* thus distress'd, our *future Eden*, made early wise by Dangers, which she feels not, would not only fix her Foot upon a firm Foundation, so as to resist a Storm Herself, but she wou'd also spread her Wings to a Capacity of shadowing Others: A *British* Colony, shou'd, like the *Roman*, carry with it always something of the *Mother's* Glory.

Excited therefore, by an earnest Inclination to establish such a Settlement, as may, by new Means, yield new Benefits, as well in Wealth, as Safety, and resolving to proceed upon a Scheme entirely different from any hitherto attempted, and which appears to promise great, and inexpressible Advantages; the Grant on which we found the Undertaking, will be seen in the following Abstract.

The underwritten Palatine and Lords Proprietors of the Province of *Carolina*, do on the Considerations herein after mention'd, grant, sell, alien, release, and confirm to Sir *Robert Mountgomry*, Baronet, his Heirs, and Assigns, for ever, all that Tract of Land, which lies between the Rivers *Allatamaha*, and *Savanna*, together with the Islands, Ports, Harbours, Bays, and Rivers on that Part of the Coast, which lies between the

Mouths of the said two Rivers to the Seaward; and moreover all Veins, Mines, and Quarries of Gold, and Silver, and all other whatever, be they of Stones, Metals, or any other Things found, or to be found within that Tract of Land, and the Limits aforesaid; With Liberty over and above to make Settlements *on the South Side of* Allatamaha *River*, which Tract of Land the said underwritten Lords do erect into a distinct Province, with proper Jurisdictions, Priviledges, Prerogatives, and Franchises, Independent of, and not Subject to the Laws of *South Carolina*, to be holden of the said Lords by Sir *Robert*, his Heirs, and Assigns for ever, under the Name and Title of the *Margravate* of *Azilia*; at and under the yearly Quitrent of one Penny Sterling *per* Acre, or its Value in Goods, or Merchandise, as the Land shall be occupied, taken up, or run out; Payable yearly to the Lords Proprietors Officers at *Charles-Town*, but such Payment not to commence, till three Years after Arrival of the first Ships there, which shall be sent over to begin the Settlement; over and above which Penny *per* Acre, Sir *Robert*, his Heirs, and Assigns, shall also yield, and pay to the Lords Proprietors, one fourth Part of all Gold, or Silver Oar, besides the Quota reserv'd to the Crown out of the said Royal Minerals: Distinct Courts of Judicature to be erected, and such Laws enacted within the *Margravate*, by and with the Advice, Assent, and Approbation of the Freemen thereof in Publick Assembly, as shall be most conducive to the Utility of the said *Margravate*, and as near as may be conveniently agreeable to the Laws, and Customs of *England*, but so as such Laws do not extend to lay Duties or Custom, or other Obstruction upon the Navigation of either of the said Rivers, by any Inhabitant of *South*, or *North Carolina*, or their free Commerce and Trade with the *Indian* Nations, either within, or to the Southward of the *Margravate*, Sir *Robert* consenting that the same Duty shall be charg'd on Skins within the *Margravate*, which at this Time stands charg'd on such Skins in *South Carolina*, and appropriated to the Maintenance of the Clergy there, so long as that Duty is continued in *South Carolina*, but the said Duty shall not be encreas'd in *Azilia*, tho' the Assembly of *South Carolina* shou'd think fit to encrease it there, nor shall it longer continue to be paid, than while it shall remain appropriated, as at present to the Maintenance of the Clergy only: In Consideration of all which Powers, Rights, Priviledges, Prerogatives, and Franchises, Sir *Robert* shall Transport at his own Expence, a considerable Number of Families with all Necessaries for making a new Settlement in the said Tract of Land, and in Case it be neglected for the

Space of three Years from the Date of this Grant, Then the Grant shall become void, any Thing herein contain'd to the contrary notwithstanding. Dated *June* the Nineteenth, 1717.

Cartaret. Palatine.
Ja. Bertie for the
    Duke of *Beaufort*.
M. Ashley.
John Colleton, &c.

A Description of the Country.

IT lies about the 31*st* and 32*d* Degree of Northern Latitude, is bounded Eastward by the great *Atlantick* Sea, To the West by a Part of the *Apalachian* Mountains, and to the North and South by the two great *Rivers*, mention'd in the Grant.

In the Maps of *North America* it may be taken Notice of, how well this Country lies for Trade with all our Colonies, and in Regard to every other Prospect, which can make a Situation healthy, profitable, lovely, and inviting; *Florida*, of which it is a Part, receiv'd that Name from its delightful, *florid*, and agreeable Appearance.

It has been commonly observ'd, that gay Descriptions of new Countries raise a Doubt of their Sincerity. Men are apt to think the *Picture* drawn beyond the *Life*, to serve the Interest of the Representer: To shun the Prejudice of this Opinion, whatever shall be said upon the Subject here, is all extracted from our *English Writers*, who are very numerous, and universally agree, that *Carolina*, and especially in its *Southern* Bounds, is the most amiable Country of the Universe: that Nature has not bless'd the World with any Tract, which can be preferable to it, that *Paradise* with all her Virgin Beauties, may be modestly suppos'd at most but equal to its Native Excellencies.

It lies in the same Latitude with *Palestine* Herself, That promis'd *Canaan*, which was pointed out by *God's* own Choice, to bless the Labours of a favourite People; It abounds with Rivers, Woods, and Meadows. Its gentle Hills are full of Mines, *Lead, Copper, Iron,* and even some of *Silver;* 'Tis beautified with odoriferous Plants, green all the Year. Pine, Cedar, Cypress, Oak, Elm, Ash, or Walnut, with innumerable other Sorts, both Fruit or Timber Trees grow every where so pleasantly that tho' they meet at Top, and shade the Traveller, they are, at the same Time, so distant in their Bodies, and so free from Underwood, or Bushes, that the Deer, and other Game, which feed in Droves along these Forests, may be often seen near half a Mile between them.

The Air is healthy, and the Soil in general fruitful, and of infinite Variety; *Vines*, naturally flourishing upon the Hills, bear Grapes in most luxuriant Plenty. They have every Growth, which we possess in *England*, and almost every Thing that *England* wants besides. The *Orange*, and the *Limon* thrive in the same common Orchard with the *Apple*, and the *Pear-Tree*, Plumbs, Peaches, Apricots, and Nectarins, bear from Stones in three Years growing. The Planters raise large Orchards of these Fruits to feed their Hogs with; Wheat Ears have been measur'd there seven Inches long, and they have Barly, Beans, Pease, Rice, and all our Grains, Roots, Herbs, and Flowers, not to speak of Numbers of their own, which we can find no Names for; Beef, Mutton, Pork, Tame Poultry, wild Fowl, Sea and River Fish, are all there plentiful, and most at lower Rates, than in the cheapest Parts of *Wales*, or *Scotland*.

The many Lakes, and pretty Rivulets throughout the Province, breed a Multitude of Geese, and other Water Fowl; The Air is found so temperate, and the Seasons of the Year so very regular, that there is no Excess of *Heat*, or *Cold*, nor any sudden Alterations in the Weather; The River Banks are cover'd with a strange Variety of lovely Trees, which being always green, present a thousand Landskips to the Eye, so fine, and so diversified; that the Sight is entirely charm'd with them; the Ground lies sloping towards the

Rivers, but, at a Distance, rises gradually, and intermingles little Hills of Wood with fruitful Plains, all cover'd over with wild Flowers, and not a Tree to interrupt the Prospect: Nor is this tempting Country yet inhabited, except those Parts in the Possession of the *English*, unless by here and there a Tribe of wandering *Indians*, wild and ignorant, all artless, and uncultivated, as the Soil, which fosters them.

Of the Form propos'd in Settling.

OUR Meaning here relates to what immediate Measures will be taken, for Security against the Insults of the Natives, during the Infancy of our Affairs; To which End we shall not satisfie ourselves with building here and there a *Fort*, the fatal Practice of *America*, but so dispose the Habitations, and Divisions of the Land, that not alone our Houses, but whatever we possess, will be enclos'd by *Military Lines*, impregnable against the *Savages*, and which will make our whole Plantation one continued Fortress.

It need not be suppos'd, that all the Lands will thus be fortified *at once*; The first Lines drawn will be in just Proportion to the Number of Men they enclose; As the Inhabitants encrease, New Lines will be made to enclose them also, so that all the People will be always safe within a well defended Line of Circumvallation.

The Reader will allow, it is not necessary, that these Retrenchments be of Bulk, like those of *Europe*; small Defence is *strong* against the poor unskilful Natives of *America*; They have accomplish'd all their bloody Mischiefs by Surprizes, and Incursions, but durst never think of a Defyance to Artillery.

The Massacres, and frequent Ruins, which have fallen upon some *English* Settlements for want of this one Caution; have sufficiently instructed us, that *Strength*, producing Safety, is the Point, which shou'd be chiefly weigh'd in such Attempts as these: *Solon* had Reason when he said to *Croesus*, looking on his Treasure —, *You are rich indeed, and so far you are mighty; But if any Man shou'd come with sharper steel than Yours, how easily will he be made the Master of your Gold?*

At the Arrival therefore of the first Men carried over, proper Officers shall mark, and cause to be entrench'd a Square of Land, in just Proportion to their Number; On the Outsides of this Square, within the little Bastions, or Redoubts of the Entrenchment, they raise light Timber Dwellings, cutting down the Trees, which every where encompass them: The Officers are quartered with the Men, whom they command, and the Governour in Chief is plac'd exactly in the Center: By these means the labouring People (being so dispos'd, as to be always watchfull of an Enemies Approach) are themselves within the Eye of those, set over them, and *All together* under the Inspection of their Principal.

The Redoubts may be near enough to defend Each other with Musquets, but Field Pieces, and Patarero's will be planted upon Each, kept charged with Cartridge shot, and Pieces of old Iron: Within these Redoubts are the Common Dwellings of the Men who must defend them; Between them runs a Palisadoe'd Bank, and a Ditch, which will be Scour'd by the Artillery. One Man in Each Redoubt kept Night and Day, upon the Guard, will give alarm upon Occasion to the others at their Work. So they cultivate their Lands: secure their Cattle, and follow their Business with great Ease, and Safety. Exactly in the Center of the inmost Square will be a *Fort*, defended by large Canon, pointing Every way, and capable of making strong Resistance, in Case some Quarter of the outward Lines shou'd chance to be surpriz'd, by any sudden Accident, which yet with tolerable Care wou'd be impracticable.

The Nature of this Scheme, when weigh'd against the Ignorance, and wildness of the Natives, will shew, that Men, thus settled, may at once defend, and cultivate a Territory, with the utmost Satisfaction, and Security, even in the *Heart* of an *Indian* Country, Then how much rather in a Place considerably distant from the Savage Settlements.

As the Numbers shall encrease, and they go on to clear more

Space of Land, they are to regulate their Settlements with like Regard to Safety, and Improvement: And indeed the Difference, as to Time, and Labour, is not near so great as may be thought, betwixt enclosing Land this Way, and following the dangerous common Method; But what is here already said will serve the End, for which it has been written, which was only to give a general Notion of the Care, and Caution we propose to act with.

It will not, however, be amiss, as you have seen the first rude Form of our *Azilia* in her Infancy, to view her also in the Fulness of her Beauty; And to that End we have affix'd a Plan of one whole *District*, clear'd, planted, and inhabited; For as the Country thrives, all future Townships will be form'd according to this Plan, and measur'd out as near Each other as the Rivers, Hills, and other natural Impediments will any way admit of.

But least it shou'd be fear'd from the Correctness of this Model, that twill be a Work of too great Difficulty, and require a mighty Length of Time to bring it to Perfection, we think it proper to declare, that *Purchasers* will not be obliged to wait this Form of Settlement, but are entitled to the immediate Profits of peculiar Lands, assign'd them, from the very first Arrival of the Colony; which Lands, being set apart for that Purpose, will be strongly enclos'd, and defended by the Lines, or Entrenchments before mention'd.

Neither wou'd we have it thought a Labour so tedious, as 'tis generally fancy'd, to establish in this manner a Colony, which may become not only an *Advantage*, but a *Glory* to the Nation: We have Prospects before us most attractive, and unprecedented, in the three tempting Points *Wealth, Safety,* and *Liberty*: Benefits, like these, can never fail of drawing Numbers of Inhabitants from Every Corner; And, Men once got together, 'tis as easy to dispose them regularly, and with due Regard to Order, Beauty, and the Comforts of Society, as to leave them to the Folly of fixing at Random, and destroying their Interest by indulging their Humour; So that we have more than ordinary Cause to expect, that in a very short Time, we shall be able to present the solid *Life its self*, as now we give the *Shadow* only, in the following Explanation.

You must suppose a level, dry, and fruitful Tract of Land, in

A Plan representing the Form of Setling the Districts, or County Divisions in the Margravate of Azilia.

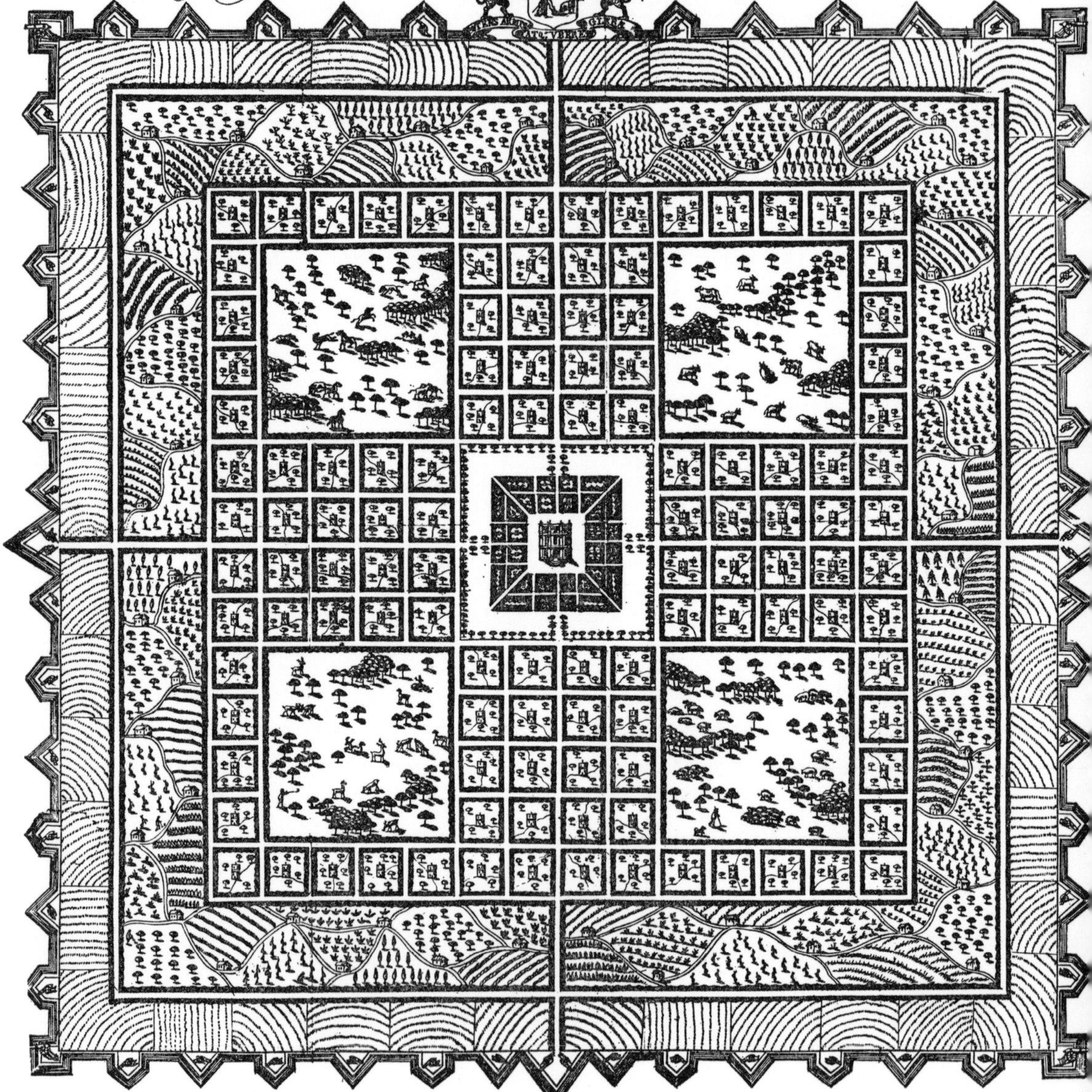

some fine Plain or Valley, containing a just Square of twenty Miles Each Way, or two hundred and fifty Six thousand Acres, laid out, and setled, in the Form, presented, in the Cut annex'd.

The District is defended by sufficient Numbers of Men, who, dwelling in the fortified Angles of the Line, will be employ'd in cultivating Lands, which are kept in Hand for the particular advantage of the *Margrave*; These Lands surround the District just within the Lines, and every where contain in Breadth one Mile exactly.

The Men, thus employ'd, are such, as shall be hir'd in *Great-Britain* or *Ireland*, well disciplin'd, arm'd, and carried over, on Condition to serve faithfully for such a Term of Years, as they before shall agree to; And, that no Man may be wretched in so happy a Country, at the Expiration of those Peoples Time; besides some other considerable, and unusual Incouragements, all such, among them, who shall marry in the Country, or come married thither, shall have a Right of laying claim to a certain Fee-Farm, or Quantity of Land, ready clear'd, together with a House built upon it, and a stock sufficient to improve, and cultivate it, which they shall enjoy, Rent, and Tax free, during Life; as a Reward for their Services; By which Means two very great Advantages must naturally follow; Poor labouring Men, so secur'd of a fix'd future Settlement; will be thereby induc'd to go thither more willingly; and act, when there, with double Diligence, and Duty; And when their Time expires, possessing just Land enough to pass their Lives at Ease, and bring their Children up honestly, the Families they leave will prove a constant Seminary of sober Servants, of Both Sexes, for the Gentry of the Colony; whereby they will be under no necessity to use the Dangerous Help of *Blackamoors*, or *Indians*; The Lands set apart for this Purpose, are two Miles in Breadth, quite round the District, and lie next within the *Margraves* own reserv'd Lands abovemention'd.

The 116 Squares, Each of which has a House in the Middle, are, Every one a Mile on Each Side, or 640 Acres in a Square, bating only for the High Ways, which divide them; These are the Estates, belonging to the Gentry *of the District*, who, being so confin'd to an Equality in *Land*, will be profitably Emulous of out doing Each other in *Improvement*, since that is the only way, left them to grow richer than their Neighbours; And when the Margravate is once become strong enough to form many Districts, the Estates will be all given gratis, together with many other Benefits, to honest and qualified Gentlemen in *Great Britain*, or elsewhere, who having Numerous and well-educated Families, possess but little Fortunes, other than their Industry; and will therefore be chosen to enjoy these Advantages, which they shall pay no Rent, or other Consideration for; and yet the Undertaking will not fail to find its own Account in their Prosperity.

The four great Parks, or rather Forrests, are Each four Miles Square, that is 16 Miles round each Forrest, in which are propagated Herds of Cattle of all Sorts by themselves not alone to serve the uses of the District, they belong to, but to store such *New Ones*, as may from Time to Time, be measur'd out, on Affluence of People.

The Middle hollow Square, which is full of Streets crossing each other, is the *City*, And the Blank, which runs about it, on the outside surrounded with Trees, is a large void Space, which will be useful for a thousand Purposes, and, among the rest, as being airy, and affording a fine Prospect of the Town in Drawing near it.

In the Center of the City stands the *Margraves House*, which is to be his constant Residence, or the Residence of the Governour, and contains all sorts of publick Edifices for Dispatch of Business; and this again is separated from the City by a Space, like that, which, as above, divides the Town from the Country.

Of some Designs in View for making Profit.

OUR Prospects in this Point, are more extensive than we think it needful to discover; It were a Shame shou'd we confine the Fruitfulness of such a rich and lovely Country to some single Product, which *Example* first makes common, and the *being common* robs of Benefit. Thus *Sugar* in *Barbadoes*, *Rice* in *Carolina*, and *Tobacco* in *Virginia*, take up all the Labours of their People, overstock the Markets, stifle the Demand, and make their Industry their Ruin, merely through a Want of due Reflection on Diversity of other Products, equally adapted to their Soil, and Climate.

Coffee, Tea, Figs, Raisins, Currants, Almonds, Olives, Silk, Wine, Cochineal, and great Variety of still more rich Commodities, which we are forc'd to buy at mighty Rates from Countries, lying in the very Latitude of our Plantations: All these we certainly shall Propagate, tho' it may perhaps be said, that they are yet but distant Views; mean while, we shall confine our first Endeavours to such easy Benefits, as will (without the smallest waiting for the Growth of Plants) be offer'd to our Industry, from the *spontaneous* Wealth, which over-runs the Country.

The Reader may assure himself, our Undertakings upon all Occasions, will be the plainest, and most ready Roads to Profit; not form'd from doubtful, and untried Conceits, nor hamper'd by a Train of Difficulties; none are more apt than we to disregard Chimerical, or rash Designs; but 'tis the Business of Men's Judgment to divide Things *plain* from Things *unlikely*.

We cannot think it proper to be too particular upon this Subject, nor will it, we suppose, be expected from us: One Example, however, we will give, because we wou'd present a Proof, that much is *practicable* there, which has not yet been *put in Practice*; we shall Pitch on *Pot-ash*, a Commodity of great Consumption in the Trades of *Dying, Glass-making, Soap-boiling,* and some others; not that this is the only present Prospect, which we build on, but as 'tis necessary we shou'd particularize *one* Benefit, that others may be credible.

And here it will not be amiss, if we describe what *Pot-ash* is, and how they make it; since, 'tis likely, some may have attempted it already, in the Forests of *America*, and miscarried, by depending upon ignorant Undertakers.

It is not very *properly* indeed call'd *Pot-ash*, not being any kind of *Ashes*, but the fix'd, and vegetable *Salt of Ashes*, which, if mix'd with Water, melts away, and turns to *Lye*; For this Reason 'tis preferr'd to all other Lixiviate Ashes, Foreign, or Domestick, which, not being perfect *Salts*, but Ashes of Bean-Straw, and other Vegetables, made stronger by the Help of Lye, bear no Proportion, as to Price, with *Pot-ash itself*, which is, as we said before, the pure *Salt* without any of the *Ashes*.

To procure this Salt, in *Russia*, and the Countries famous for it, they burn great Quantities of *Oak*, *Firr*, *Birch*, and other Woods, cut down, when flourishing, and full of Sap; The Ashes they throw into Boilers, or huge Caldrons full of Water, and extract a thick, sharp Lye by boiling; They let this Lye grow clear by settling, and then draw it off, and throw away the Ashes left at Bottom.

This Lye, so clarified, they boil again, and as the Watry Part evaporates apace, they supply the Waste thro' a small Pipe, from another Vessel of the same Sort of Lye, set higher than the Boiler; At last, by a continued Evaporation, the whole Vessel becomes full of a thick brownish Salt, which being dug out in Lumps, and afterwards calcin'd, compleats the Work, and gives a Colour to the *Pot-ash*, like a whitish Blue, in which Condition it is barrell'd up, and fit for Merchants.

Nothing can be plainer, or more easy than this Practice in our intended Settlement; As to the *Boilers*, which have ever been the great, and terrifying Expence and Encumbrance of this Work, we shall extreamly lessen, and reduce that Charge almost to nothing, by some *new Methods*, being an experienc'd Invention, wherein we use neither Copper, Lead, Iron, nor other Mineral whatsoever, and (that excepted) there is no Material necessary, but *Wood only*; For Wood cut down, and burnt upon the Ground, affords the *Ashes*; The Rivers every where abounding in that Country furnish Water; Ashes, and Water boil'd together, yield the *Lye*; The Lye evaporated, leaves behind the *Salt*, and that very Salt calcin'd, becomes the *Pot-ash*, and it is pack'd, and sent away in Barrels, made and hoop'd there also.

From due Consideration of these Circumstances, it appears, that this must be a rich, and gainful Undertaking in a Country where the greatest Quantities of Timber, and the finest in the World, cost nothing but the Pains of cutting down, and burning, on the Banks of Navigable Rivers; where the enlivening Influence of the Sun prepares the Trees much better for this Practice, than in colder Climates, and where stubbing up the Woods, which cover all the Settlement, will give a sure, and double Benefit; for first they yield this valuable Traffick *Potash*, and afterwards leave *clear* the Ground, they grow on, for producing yearly Crops of such Commodities, as are most profitable, and fittest for the Country.

Thus, having faintly touch'd the outward Lines, and given some Prospect of our Purpose, we proceed to the Conditions, upon which we will admit of Purchasers.

The PROPOSAL.

NOTE that, for the Purchasers Security, and effectually making good their Claims, as well to the Land, which they shall buy, as to all the other Benefits propos'd in the following Articles, The whole Country, and its Improvements in all Times to come, is settled as a Mortgage and made liable in manner, as here under recited, in which such unusual, and equitable Regard has been had, for avoiding all Charge, or Delay, in Respect to the Distance of Countries, and the Difficulties, which might thence be suspected to arise, in obtaining Satisfaction by the ordinary Course of the Laws, that nothing of *Form*, or *Expence* will be necessary; but, on the first Breach of Covenant, an Easy and immediate Possession may be taken of the forfeited Province, and for ever maintain'd against all kinds of Pleas or Pretences for the use of the *Purchasers*. And, that perpetual and unobjectionable Testimony may remain, for the more absolute securing the Rights of the Purchasers, the following Deed, together with the Articles themselves, stands enrolled in the High Court of Chancery.

To All to whom these Presents shall come I *Robert Mountgomry* of *Skelmorley* in the *Sherifdom* of *Aire* in *North-Britain* Baronet send Greeting. Whereas His Excellency the Lord *Carteret Palatine*, and the Rest of the true and absolute Lords Proprietors of the Province of *Carolina* in *America* have by their Grant, bearing Date the Nineteenth Day of *June* last, bargain'd, sold, alien'd, releas'd, enfeoff'd, and confirm'd to Me the abovemention'd Sir *Robert Mountgomry*, my Heirs, and Assigns all that Tract of Land in their said Province, which lies between the Rivers *Allatamaha* and *Savanna*, and erected the said Tract into a distinct Province, with proper and independant Jurisdictions, under the Name and Title of the *Margravate* of *Azilia*, to be held of them the Lords Proprietors of *Carolina* by me, my Heirs and Assigns for ever; and whereas for better carrying on my design of transporting People, and making a new Settlement in the said *Margravate*; I have made and caused to be publish'd the Proposals hereunto annex'd, Now Therefore for securing the Advantages proposed in the said Articles to all, who shall or may Subscribe any Sum or Sums of Money for the Purchase of Lands and Profits in the *Margravate* of *Azilia* aforesaid, and shall on their parts, make good the Payments and Conditions mention'd in the Articles, I the abovenamed Sir *Robert Mountgomry* do, by these Presents to be enroll'd in the High Court of Chancery, in perpetual Proof and Testimony of the Security hereby design'd to be convey'd, engage, bind, mortgage, assign, and firmly make subject the said Grant, Lands, and benefits for making Good the Uses in the said Articles express'd in Manner, as at large herein under describ'd: And I do hereby declare and consent, that the Instruments sign'd by my Hand writing as recited in the seventh Article, shall be deem'd, and they are by virtue of these Presents declar'd to be, a firm, and sufficient Proof of Title to the respective Claim therein mention'd, to be convey'd, by and upon the Security by these Presents provided; And I do hereby authorize and appoint *David Kennedy*, Esq; in my Absence, to fill up, and deliver the said Instruments with all effectual Authority, and irrevocable Right of Representation, which by Letter of Attorney, or by any other

Form or Means whatever, can or might be deputed to Him, And I declare my self obliged, as to the sufficiency of the Writings delivered by such Act of the said *David Kennedy*, Esq; as firmly as if I had in Person fill'd, and deliver'd the said Writings; And in Case that I Sir *Robert Mountgomry*, or my Heirs, or Assigns, or any claiming Right, or exercising Power by, from, or under me, shall at any time hereafter refuse to submit to the said annex'd Articles or to any of them, or shall under any unjust Pretence whatsoever forbear the Cultivation of the Purchasers Lands, or consign the annual Products, arising therefrom, or any Part of the same, to any other Person, or Persons, than to the Factor, or Factors, who shall be appointed by the Purchasers, or to Persons approved by them, or shall refuse, or deny admission, Residence, or ocular satisfaction on the Spot to any Agent, whom the Purchasers may at any time think fit to send over for that Purpose; In any of these Cases the Purchasers shall, by virtue of these Presents (any Form of Law, Usage, Custom, or Pretence to the contrary notwithstanding) have a warrantable, and incontrovertible Right, and Authority, to procure, and obtain present Justice to themselves in Manner following, That is to say—Upon such Breach of Covenant the said Purchasers shall, or may meet upon the Summons of the Party injur'd, or of any other Person interested, and by a Majority of the Voices present elect a Committee of Three, which Committee shall draw up a State of the Case they complain of, And present it to me, or my Heirs or Assigns, or to any Agent acting for me, or them, or any of them in *London*, or elsewhere, and if within ten Days after such Presentation they receive not due Satisfaction from such Person, or Agent, they shall leave Notice in Writing at the Place of his dwelling, or publish in the Gazette, or other Authentick News Letter, that on some day therein to be named, they design to lay the State of their Case before the *Kings Attorney General*, and *Solicitor General* in *London* for the Time being, in order to have their Opinion, whether the Fact they complain of be, or be not a Breach of any Part of the Articles hereunto annex'd, that so the said Person, or Agent may attend, if he shall have any thing to offer, in Defence of the Matter complain'd of, And if upon the Question, the *Attorney* and *Solicitor General* shall joyn in Opinion and give it under their Hands, that the Cause of Complaint does plainly appear in their Judgements, to be a Breach of the Articles subscribed to, and such Person, as above described, or some Agent acting for Him, shall not forthwith make due satisfaction, such Forbearance to do Justice in the Case, shall after

Thirty Days next following the date of the said written Opinion, become an Absolute Forfeiture of the Grant, and from thenceforth all Lands, Prerogatives, Priviledges, Powers, and Benefits, whatsoever held, claim'd, or enjoy'd by virtue of the said Grant, shall be taken Possession of for the sole future Use of the Body of Purchasers, and shall be carry'd on to their general Advantage, and according to their Orders, and Direction, by any Person, or Persons, whom they shall chuse by a Majority of their Voices, and send over to that Purpose: And that no possible Let, or Impediment, on my Part, or the Part of my Heirs, or Assigns, may in any sort incommode, or prevent the most strict, and immediate Performance of this Covenant, I the said Sir *Robert* do hereby renounce for my self, and all claiming from me, all Pleas, Prerogatives, Priviledges and Pretences whatsoever, which I, or they, may by the said Grant, or by any Form, Custom, or Mode of Proceeding at Law be possess'd of, or entitled to; And I do consent, and declare, that when the written Opinion abovemention'd of the *Attorney*, and *Solicitor General* in *London*, shall be produc'd to the Lords Proprietors of *Carolina*, and sent over to their Deputies at *Charles Town*, and be enter'd in their Journal, It shall stand as a determinate Judgment recorded against me, or them, after which no Appeal shall be lawful, and possession shall be given immediately, that is to say, no other Process shall be needful than twenty Days Notice from the Governour, and Council at *Charles Town* abovemention'd: From which Time for ever, if full satisfaction be not made within the said twenty Days, as well in the Matter complain'd of, as by Payment of all Costs, and Damages sustained by the Complainants, the Purchasers shall in Right of themselves, and by Virtue of these Presents, possess, occupy, and enjoy all Manner of Authorities, Territories, and Advantages of what kind soever, arising from the Grant abovesaid, and I the said Sir *Robert Mountgomry*, my Heirs, and Assigns shall effectually stand excluded, both in Law, and in Equity, to all Intents and Purposes, as if the said Grant had never been made. In Witness whereof, I have hereunto set my Hand and Seal this Fifteenth Day of *July*, in the Third Year of the Reign of our Sovereign Lord *George*, by the Grace of God, of *Great-Britain*, *France* and *Ireland*, King, Defender of the Faith, &c. *Annoq*; *Domini*, 1717.

R. Mountgomry.

ART. I. The first fifty thousand Acres, which shall be run out, set-tled, or planted, shall be always kept, as a distinct Division, separate from the rest of the Margravate, and shall all be clear'd, and improv'd before any other Settlement is made, or suffer'd in any Part of the Margravate, and a Right will be sold by Virtue of the propos'd Subscription, to all the Profits arising from twenty five Thousand of those Acres, when the fifty Thousand shall be clear'd; and in the mean time to half the yearly Amount of the whole Profit which shall be made by the Colony, which Sale will be made in Acres, (more or less at the Discretion of the Buyer, only nothing less than five Acres) at the Rate of forty Shillings *per* Acre: And tho' the whole shou'd not be purchased, yet the Books shall, notwithstanding, be shut up forthwith, that so no Time may be lost, and the then Number of Purchasers, be they never so few, shall compose the Body, and enjoy their Proportional Benefits, as fully as if the whole had been compleated.

ART. II. The land thus bought, is not to be cultivated at the Charge of the Buyer; but the yearly Profits of it shall for ever be brought Home to the Purchasers, their Heirs or Assigns, in the Ships of the Margravate, and paid them in regular Dividends.

ART. III. The Purchase Money, that is to say, the forty Shillings *per* Acre abovemention'd, shall be paid one half down, and the other half, not till the first Return of the Shipping, and after a Dividend of Profit made among the Purchasers, by Sale of such Goods or Products as the said Ships bring over with them.

ART. IV. This first Return, and the whole yearly Produce for ever, of the first settled fifty Thousand Acres, or so much thereof, as shall at any Time be clear'd, and cultivated, shall always come consign'd to the Purchasers Factors, for the Time being, or their Agents, or to Persons of their Appointment or Approbation, and shall be sold by them, or by Brokers of their chusing, which Brokers shall account with them the said Factors or their Agents, for the Purchasers Half the Profits, and with the Agents of Sir *Robert Mountgomry*, or his Assigns, for the other Half. Pro-vided always that a Preference be given to any Buyer nam'd by the said Sir *Robert*, or his Assigns, or his or their Agents, on Condition however that such Buyer shall give a better Price than has before been offer'd.

ART. V. That on the Death, or Surrender of the Factors, or upon Dislike of their Management, it is always to be understood that a Majority of the Purchasers shall have Power to chuse new ones in their Places.

ART. VI. That on closing the Book of Subscription, due Notice shall be given, and the Purchasers shall meet, and chuse by Majority of Voices, (every twenty Acres entitling to a Vote) such Person or Persons as they think best qualified to act, as their Factors, in the Trust abovemention'd, and such Factor, or Factors, shall in Consideration of their Trouble, be allow'd over and above their necessary Charges in the Management, such Gratuity as the Purchasers think reasonable out of the respective Dividends, which they from Time to Time, shall pay to the said Purchasers.

ART. VII. On Payment of the first Half the Purchase Money, the Purchasers shall severally receive an Instrument in Form following.

This witnesseth, that A. B. did on this —— Day of —— 1717. Subscribe the Sum of —— Pounds, towards Establishment of a new Colony, in the Margravate of *Azilia* in *Carolina*, and paid down one half of the said Sum, in Consideration whereof, and of the remaining Half to be paid, as by the Articles provided, the said A. B. is for himself, his Heirs, or Assigns admitted as Proprietor of —— Acres of Land in the said Margravate, The whole Rents, Products, Profits, and Advantages of which —— Acres are absolutely vested in the said A. B., his Heirs, or Assigns for ever, as they shall arise, and accrue yearly, by virtue of a General Management, as by the Articles provided, at the Cost of Sir *Robert Mountgomry*, or his Assigns, without Charge, or Trouble to the said Proprietor under the Penalties express'd and covenanted in a Deed to that End executed and enroll'd in the High Court of Chancery, for perpetual Proof of the Security therein provided. In Witness whereof, I the abovemention'd Sir *Robert Mountgomry*, have hereunto set my Hand, the Day and Year first above-written.

R. Mountgomry.

ART. VIII. And for Encouragement of those, who shall considerably Interest themselves in this Affair. Whoever shall Subscribe the Sum of Five Hundred Pounds, for Purchase of two hundred and fifty Acres, as abovemention'd, shall, over and above his yearly Profits from the said two Hundred and Fifty Acres, be entitled to one of the Estates of a Mile Square, or 640 Acres, in the first District, which shall be settled, as in the Cut describ'd. And shall for himself, his Heirs, and Assigns for ever, be put in Possession of the said Estate of 640 Acres, together with a House built on it, and the Ground ready clear'd to his Hand, without any Charge to him, or his Assigns, as soon as such first District shall be measur'd out, and settled; The said Estate to be cultivated at his Pleasure and for his Profit, by Himself, or his Agents, on Condition only, that if he shall not himself think fit to go over, and inhabit it, The Person he sends over in his Stead, shall be no ordinary Overseer, but a Gentleman well qualified, of a liberal Education, who is married, and carries with him a genteel, and well bred Family.

ART. IX. Over and above the Regard, which may naturally be expected to the Recommendation of Purchasers, in Disposal of Offices, and furnishing the various Supplies from Time to Time needful; it will be fit that some particular Encouragement be given to such, as shall be early Promoters of the Undertaking; because in this, as in all great Affairs, Expedition is the main Life of Business, and the necessary Preparations will require so much Time, that if the Subscription is suddenly compleated, it will turn to the extraordinary Benefit of the Design, and all concern'd in it; It is therefore hereby made an Article, that the first hundred Subscribers (to be known by the Numbers on their Instruments) whether they Subscribe more, or less, shall have, and be firmly entitled in all Dividends, to an additional Share of Profit, after the Rate of one Acre over and above every ten Acres they buy, and so for more or less in Proportion; to be paid them out of the Undertaker's Part of every Dividend by their own Factors or Agents: As for Instance, a Purchaser of 100 Acres, if his Ticket of Purchase bears any Number from 1 to 100, shall not, at the Dividends, receive in Proportion to the 100 Acres he bought, but as if they were 110 Acres: by Virtue of the 10 Acres additionally annex'd to his Quota by Virtue of this Article. And so it shall be understood of any different Quantity purchas'd, from five Acres upwards.

A more particular Explanation of the Benefits of this Proposal.

'TIS impossible to give a firmer Title, than is hereby made, both to the Lands, and their Profits, since the whole Country, with all its Improvements, in all Times to come, is engag'd as a Mortgage, and will be forfeited into the Purchaser's Hands on Non-performance of the Covenants, and as to the Rate of the Purchase, 'tis the cheapest that ever was heard of: For it must be observ'd, that the Forty Shillings *per* Acre is not a Consideration for the *Land only*, to be cultivated afterwards at the Charge of the Buyer, but on the contrary, it is the first, and last Expence, not only of the Land, but its perpetual Profit; so that for what is once laid out, a Man has, every Year, brought Home to his Door, by other People's Care and Charge, and without the least Trouble to Himself, but That of receiving the Money, the Produce and Profit of so many Acres of the finest Land in the World, as he thus pays Forty Shillings a piece for; and this is to continue, not only during his own Life, but to Descend for ever to his Heirs, or those, to whom he shall assign his Interest. And, that the Benefits of this Proposal may as well reach those who are willing to spare but a *little*, as those who shall incline to Subscribe *large Sums*, we have therefore fix'd the lowest Quantity at five Acres; By which Means People who cannot, or who care not to venture much, may become concern'd for only five Pound down, and five Pound more after the first Dividend of Profit, at Return of the Shipping; and this will we hope be of General Advantage, since the Benefit being made diffusive, will reach Numbers who had else been shut out: And with that View we have permitted it against the Opinions of a few: Since a Man who is able to spare but 10 or 20 *l.* and does afterwards sell his Interest for two or three hundred, will much more feel the Benefit than one, who being able to subscribe larger Sums, makes a Profit in Equal Proportion.

And here, tho' we utterly disapprove all swelling, and overrated Computations, it will be some satisfaction to give as rational a

Guess, as Things to come admit of, after what proportion Purchasers may calculate their Profit, by the most modest Expectation; for tho' tis impossible exactly to state these Accounts, before they are put to the Trial, yet such Computations as are fairly, and impartially Drawn, are at least so far Useful, as to give some Idea to the Reader, of what he may otherwise perhaps be utterly ignorant in the very Nature and Meaning of.

It will be allow'd without Argument, that Three working Men may be carried over, and maintain'd one whole Year round, for every Hundred Pound in the Stock; And so a purchaser, for every Hundred Pounds, he subscribes, will the first Year be entitled to Half what is gain'd by Three Mens constant Labour the whole Year about, The other Half remaining to the Undertakers, to supply Encrease of People, and the necessary Charges of their Maintenance, and Government.

The Practice of our Colonies all over *America*, has made it undeniable, that the Labour of a Man, for one Year, no otherway employ'd, will clear, at least, four Acres; It must be observ'd, that we do not suppose him to *cultivate* the four Acres, but only to cut, and burn down the *Trees*, which grow there; By this Account such a Purchasers first Years Claim will be the Profit of Six Acres (Half Three Mens Labour for That Year) And his Second Year advancing in Proportion, after Allowance for all Kinds of Hazard, there arises a great, and uncommon Advantage. For not to urge that the Designs, we shall employ our Men in, are such, as may be fairly expected to produce far greater Profit, than the overstock'd and beaten Practices, in Use at Present, we will take as our Example, the most common, known Product of *South Carolina* Herself, and That is *Rice*; This is, at least, one Crop with another worth Six Pounds *per* Acre; we will state it, however, but at four Pounds, and out of That allow Deduction of one Pound for Freight Home, and Duty; so the Purchaser receives but Three Pounds neat from each Acre.

Thus, all the Land clear'd, a Man, whose Purchase Money was a Hundred Pounds, for fifty Acres, must receive a Hundred, and fifty Pound *per Annum* for ever, as the Profit of it; but we are not desirous of laying more weight than the Reader, on the Exactness of such Calculations; A Thousand Accidents, not easily foreseen, will still vary these Events, sometimes for the better, sometimes for the Worse; we leave Peoples Expectation to be determin'd by their Reason, tho' even Men of Diffidence will we think be asham'd to disallow a Computation so low, as *Three Pounds per Acre*, from such Land in such a Climate.

But it may be objected that we compute on a Supposition of all the Land clear'd, and improv'd by Cultivation, whereas it may be some Years before the Woods, which over-run it, are Fell'd, and the Earth fit for Sowing; 'Tis true, to clear all the Land will require some Time, But while That is doing we make all our *Potash* before-mention'd, of the waste Wood cut down, to clear the Land, and the Profit from an Acre that way, will be so much greater, than from any yearly Crop, that Purchasers may reasonably expect as large gain the very first Year, from a few Acres only, as afterwards from all their Land, clear'd and cultivated.

A word or two, to explain this Assertion, which may look like a Mystery, and we shall draw to a Conclusion.

When Workmen have nothing to do, but fell Great Trees cross one another, and as soon as dry, set Fire to them, that they may be burnt to Ashes, tis demonstrable beyond all Dispute, that Three Men so employ'd, in Twelve Months constant Work, must cut down more Wood than can grow on Twelve Acres.

If therefore we state it but at Twelve Acres, it is a Rate of computing which can admit of no reasonable Contradiction; And to shew how much *Potash* this will yield, it is plain from Experience and any Reader who doubts, may examine it at his Pleasure for the Charge of a Faggot, That the Weight of any good Wood Ashes amounts to about a Sixteenth of the Wood, they are burnt from; and the Weight of the *Potash*, which will be produc'd from those Ashes, is from a Sixth, to an Eighth of the Weight of the Ashes; But allowing at large, for loss, waste and Accidents, call the Sixteenth a *Twentieth*, and the Sixth a *Tenth* only.

For Quantity of Wood, say there grows on an Acre, so cover'd with huge Timber Trees, but four Hundred Tun; we have often much more (Bark, Timber, and Brushwood) on an Acre in *England*; It is therefore an unexceptionable Computation for *America*, where the date of the Woods, instead of *Years*, must be reckoned by Ages. Then the Wood of an Acre yields two Tun of *Potash*, and the whole Years Labour of Three Men employ'd in cutting down, and burning on Twelve Acres, and boiling and managing the Ashes, will produce 24 Tun of *Potash*, which being a Commodity of Universal Consumption, cannot easily over stock Markets, at least not from far greater Quantities of Wood Land, than we are here talking of.

The general Price of such *Potash*, being the Richest, and Best, is from Forty to Sixty Pounds Sterling *per Tun*, but we will reduce it to Twenty, for Arguments Sake, tho' such a Fall is improbable for such a Commodity, (Some of our *own English Ashes*, which have not a *4th* Part good *Potash*, yielding that Price or more) The 24 Tun will then sell for four Hundred, and Eighty Pounds; If out of this Sum we allow for payment of Freight, and Custom House Duties, *&c.* at the most extravagant Reckoning, we may deduct on that Score one Hundred and Eighty pounds, and then out of the remaining Three Hundred, *One Hundred and fifty Pounds* will be due to the Purchaser in *England*, as the first Years clear *Profit* of his *Hundred Pound Venture*, and That Profit will be every Year growing greater, and greater.

We repeat here once again, that we wou'd not impose the punctual Exactness of such Calculations, as a Matter of Infallibility; The utmost, Men can do in these Cases, is fairly to lay down Probabilities, and That we have done undeniably, notwithstanding the Giant-like size of the Benefit; and we shou'd perhaps far more Surprize, if we varied the Subject, and computed on some other of our Intentions: A Man wou'd make but a very indifferent Use of his Caution, who shou'd neglect an uncommon Advantage, without some better Reason against it, than that the Prospect of Profit was *too Great to be credited*; But be that as it will, Here is Room enough for Profit, let Men reduce it, as they please, nor indeed is Profit, how Greatsoever, the only Motive to Men of Noble Minds; There is in an Attempt of this Nature, something *more* to recommend it, to all those, who take a Pleasure in Things publick Spirited, and Useful to Posterity.

If then what we *have said* is not sufficient Encouragement, whatever we *can say*, will be said to no Purpose, so we only shall add our most earnest Entreaty, that every Reader would narrowly *scan* both the Facts, and the Reasonings here offer'd, and let it be done with the sharpest Attention, and Severity of his Judgment; for we are justly convinc'd, that They, who examine them most, will most firmly believe them.

POSTSCRIPT.

THO' all, that I think can possibly be expected by a reasonable Reader, has been said in the short Tract foregoing, I find my self advis'd to add a Word, or two by way of Postscript, for Satisfaction of some, who may be apt to object, that *tho' the Lands, which are bought, will be more than an Equivalent for the Money Subscrib'd, when those Lands shall be settled, and planted, yet as they are of no such Value in their present Condition, and as the Subscribers should have all possible Security, that the Settlement shall really be made, as propos'd, they may therefore expect, that over and above the Assignment of the Lands, the Money they subscribe, shou'd, instead of being paid into my Hands, be deposited in those of Trustees, for the Uses intended.*

Tho' I cannot but hope, that such kind of Suspicions will never disturb any Person, to whom I am known, yet I thought it but reasonable to *State* the Objection, and *Answer* it, for the Sakes of such Readers, who, being equally Strangers to my Person, and Character, may justly enough, entertain the Distrusts, which are common, and allowable in Matters of Money, and Bargainings.

It will be granted, that it signifies little into whose Hands the

Money is paid, if it is but apply'd to the Purpose intended; and as I neither expect, nor Desire the Subscription of any, but such, who, by weighing the Design, are fully convinc'd, that it is *well founded*, and *profitable*, so it follows, as a necessary Consequence, that *all such* must think their Money best placed in his Hands, whose Profit, Honour, and Success must depend upon That of the Undertaking, and who may therefore be naturally suppos'd more careful, and diligent than others wou'd be, in the Application of the Money, *because always most interested in the Effect of that Application.*

This Reason is so good, that it might alone be sufficient, if there was not another as considerable, which arises from the following Reflection.

Where Trustees are to act in Matters of Care, Form, or Equity, it must be confess'd, they are not only useful, but necessary; But when they are trusted, as in our Case they would be, with a Deposite of Money, and a Power to see it apply'd to a Purpose, in which they are no otherwise concern'd, than as Adventurers among others, (to say nothing of the Impossibility to chuse such, as would be equally agreeable to all) the Temptations are many, and but too well known, which may make it their Interest to find means of Cavil under plausible Pretences for delaying the Business, and Detainment of the Money, as long as the Managers shall see it convenient for their private Advantages.

A wise Man will therefore very easily discern, and approve of my Reasons for not dividing the Power of the *Money*, from the Power of the *Management*, since on this only Rock might be split a more promising Adventure, than was ever undertaken.

If I did not believe, that every Body's Experience can furnish him with Instances enough, in the daily Destructions of well laid Designs, through the idle Disputes, and Disagreements of those, who are carrying them on, it were easy to illustrate the Fact by a thousand Examples.

But, as none, I presume, will deny a known Truth, I will Instance but *One*, which is the fitter for my Purpose, because it is taken, not only from a Parallel Case, but was acted in the very next Country to that, which is the Scene of our Settlement.

The first Attempts, which were made for the settling an *English* Plantation in *Virginia*, were carried on by the private Subscriptions of Gentlemen and others, who thought it their Interest by Way of *Security*, to entrust the Disposal of their Money, to certain Men of the best Publick Credit among them, who were chosen Trustees, and transacted all Matters at Home in the Name of the Body. Mean while, the Command of their Colonies was committed to such Great, and Brave Men, as Sir *Walter Raleigh* and others, who went over, and settled the Country, with all the Appearance of a promising good Fortune; but just in the Crisis, when their Houses were Built, Lands prepar'd, and nothing was wanting, but the expected Arrival of Ships with the necessary Supplies of Ammunition, and Provision, they were all *Starv'd to Death*, or cut off by the *Indians* with a shocking Barbarity. For the Gentlemen in *England*, while they shou'd have laid out the Money subscrib'd, and sent over the Supplies abovemention'd, were quarelling with one another, who should make most Advantage, by furnishing such Goods, as were wanted, or helping others to do it; In which, and the like kind of Follies, they wasted sometimes two, three, or more Years, till their poor starving Colonies fell a Sacrifice to their Inhumanity and Avarice.

Nor was this Game play'd but once, and then mended; on the Contrary, from the Reign of Queen *Elizabeth*, to that of King *Charles* the First, they repeated the Extravagance in numberless Trials, and lost six, or seven different Colonies, not to mention the Money, they had so warily ventur'd, into the Bargain, by no other Error, or Miscarriage, than that the Disposal of their *Stock* did not lie in the same Hands, which had the Management of their *Authority*; and this was so visible a Truth, that K. *Charles* abovemention'd, as a Punishment of their Indiscretion, depriv'd them of their *Charter*; and ever after that, the Purse, and the Power being join'd, as they ought, *Virginia* throve apace, till it grew the most flourishing, and mighty of all our Plantations in *America*.

This remarkable Instance ought to serve, as a Warning to all, who embark in these noble Designs, not to *run into* Losses by mistaken Endeavours, and ill-guided Cautions to *avoid* them; The

Reader may apply the Advice, as he pleases, But we would have none concern'd with us, whose establish'd Opinion of the Nature of this Undertaking does not set him above all mean, and unnecessary Jealousies.

R. Mountgomry.

The Subscription Book will be open'd at the *Carolina* Coffee-House in *Birchin-Lane* near the *Royal-Exchange*, on *Thursday* the First Day of *August* next, and Attendance will be given from 9 to 12, and from 3 to 6 Daily.

Finis.

A Description of

the *Golden Islands*, &c.

A

DESCRIPTION

OF THE

Golden Iſlands,

With an Account of the Undertaking now on Foot for making a Settlement there :

EXPLAINING,

1ſt, The Nature of that Deſign, in general

2dly, The Meaſures already taken : And,

3dly, Thoſe intended to be taken hereafter.

LONDON:

Printed and ſold by *J. Morphew* near *Sta-
tioners-Hall.* 1720. Price Six-pence.

A Description of
the *Golden Islands, &c.*

HE Gentlemen, who manage this Undertaking, are indifferent what Opinion the Generality of Mankind may have of it. But, being desirous to stand right in the Eye of the Judicious, they publish these few Sheets to distinguish themselves from that shadowy Tribe of Nothings, now lately deceas'd, and to demonstrate with what Reason they depend on due Protection and Encouragement.

It gives them no Pain to be number'd among *Bubbles*; though, on Purpose to prevent it, they delay'd their Appearance till now, when nothing wou'd chuse to appear, that cou'd not depend on its Stability. They never proposed to support their Undertaking by the feeble Arts of the Alley, having establish'd it on so solid and lasting a Foundation, that they have nothing to hope or fear, from the Rise and Fall of Opinions.

There are but two safe Bottoms (in Designs of this Nature) on which Men may build Expectations of Profit. One of these is *Land*; the other *Trade:* If either of them, separate, is an unquestionable Foundation: Nothing sure can be objected against Both join'd together. And such is the Security and Ground-work of this Undertaking.

Carolina is well known, as to Temperature of Climate, Richness of Lands, and Commodiousness of Living, to be the finest *English* Plantation in *America*. But as to certain Disputes and Uneasinesses within themselves, they have been remarkably *unhappy*; and were so weakened, by Effect of their Animosities, that the late *Indian* War broke in upon the Settlements, at a Time, when they were altogether unable to defend themselves; and therefore made united Application, for Assistance, to the Lords Proprietors; who hold that Province, under Right of a Charter from King *Charles* the Second, to them, and their Heirs and Assigns for ever.

The Lords Proprietors, commiserating the Distresses of their Colony, and desirous to strengthen and assist them, as much as possible, did, in the Year 1717, make the following Grant to Sir *Robert Montgomerie*.

Abstract of the Grant.

The under-written *Palatine*, and Lords Proprietors of the Province of *Carolina*, do, on the Considerations herein after mention'd, grant, sell, alien, release, and confirm to Sir *Robert Montgomerie*, Baronet, his Heirs and Assigns for ever, all that Tract of Land which lies between the Rivers *Allatamaha* and *Savanna*, together with the Islands, Ports, Harbours, Bays and Rivers, on that Part of the Coast which lies between the Mouths of the said two Rivers to the Seaward; and moreover all Veins, Mines, and Quarries of Gold and Silver, and all other whatever, be they of Stones, Metals, or any other Things found, or to be found within that Tract of Land, and the Limits aforesaid; with Liberty over and above to make Settlements *on the South-Side* of *Allatahama River*, which Tract of Land the said under-written Lords do erect into a distinct Province, with proper Jurisdictions, Privileges, Prerogatives and Franchises, independent of, and not Subject to the Laws of *South Carolina*, to be holden of the said Lords, by Sir *Robert*, his Heirs and Assigns for ever, under the Name and Title of the *Margravate* of *Azilia*; at and under the yearly Quit-rent of one Penny Sterling *per* Acre, or its Value in Goods or Merchandize, as the Land shall be occupied, taken up, or run out; payable yearly to the Lords Proprietors Officers at *Charles Town*, but such Payment not to commence, till three Years after Arrival of the first Ships there, which shall be sent over to begin the Settlement: Over and above which Penny *per* Acre, Sir *Robert*, his Heirs and Assigns, shall also yield and pay to the Lords Proprietors One fourth Part of all Gold or Silver Oar, besides the *Quota* reserved to the Crown, out of the said Royal Minerals. Distinct Courts of Judicature to be erected, and such Laws enacted within the *Margravate*, by and with the Advice, Assent, and Approbation of the Freemen thereof in Publick Assembly, as shall be most conducive to the Utility of the said *Margravate*, and, as near as may be conveniently, agreeable to the Laws and Customs of *England*; but so, as such Laws do not extend to lay Duties or Custom, or other Obstruction, upon the Navigation of either of the said Rivers, by any Inhabitant of *South* or *North Carolina*, or their free Commerce and Trade with the *Indian* Nations, either within, or to the Southward of the *Margravate*; Sir *Robert* consenting, that the same Duty shall be charg'd on Skins within the *Margravate*, which, at this Time, stands charg'd on such Skins in *South Carolina*, and appropriated to the Maintenance of the Clergy there, so long as that Duty is continued in *South Carolina*, but the said Duty shall not be encreas'd in *Azilia*, tho' the Assembly of *South Carolina* shou'd think fit to encrease it there; nor shall it longer continue to be paid, than while it shall remain appropriated, as at present, to the Maintenance of the Clergy only. In Consideration of all which Powers, Rights, Privileges, Prerogatives and Franchises, Sir *Robert* shall transport, at his own Expence, a considerable Number of Families, with all Necessaries for making a new Settlement, &c.

Carteret, Palatine.
Ja. Bertie, for the Duke of *Beaufort*.
F. Skipwith, for the Lord *Craven*.
M. Ashley.
John Colliton, &c.

What Approbation the Design of settling this new *Margravate* met with, as well in Council as at the Board of Lords Commissioners for Trade and Plantations, and from his Majesty's Attorney General, may be seen by the Report, a Copy whereof follows:

To the King's most excellent Majesty.

May it please your Majesty,

In humble Obedience to your Majesty's Commands signified to me by the Duke of *Roxburgh*, I have considered the annex'd Petition of Sir *Robert Montgomerie*, Baronet, setting forth, that he being duly entitled, by the Lords Proprietors of your Majesty's Province of *Carolina* in *America*, to a Tract of Land within their Limits, to the Southward, near the *Spanish* Part of *Florida*, to which Tract they have given the Name of *Azilia*; he the said Petitioner does design to transport and settle there, a considerable Body of your Majesty's Subjects. Which Design has already been approv'd, in a Report on that Occasion made, to your Majesty, by your Board of Commissioners for Trade and Plantations, as what may cause Encrease of Navigation, and become a Strength to all your Majesty's Colonies on the northern Continent of *America*, and most especially to *Carolina*, much oppress'd and weakened by an *Indian* War. But, by Reason of such War, the Petitioner having found it necessary to be at Expence, beyond his Expectation, does most humbly presume to represent to your Majesty, That it appears on Record, that when *Virginia* was first planted by the *English*, and oppress'd by Savage Enemies, as *Carolina* is at present, your Majesty's Predecessor King *James* the First, of happy Memory, then reigning, did, in the Year 1612, out of his Royal Bounty, and a Princely Regard to the Welfare of his Subjects, grant Licence for a Lottery, in Aid of the said Settlement, to be publickly drawn in the City of *London*. The Profits of which Lottery were to be apply'd by the Grantees for Support of the then new Plantation of *Virginia*. Encourag'd by the Precedent, and humbly conceiving, that the Act concerning Lotteries, as it was made by an *English* Parliament, long before the happy Union of the two Kingdoms, does not extend to your Majesty's Dominion of *North Britain*, The Petitioner therefore most humbly Prays your Majesty, That your Majesty taking into your Royal Consideration the general Usefulness of the Petitioner's Design, will be graciously pleas'd to grant to him the said Petitioner, and his Assigns, your Royal Licence for proposing, establishing, and causing to be drawn (within twelve Months from and after the Date of the said Licence) a Lottery in your Majesty's City of *Edinburgh*, or in any of the Royal Boroughs of *North Britain*, to be drawn openly, and in the usual and most publick

Manner, with, and under the Inspection of the Magistrates of that City or Borough, wherein it shall be drawn, who shall be satisfied for their Care, Trouble, and Inspection by the Petitioner, or his Assigns, as may be agreed betwixt them; and that the Petitioner, or his Assigns, may cause to be prepar'd and deliver'd out, by some Bank or Society of sufficient Credit, One hundred thousand Tickets, at the Rate or Price of forty Shillings *per* Ticket; The Money to be kept in Trust by the said Bank or Society, and paid out on Demand, to the Fortunate, that is to say, to those, whose Tickets, in the Chance of Drawing, shall entitle them to Prizes, the highest Prize being Ten thousand Pounds, and the rest, at the Discretion of the Petitioner, or his Assigns; provided always, that the general Proportion of Blanks to Prizes shall not be more, than Four to One, and that the Amount of Prizes, in the whole, shall be equal to the full Sum, which shall arise by Sale of the said Tickets, at the said Rate of forty Shillings for each; only a Deduction shall be made of a Sum, not exceeding fifteen *per Cent.* on every of the said Payments of Prizes, which Sum, so deducted, shall be paid, and allowed to the Petitioner, or his Assigns; to be apply'd in Discharge of Expences, and supporting the Settlement abovemention'd.

And I do most humbly certify your Majesty, that the Petitioner has produc'd to me certain Indentures of Lease, and Release, bearing Date respectively, the eighteenth and nineteenth Days of *June*, in the third Year of your Majesty's Reign and mention'd to be made between his Excellency, *John* Lord *Carteret*, Palatine, the Honourable *James Bertie*, and the Honourable *Doddington Grevill* Esquires, as Guardians, and Trustees to *Henry* Duke of *Beaufort*, Sir *Fulwar Skipwith*, as Guardian and Trustee to *William* Lord *Craven*, the Honourable *Maurice Ashley*, Esquire, Sir *John Colliton*, Baronet, *John Danson*, Esquire, and the rest of the true and absolute Lords Proprietors of the Province of *Carolina* in *America*, of the one Part, and your Petitioner, Sir *Robert Montgomerie*, of the other Part; and which appear to have been duly executed by the said Lord *Carteret*, Palatine, *James Bertie*, Sir *Fulwar Skipwith*, *Maurice Ashley*, and Sir *John Colliton*, whereby the said Lords Proprietors, in Consideration of the great Expence, the said Sir *Robert* is to be at, in transporting a considerable Number of Families, and making new Settlements in the aforesaid Province of *Carolina*, and other good Considerations therein mention'd, have granted and conveyed unto your said Petitioner, Sir *Robert Montgomerie*, his Heirs and Assigns, a Tract of Land, which lies between the Rivers *Allatamaha* and *Savanna*, together with the Islands, Ports, Harbours, Bays, and Rivers, on that Part of the Coast which lies between the Mouths of the said Rivers to the Seaward, with every of their Appurtenances; And in, and by the said Indenture of Release, your said Petitioner Sir *Robert Montgomerie* hath covenanted with the said Lords Proprietors, that he wou'd immediately transport, at his own proper Costs and Charges, a considerable Number of Families, with all necessaries for making a new Settlement into the said Province or *Margravate* of *Azilia*. And I do further certify your Majesty, that your Petitioner, Sir *Robert*, by his Affidavit hereunto annex'd, hath sworn, that he doth really, and *bona fide*, design to make such Transportation, and Settlement as aforesaid; And I find, that the Lords Commissioners of Trade and Plantations by their Report (which is also hereunto annex'd) have represented to your Majesty, that the propos'd Settlement wou'd be of Advantage to *Carolina*, and might defend the Plantations on that Continent against the Incursions of the *Indians*. I have also considered the Act pass'd in the tenth and eleventh of his late Majesty King *William* the *Third*, intituled, *An Act for suppressing of Lotteries*, and am humbly of Opinion, that the same does not extend to *Scotland*, and by Consequence, will be no Objection in Point of Law, to your Majesty's granting your Royal Licence to the Petitioner, for a Lottery in the City of *Edinburgh*, or in some of your Royal Boroughs of *North Britain*, there not being, as appears to me, any Law in Force in that Part of great *Britain* against the same. On all which Considerations, I am humbly of Opinion, that your Majesty may lawfully gratify the Petitioner, in his Request, if your Majesty shall be so graciously pleas'd.

All which, &c.

N. *Lechmere* 15 *Nov.*

It may, in some Measure, be gathered from the foregoing Report, what Assistance, and Encouragement the Proprietors have Reason to hope for from the Government; And the Profits of the Lottery, as above-petition'd for, will, as soon as procured, be apply'd by the Trustees, for the common Benefit of the Settlement, and Advantage of the whole Body of Proprietors.

The Reader is to take notice, that the *Golden Islands* are a Part of the *Margravate* of *Azilia*, lying four or five Miles from the main Continent, and containing about one Hundred thousand Acres of fine rich Land, besides Sand Hills and Marshes; of which Hundred thousand Acres, Sixty thousand are rich Plain clear'd Ground, ready prepared for the Plow, and the rest close Thickets, and Woodland.

It is for Conveniency of this ready clear'd Land, and certain other Advantages to be found upon the Islands, that the Settlements are begun there; But they will, in a little Time, be extended to the Main-land, and the Present Proprietors will then have Preference to all other Persons, as the Fund comes to be enlarged for that Purpose.

The *Golden Islands* are four; Their Names are St. *Symon, Sapella,* or *Sapola, Santa Catarina,* and *Ogeche,* now called *Montgomerie;* They have excellent Harbours, are very finely water'd, abound with great Plenty of wild Deer, Fish, and Fowl; have high, healthy, fruitful Land, and lie within a Days rowing of the *English* Habitations in *South Carolina;* And now lately, the Government have appointed an Independent Company of one hundred fourteen Men, to go over, and keep Garrison to the Southward, between these Islands, and the *Spaniards* and *Indians.*

They took the Name of *Golden Islands* from the *Spaniards,* who made many fruitless Expeditions into these Parts of *Florida,* in search of Gold, and Silver Mines, excited by a View of the prodigious Quantities, which their Countrymen brought out of *Peru,* about that Time.

Sir *Robert Montgomerie* by Indenture, the third of *May* last, made Sale of the *Golden Islands* above-described, in one thousand Allotments, each Allotment containing one hundred Acres, at twenty Shillings *per* Acre, twenty-five *per Cent.* only to be called in, for beginning the Settlement; he receiv'd not any of this Purchase Money, but subjected it all to be call'd in, and apply'd from Time to Time, as shall be necessary, in Improvement of the said hundred thousand Acres of Land, by Trustees, in the said Indenture nam'd, for the common Benefit of all, and every the Proprietors; their Executors Administrators and Assigns; so that they buy not only the *Land,* but the *Profits* of it for ever.

And in Consideration of his Conveyance of all these Lands and their Benefits, he reserv'd only a Right to two hundred of the said Allotments exempted from the first Payment of twenty-five Pounds *per Cent.* but subject to all further Calls, as the Rest of the Proprietors.

The Trustees, by the Indenture, are to make a Dividend of Profits, within eighteen Months from the third of *May* last, or the Proprietors have Power to appoint, from among themselves, an equal Number, to act for them.

They account for all Sums, call'd in, and divide Returns of Profit, in Proportion to the Claims; And the Claims are distinguish'd by certain Notes of Allotment, sign'd by Sir *Robert Montgomerie*, and running all to *Bearer*.

Note, the Title to the Lands was not meant to be conveyed by these Notes of Allotment, but was done in due Form of Law, by the general Indenture, to which the said Notes do therefore referr, and the Indenture to the Notes; for it had been tedious, if not impracticable, to have recited over and over, so many hundred Names, within the Compass of an Indenture.

This being the Nature and general Foundation of the Design, it remains to describe the Country, where the Settlement is to be made, and from the Products whereof, the Proprietors are to expect their Profits.

Azilia contains, in breadth, about one hundred *English* Miles, being all the Land, that lies between the two great Rivers, *Allatamaha* and *Savanna*. It's length from the Sea-Coast, on the East, to the Mountains on the West, is three hundred and twenty Miles, or upward; It is all a Plain Tract of Land, well water'd, with noble Rivers, stor'd with many useful Minerals, and cover'd in almost every Part, like one continued Forest, with Oak, Cedar, Cypress, Mulberry-Trees, Walnuts, Pines, and infinite Variety of most excellent Timber; abounding with large Herds of Deer, wild Buffalo's, and most kind of Beasts, Birds, and Sea and River Fish, to an incredible Degree of Plenty.

But the best, and most authentick Account, which can be given of this Country, may be gathered from the following Letter, which was written by Colonel *John Barnwell*, of *Carolina*, who is now in *London*, to Sir *Robert Montgomerie*.

SIR,

The *English* on our Side the Ocean, heard with Pleasure and Expectation, of your worthy Design of planting *Azilia*, and it gives me particular Satisfaction to find, on my late Arrival from *Carolina*, that you are pursuing it with Vigour.

Every Thing that the *French* have proposed to themselves, by their new Colonies in *Missisippi*, may, with greater Ease and Conveniency, be produced to the *English*, out of your Settlement; for all Ships bound from *France* to *Missisippi*, must go almost round *Cuba*, pass by *Hispaniola*, and very near *Jamaica*, and return through the Gulph of *Florida*; which Navigation all, who are acquainted with, know to be both tedious and dangerous; whereas the direct Passage to *Azilia* is as easy, short, and safe, as a Voyage to *Virginia*.

We may be furnished from *Azilia* with many Commodities, that are now brought from the Coasts of the *Mediterranean*, and other Countries, in, or near the same Latitude; for by Trials, which have been made there, by myself, and my Neighbours, *Azilia* produces *Rice, Silk, Indigo, Cochinele, Masts for Ships, Cedar, Myrtle Wax, Walnut-Tree, Dying Woods*, and great *Timber, Pitch, Tar, Turpentine, Rozen, Hemp, Flax, Pot-Ashes*, and *Cotton*; and had we *Olive-Trees* and *Almonds*, as we have *Oranges, Pomgranates, Peaches, Figs, Apples*, and *Pears*, they would, undoubtedly, do as well: And it is very reasonable to believe many more *Fruits* and *Drugs*, growing in *Persia*, in *India*, about *Lahore*, in *China*, and in *Japan*, Places lying in the same Climate, would thrive there, to the great Advantage of the *British* Nation, were proper Methods taken to procure the same.

You will never have Occasion to provide Fodder for black Cattle, Horses, or Hogs; the Winter being so mild, that in few Years they will encrease prodigiously, as they have done in *Cuba* and *Hispaniola*, where they kill them only for their Hides and Tallow; as is also at this Time practised in those Parts of *Carolina* bordering on your Settlement.

As for the *Indian Trade*, which takes off a great Quantity of our Woollen Manufacture, in Exchange for Buck-Skins, and other valuable Furs and Peltery, all this Trade must, of Necessity, center with *you*, as not only being nearer to the *Indians*, who deal most, but also having Water-Carriage to within a little of their Towns. These Advantages will soon oblige all our *Indian Traders*, to take up their Residence in your Settlements.

I must not omit hinting to you the Advantage, that might accrue by a well regulated Commerce with the *Spaniards* of St. *Augustine*, St. *Joseph*, and *Pansecola*, so very near your Islands, that most of their Money may pass through, or center there. *Carolina*, at greater Distance, makes considerable Profit by this Traffick.

You may, in few Years, supply the West *Indian* Islands with *Lumber* and *Provisions*, cheaper than all the rest of our Colonies on the Main of *America*, lying several hundred Leagues nearer to them, and being never liable to have your Harbours or Rivers frozen up, but approachable by Shipping, at all Times of the Year, which can't be done at *New England*, *New York*, or *Pensilvania*.

In Case of War with *France* or *Spain*, as you are seated just at the Mouth of the Gulph of *Florida*, a few Ships cruising there, would make it difficult for the *Plate-Fleet*, or the trading Vessels of either of those Nations, passing through that Gulph (which they must always do) to avoid being taken, between your selves on one Side, and the *Bahama Islands* on the other.

As to the four Islands which you have assign'd to the Purchasers, who are concern'd in your Settlement, they are called St. *Symon*, *Sapella*, St. *Catarina*, and *Ogeche*; to which last, before I came thence, I left the Name of *Mountgomery*. You have given them a general Denomination, which, I think, they may well deserve, of the *Golden Islands*; for as to convenient Pasture, pleasant Situation, profitable fishing and fowling, they surpass any Thing of that kind in all *Carolina*. They have all a Number of Sand-Hills, or Downs, on the Sea-Side, and the Way between these Sand-Hills and the Sea, is so plain and smooth, that it is a very great Pleasure to travel upon it. Here and there run in among these Sand-Hills, small Creeks of the Sea, replenish'd with great Quantity of several Sorts of Fish, which are easily taken, and great Flocks of wild Fowl. There are very good *Harbours* among these Islands.

They are almost *clear* of *Wood*, and by their Distance from the Continent, secured against any insult of the *Indians*. The four Islands above-named, contain above threescore thousand Acres of good Land, besides the Downs, very fit for Corn and Pasturage, and, as I said, almost *void* of *Woods*, so that it is ready, without Labour, for the *Plow*.

In the four or five other Islands, belonging to these, there are above twenty-six thousand Acres more, very good Soil, and full of close Thickets and Woods, very proper for *Ship-building*.

This being an exact Description of your *Golden Islands*, it is easy to infer, how fit they are for the Place of your Settlement. You may first stock them with Cattle, from the main Land of *Carolina*, and then, they will prove an inexhaustible Source of Provision, better than ten Times that Quantity of Land on the Main, the Stocks being kept entire, secure from Beasts of Prey, and without Possibility of Mixture.

I had Thoughts of informing you of several other Matters of Consequence, not here enumerated, but I have already exceeded the Bounds of a Letter; I shall therefore only add, that I shall be ready to vouch the Truth of whatever I have herein advanced, whenever you shall find it necessary to undeceive any Person, who may question it; wishing you Success in an Undertaking, which, I am sensible, is so much to the Advantage of his Majesty, and his Dominions, and to the Welfare of your Neighbours in *Carolina*, (who, I am well assured, will do all they can to assist and support your laudable Undertaking.) I conclude, with very great Respect,

Your Most Obedient Servant,

John Barnwell.

P. S. I am generally
   once a Day at the
   Carolina Coffee-
   house in *Birchin-*
   lane.

From the Description contain'd in this Letter, and what has been said in the foregoing Pages, may be easily inferr'd the Sufficiency of the Ground-work: It remains now to say something concerning the design'd Method of proceeding, to make the Best of these Advantages.

The Shipping lately bought by the Trustees, for the Service of this Undertaking, as also the Preparations they have for some Weeks been making, of Arms, Ammunition, and other necessary Stores of all Kinds, are in order, forthwith, to Form the first Settlement, and raise a Fort on the Island *Santa Catarina*, for Defence of themselves, and all After-comers; for tho' there is no probable Appearance of Danger, they think it but prudent to be provided against it. But this they do with a considerable Difference from what has usually been practis'd in Cases of like Nature. For instead of maintaining an idle Garrison of Soldiers, at a fruitless Expence to the Proprietors, they form all the Labouring-Men they send over, to be capable, by good Discipline, of defending themselves, on all Occasions; to which End they divide them into regular Companies, and cloath them handsomly and uniformly, in blue Cloth, fac'd with White, and arm them with *Fuzee's*, with *Bayonets*, *&c.* And they are exercis'd and commanded in their Military Services, by the very same Officers, who are Directors of their Labour in the common Employments they will be set about: So that to *fight* is their extraordinary, and to *work* their ordinary Occupation.

The following Extract, from their Minute-Book, will better explain the Nature of the Agreements they make with the Men, whom they take into their Service.

At a Meeting of the Trustees for planting and improving the Golden Islands, *to the South of* Port-Royal *in* Carolina, *at their Office in* Lothbury, *on Tuesday the* 13*th of* September, 1720.

Resolved that all *Husbandmen* and *Labourers* who are sent over, shall enter into Articles to work, as Covenant-Servants, in tilling the Ground, or on any other Employment which may be appointed them, for the Space of five Years from their Arrival in the Islands, during which Time they shall also be subject to a regular Discipline, and made capable, by frequent Exercise, to handle Arms in a soldierly Manner, and defend themselves well upon Occasion.

That Cloaths, Provision, Bedding, and other necessaries shall be furnish'd them, at the Expence of the Proprietors; their Cloathing consisting of the following Particulars, a Coat, a Wastcoat, two Pair of Breeches, a Frock, four Shirts, four Neck-cloths, two Pair of Shoes, a Pair of Buckles, two Pair of Stockings, a Hat: Besides all which, they shall receive Pay, after the Rate of six Pence *per* Day *English* Money, to be paid, either in the *Islands*, or to their proper Attorney in *London*.

That they shall also be furnish'd with proper Arms for their Defence, at the Expence of the Proprietors.

That, after Expiration of five Years (being the usual Term of Service in those Countries) each Husbandman or Labourer, shall have a House, and ten Acres of Land, all ready clear'd for the Plow, and consequently of much more Value, than such Land as is usually assign'd in the Plantations; to have and to hold the said House and Lands for three Lives, being furnish'd for the first Year, with Stock, and all necessary Materials, at the Charge of the Proprietors; and allowing only to the said Proprietors a fifth Part in Kind of the Product of the said Lands, *per* Acre.

Resolved, That for the Encouragement of all *Handicraft Tradesmen* of good Character, they shall be appointed *Overseers*, be cloath'd, arm'd and provided for, as the rest, and receive Pay over and above, after the Rate of *eighteen Pence* per *Day, English* Money, to be paid either *there*, or in *London*.

That, after Expiration of the five Years, each such *Handicraft Tradesman*, or *Overseer*, shall have a House; and twenty Acres of clear'd Land for three Lives, on the same Conditions, as above resolv'd for the Parcels of ten Acres.

T. Darling, Secretary.

It may be proper to observe, that the Companies are to consist but of five and twenty Men; One of whom is a Gentleman, to command, and supervise the whole Company: Four are *Handicraft Tradesmen*, such as *Smiths, Carpenters, &c.* who are also to act as under Officers and Overseers: And the other twenty are stout labouring Men, so that each Overseer has five working Men immediately under his Care; and All, together, are accountable to the Supervisor of the Company; As the Supervisors to the President, or Chief Director of the Colony.

The whole Scheme may be reduc'd to this—The Men, who are sent over, going as Covenant-Servants, work five Years, for the Benefit of the Proprietors. In all which Time, whatever the Product of their Labour will sell for, more than the Charge of their Maintenance, is clear Profit to the Undertakers: After the Expiration of their Term of Years, each Man has Claim to a stated Parcel of ready-clear'd Land, allowing a fifth Part in Kind, of their yearly

Product, *per* Acre. So, from Time to Time, supplying the Place of old Servants, with new ones, out of *England*, or from the Plantations, the *Old*, instead of *Servants*, will become *Tenants* to the Proprietors. And thus, the Profits of this Colony, will not only be settled for ever, but encreasing, every Year, upon a solid Establishment.

Over and above all which, a very large and certain Gain must arise from the Inclination, which Gentlemen, out of the neighb'ring Plantations, will find, to remove themselves and their Families, to so rich and fine a Soil, all ready-clear'd, and under Protection of a Fort, so well defended. Every Body knows the Advantage of *clear'd* Land, in the Plantations; one Man's Labour on such Ground, being worth ten, in other Places.

To this End the Trustees have resolv'd to grant Estates, on such clear'd Land, to any Gentlemen, who are desirous of settling there, to them and their Heirs for ever; receiving no Purchase-money, or stated Rent for the same, but only one yearly fifth Part, in Kind, of their Product *per* Acre: Each such Gentleman maintaining a proper Number of working Hands, as shall be agreed, in Proportion to the Lands, which shall be assign'd him, and applying the said Lands to whatever Use he thinks fittest.

It is easy to infer, that the Amount of this Profit must be very considerable, in a Climate, where the Produce of Lands is of infinitely more Value, than in *England*; and the Proposition is in general so acceptable, that not only many Gentlemen from the other Colonies, will come readily into it, but several, from our own Country, have now actually resolved to go over, on those Conditions, to settle Plantations for themselves; and are making Preparations accordingly.

For the stronger Inducement to such Gentlemen, and others, to make Settlements on the Proprietors Lands, the Trustees have it under their Consideration, to prevent one considerable Inconveniency, which is almost general, in the Plantations; where few Men, having Stock large enough to maintain Ships, or freight them wholly, with the Product of their own Estates, they are expos'd to the Combination of Factors and Merchants, whose Business is to buy up Goods from the Planter; and who will neither purchase them, but at a Price much below their real Value; nor agree for any other Species of Commodities, than the common Staple of that Colony, which they reside in; and this Want of current Vend for any, but the common Product, is the Chief, if not the only Reason, why we are not supply'd with many very rich and very profitable Commodities, which our Plantations are more fit for, and which they wou'd get much more by producing, than they now gain by the *Tobacco*, which often overstocks the Markets, from *Virginia* and *Maryland*; and the *Sugar*, which does the same, from *Barbadoes*, *Jamaica*, and all the *Leeward* Islands.

For Remedy of all this, it is design'd by the Trustees, in their Settlement of the *Golden Islands*, and of all *Azilia* in general, to fix a stated, known, and unalterable Price, for all Sorts of Commodities, which any Planters shall produce, by Cultivation of the Lands, they agree with them for settling on. And they will establish, from Time to Time, a Fund sufficient to take off the said Products from the Planters Hands, at the known and declared Rates, as fast as the said Planters shall be able to raise them; by which Means two infallible Benefits must arise to both Parties: The *Planters*, when they find, that they are sure of a Market, will apply themselves, with Pleasure and Vigour, to raise Products of different Kinds, and so their Estates will not rival, and run down the Value of each other. And the *Proprietors*, on their Part, becoming the common Buyers, and Exporters of all Goods from their Country, will unite three Considerable Benefits to their Advantage; 1st, The Fifth of all Products, which will be paid them, as a Quit-Rent; 2dly, The Profits of the Merchant, upon buying the other four Parts; And, 3dly, The Gain of Freight, by exporting the said Commodities in Ships of their own Building.

As to the particular Improvements, which are propos'd to be gone upon; it will not be expected, that any Thing of that Nature shou'd be made publick, in this Manner; In general, it is resolv'd by the Trustees, that the most easy, and most certain, are the best to begin with. Many noble Experiments will be made, which may open the Way to great Things hereafter; but the *safest* and most *beaten* Tracks are thought properest, for the first Application.

The Reader can scarce Doubt a considerable Benefit, if he reflects, that little more than a Third of the Hundred thousand Acres is *Wood-land*; above Sixty thousand Acres lying as clear, and as plain, as the finest Pastures in *England*.

And as to this *Wood-land* itself, certain Methods will be taken, to make it of equal Value, if not much more, than the other; to which End proper Persons are sent over, skill'd in making and managing, to the best Advantage, some rich and merchantable Commodities, which none but such thick wooded Countries are fit for.

But, to form a true Judgment, concerning the Value of the Sixty thousand Acres of *ready-clear'd Land*, so commodiously seated, it need only be remember'd, what a Noise has been made about the Thirty thousand Acres of clear'd *French* Lands, in the Island of *St. Christophers*, which were given up by an Article, in the Treaty of *Utrecht*. Every Body knows, that it has been represented to the Parliament, that these Lands might be sold, at the Rate of ten Pound an Acre, and find Plenty of Purchasers, from the neighbouring Plantations: It is easy then to draw Inferences, to the Advantage of twice that Quantity of much richer Land, much better clear'd, and in a better Situation; for the Climate of *Azilia* is not only capable of all the Products of the Other, but also of *Pitch, Tar, Corn, Wine, Oil, Provisions*, and many more such, which the other is not fit for.

This then is a Foundation, which must be acknowledg'd Equal to much higher Expectations than have probably been yet rais'd among the Gentlemen, concern'd in the Undertaking.

It has been objected, that the utmost Extent of the Stock, being but One hundred thousand Pounds, will prove too little, to supply the Expence of so considerable a new Settlement; it is answered, that the Trustees have taken their Measures with so much Caution, as to assure the Proprietors, they will make no new Call, till after a Dividend of Profit, at which Time the Books will be laid open to the strictest Examination, that all Persons, interested, may be convinc'd, that the Money divided, is the neat Proceed of the Trade; and if it then shall be thought properest to encrease the Stock gradually, by Deduction from the Dividends, easy Means may be found to support the Undertaking in its utmost Extent, without Calling in any Part of the hundred Pound, Purchase-Money, upon each Allotment, further than the 25 *l*. already paid by the Proprietors.

The only Reason for publishing any Thing at present concerning this Design, is to vindicate it from Mistakes and Misrepresentations: Which are the natural Consequences of Men's Disappointments; and fall, commonly, without Distinction, on the *Solid* and *Chimerical*.

It has already been demonstrated, in several printed Abstracts, that the Powers, proceeded by, are authoriz'd by Royal Charter, so far as to enable the Proprietors of Allotments, and their Assigns, for ever, to sell and buy Shares, as they think fit, in the Lands, and Profits of these Islands, without incurring any of the Penalties, in the late Act of Parliament, for suppressing Publick Subscriptions, *&c.* detrimental to the Trade, and Benefit of the Kingdom.

It is a Wonder, indeed, how any Doubt, of that Kind, cou'd find Place in Men's Judgment! What most encreases Export and Import, is the most beneficial Trade to the Nation: And nothing does either, in any Degree equal to such a Settlement, as is the Foundation of this Undertaking.

And this, naturally, introduces a remarkable Advantage, with which these Pages shall conclude: Which is, a Privilege, granted by the Crown, for Encouragement of certain rich Products from these Parts: To which End Liberty, Power, and Authority, is given to import, from that Province, *Silk, Wine, Currants, Raisins, Capers, Wax, Almonds, Oil,* and *Olives:* Without paying any Custom, or Duty, for the first seven Years: Any Law, Act, Statute, Prohibition, Matter, or Thing, made, or to be made hereafter, in any wise notwithstanding.

Postscript.

WHEREAS a small Number of Allotments have been kept, on the earnest Request of some Proprietors, for their Friends in the Country, and those Persons have not yet made their Payment, Notice is hereby given, that if they do it not forthwith, the said Allotments will be dispos'd of, at the first Price, to any other Persons, who shall pay in upon them.

Any *Husbandmen, Labourers,* or *Handicraft Tradesmen,* of good Character, may have Proposals for their Encouragement, at the Office for the *Golden Islands;* which is kept *at the Great Yellow Gates,* over-against the *Church* in *Lothbury.*

Finis.

Memorial of
Jean Pierre Purry

MEMORIAL

presented to His Grace
My Lord the DUKE OF NEWCASTLE,
Chamberlain of his Majesty King George, &c.,
and Secretary of State:
upon the present condition
of

CAROLINA,

and the Means of its Amelioration:

BY

JEAN PIERRE PURRY,
of Neufchâtel, Switzerland.

———————

PRIVATELY PRINTED.

———————

AUGUSTA, GEORGIA.
1880.

Memorial of

Jean Pierre Purry

MY LORD: Although the English, who possess Carolina, are fully persuaded that it constitutes one of the richest countries in the world, Jean Pierre Purry of Neufchâtel, Switzerland, —formerly Director General in the service of the India Company in France,—seriously doubts whether they have properly investigated the true cause of its fertility, and the methods by which it may be developed to the greatest possible extent.

Hence the reason why he takes the liberty of memorializing you, my Lord, in the following concise and graphic manner.

I. *The boundless wealth* which might be obtained from Carolina not only on account of the extent of its territory,—which is immense,—and the fertility of its soil,—which is remarkable,—but also by reason of its situation, excellent in many respects.

II. *The facility* with which, without depopulating England,— this country could be peopled with good inhabitants from various nations,—Switzerland, France, Germany, and other countries,— all professing the Protestant religion.

III. Finally, there is perhaps, nothing more *important* to the State, more worthy of public attention, or more likely to enhance the general wealth of England, than the consummation of an enterprize such as this.

In proof of this, it is only necessary for us to observe, in the first place, that it is quite impossible for us to reflect upon the system of our Globe, and its natural productions,—varying with climates and seasons,—without admitting that it is the Sun alone which animates all things and causes them to fructify; since they languish and die or acquire vitality just as this heavenly body withdraws itself from or approaches the earth. For, as all the countries of the world which are not located on the same parallel possess degrees of heat differing the one from the other to a greater or less extent, and as from the Equator to the Poles there is no degree which corresponds exactly with another, it necessarily follows that there must be one which is the best of all. Behold a fixed principle which none can doubt.

Now this principle, upon which depends our whole system, being once well established, it will be very easy to ascertain which one of these degrees of heat and of the temperature of the air is best adapted to evoke abundantly from the earth,—and that without much labor or expense,—everything essential to life. When we consider the fact that the longest days of Summer are twelve hours on the Equator, and twenty-four hours on the Polar Circles, and take the mean of these two extremes,—that is to say counting from the first degree to the half of 66½ degrees, which is 33¼ degrees,—we will find that the best countries of the world ought to be on or about the 33rd degree of Latitude. This is moreover verified by experience; and all the countries of our Globe, as Barbary, Syria, Egypt, Persia, Mogolistan, China, Japan, and, generally speaking, all others are rich and productive only in proportion to their proximity to this degree, unless, indeed, they should here and there be found of sandy, marshy, or rocky character, or of no value, where fruit-bearing plants cannot come to perfection. We must note this carefully.

In accordance with this principle it follows necessarily that Carolina and New Mexico on the Northern side, and Chili and Rio de la Plata on the Southern, are, regarded as a whole, the best countries in America because they are situated on or about the 33rd degree of Latitude. This conclusion cannot be questioned. Even if

we had never heard Spain described, we would never weary in asserting that Andalusia must be the best of her provinces because it
approaches nearest to the 33rd degree. Provence and Languedoc
must be superior to all the other provinces of France because they
are the most southern. For the same reason Sicily and the Kingdom
of Naples ought to be more fertile than the rest of Italy. Thus
might we distinguish between the other countries of the world,
known and unknown. In truth, it is only necessary to affirm that it
is the Sun which causes differences in countries and climates.

The undersigned, Jean Pierre Purry, dares to maintain without
presumption that he believes himself to have been the first who
located the best climate at the 33rd degree of Latitude; and he will
persist in this opinion until he finds some one who will convince
him that he is mistaken in his calculations. While waiting, he re-
quests persons, learned on such subjects, to name to him a single
country in that degree (always supposing that the soil is neither
sandy, nor marshy, nor rocky,) which does not constitute one of
the most fertile regions in the world. He also ventures to assert,
without desiring to give offence to any one, that historians and
geographers have all attributed the change to nature and to a diversity of climate. When they speak to us of the degrees of heat
and cold which characterize each country, when compared with
others, they always base their opinions upon that false principle,
knowing that countries which are situated in the center of the Tor-
rid Zone are the warmest, and that the others differ in heat in proportion as they are nearer to or farther removed from this center.

The same error is observable when we note the conduct of Europeans in the explorations which they have conducted up to the
present time in remote countries. Assuredly they did not know
where the best climate was to be found. The French, for example,
who pride themselves [for what substantial reason I am at a loss to
say] upon having outstripped all other peoples in the knowledge of
Cosmography, have been established for more than a century in
the more northern regions of Canada. They resemble a man who,
having a selection of many good viands on a table amply furnished
and spread before his eyes, should decide, in the exercise of a ridic-

ulous and ill-advised prudence, to choose that which was least attractive. For it is certain that Canada now is, and, because of its situation, always will remain one of the poorest countries in America. The English have been established in Carolina only since about the year 1664; and when before that time they had advanced their settlements as far as Virginia, they found indeed that the country was good, but it does not appear that they then realized, as perchance they do not now comprehend, the reason why. The Dutch, in like manner, did not establish themselves at the Cape of Good Hope until they had voyaged for fifty or sixty years in the East Indies.

But what is most remarkable in this connection is that the Cape of Good Hope, with the exception of the *Terre Natal*,—which is still occupied only by savages,—was the sole place where one could form a desirable settlement for the Great Indies:—one which would serve not only as a store-house and granary, but also as an excellent *entrepot* and place for refitting ships. Notwithstanding all these advantages neither the Spanish, nor the Portugese, nor the English, nor any other peoples desired to form a settlement there until more than one hundred and fifty years had elapsed after the discovery of such an attractive country. To-day however, the Dutch, well recognizing the utility, not to say the absolute necessity of this settlement, declared they do not know how they can, from this time forward, dispense with it.

In all good faith it should be admitted that such mistakes were caused either by a want of knowledge of the nature of climates, or by false ideas entertained on this subject. So true is this, that when they chanced upon a good country one would be justified in asserting that they did so blindly, since they followed routes directly contrary to their plans.

This is very evident from the testimony of Dampier himself,—one of the most famous voyagers of his day. We will see what he thought of the *Terres Australes* and *La Nouvelle Hollande:* "For," says he *, "if I had been asked why, the first time I came on this side, I did not traverse it towards the South, and why I did not

* Dampier. Voyage to *Terres Austral*, volume v., p. 3.

endeavor to extend my voyage to the East of *La Nouvelle Hollande* and of *La Nouvelle Guinée*, I would have answered that I was unwilling to lose more time than was absolutely necessary in the higher latitudes, being fully persuaded that the countries on that side were not so worthy of exploration as the regions nearest to the Equator and more directly under the influence of the Sun." Now nothing can be more false than such a statement. Because, of all *La Nouvelle Hollande* no section can be better than that which lies on the Southern side and which is called *Terre de Nuits:*—the residue being always poorer as it approaches the line; or, to make use of proper terms, as it stretches out under the more direct influence of the Sun. Let us apply this principle to Carolina, and the adjacent countries from the Northern Sea even to the Southern. It certainly embraces, and without exception, the best parts of North America, extending on this same parallel of the 33rd degree of Latitude not less than from five to six hundred leagues. This degree is the par excellence of heat and of temperature, causing a fertility of soil, and contributing to the happiness of all who there inhabit, no matter from what quarter of the world they may have come. All other regions are less desirable in proportion to their remoteness from this degree.

In proceeding it is proper to remark that Carolina, situated in the degree named, has very few mountains,—that it is a land of plains,—of hills,—and of gentle declivities, that the soil is for the most part very rich, requiring only good cultivation at the hands of man, that it abounds in game, deer, and wild bulls, that it is watered by numerous beautiful rivers teeming everywhere with excellent fishes, and that within its limits,—which are narrowest from east to west,—it includes all that vast extent of country which once bore the name of *Florida*, for some time however, called by the French *Louisiana*, and which the English could more appropriately name *Georgia* or *Georgine* in conformity to the two charters granted to the *Concessionaries* in 1664 and 1666 during the reign of Charles II. The propriety of this latter appellation could be easily demonstrated.

It is true that the French have possession of the mouth of the

Mississippi river; but, with the exception of the land adjacent to the mouth of this river and for a distance of some sixty or eighty leagues into the country, the region is very poor. If they should purpose to prevent the English from descending the river and entering the Gulf of Mexico by that route, they, in turn, by virtue of the right of original occupancy, having securely established themselves on that same river in the vicinity of the 33rd degree of Latitude, would not permit the French to ascend higher. It would not be less ridiculous in the French to imagine [and a more chimerical pretension I cannot divine], that all the country belonged to them, than it would be in the Dutch to idly claim all lands situated along the Rhine or the Meuse, upon the pretext that they were the owners of the territory surrounding the mouths of those rivers.

But let us consider the case under the worst possible circumstances. Let us suppose for a moment that the French should be strong enough to prevent the English from descending the river. In that event they could then transport their silks, furs, indigo, and, generally speaking, all their most valuable products, upon mules and horses and in conveyances to their licensed ports, as is the common practice in Persia, in Arabia, and in different countries in the East: whereas, if the French possess only the lower part of the country, which is worth nothing, and are not able to ascend the river and carry on their commerce with the Spaniards of New Mexico and with the natives, the mouth of this river would no longer prove of any utility to them unless indeed, to furnish a spot wherein to bury immense sums as surely as if they had thrown them into the sea. Such truly has been the case, either through ignorance or otherwise, for nearly twenty-five years;—in fact, ever since they have been occupying that locality.

However, to obviate all difficulties and relieve the English of all apprehensions they can have on this score, it is manifestly their duty to people the country, and advance, year by year and little by little, towards the river in order not only to defend themselves, but also, if circumstances rendered it necessary, to attack their enemies. This action becomes all the more important because the wealth and fertility of a country can be developed only by the cultivation of the soil and by the great increase of its population, and because they possess the means of colonizing it far superior to the French by reason of their greater number of vessels, and the proximity to Carolina which exempts them from passing through the dangerous strait of Bahama, and facilitates their return to Europe. Add to all this the ease with which they may, without depopulating England, secure colonies of good Protestants who will prove neither vagabonds nor idlers, [as is the case with the most of those whom the French send to their falsely claimed Louisiana] but rather excellent laborers, the sons of peasants, the majority of them married, each possessing a suitable calling, and specially skilled in the cultivation of the soil. Hence we conclude that the country being well peopled, as it would be in a very short time, one would find himself entirely safe, and free from all apprehension on the score above alluded to.

Never perhaps, have circumstances been more favorable than at the present time for enlisting excellent colonists in Switzerland. How many families are today, in that country, in debt through the misfortunes of the times and the stagnation of trade! How many young men are there who do not know what to do, or upon what matter to bestow their attention, and who have no means of support save the profession of arms! How many are there who refrain from marriage for fear of bringing more unhappy souls into the world, of whom there are already too many! This arises from the fact that the population of Switzerland is too dense, considering the sterility of its soil:—that peace has obtained in Europe for the past twelve or thirteen years:—that there is no longer any demand for cattle, and the peasant can no more find a market for his horses. It is not well that Switzerland should be as thickly populated as it is. Nearly eighteen hundred years agone, the inhabitants of this nation, *en masse*, formed the resolution to burn their dwellings and go in search of another country where they hoped to find habitations pleasanter and more spacious than those which they possessed among their barren mountains.

Moreover, of late years, a pestilence having ravaged some countries in the North, and a report having been circulated in Switzerland that lands would be given to all who would go thither, although the soil was poor, people flocked there from all quarters. But these deluded persons, when they arrived in those parts, finding nothing equal to what they had been led to expect, and knowing not in what direction to look for assistance, were constrained to return in confusion to their own homes.

It happens every day [very much after the fashion of bees when they find themselves overcrowded in their hives] that many young people leave Protestant Switzerland who have, so to speak, no resource other than to go into service in France, Spain, Italy, Savoy, and other Roman Catholic communities in their neighborhood, where most of them change their religion in order to maintain themselves and ameliorate their condition. Thus we see the poor Calvinists of the Palatinate betaking themselves into Hungary,—although there at the mercy of the Turks or of the Jesuits,—not knowing where else to go. Likewise many Protestants remain in France, enduring tyranny and persecution, influenced much less by a just horror of the idolatry which they there behold and frequently have the misfortune to commit, than by the helping hand which, in drawing them into such a dangerous snare, at the same time offers a sure and honest retreat where they may, by cultivating their own lands, guard themselves against poverty, and dispense with the charity of their brethren. So much may be said without in any manner excusing them.

In order to attract them hither, it would only be necessary to distribute circulars in all directions assuring them of a truth that there is no region in France, in Spain, in Italy, or in fine, in the whole of Europe, which equals Carolina in attractiveness: that just as much land as they can possibly cultivate will be given to such as desire to establish themselves here:—especially to those who are suffering persecution because of their religion;—that all will be furnished with free passage across the sea in the King's ships; and, finally, that His Britannic Majesty will extend to them all the charitable aid which they could hope from his royal bounty in order that they may enjoy happy lives and form prosperous settlements in this country.

It is proper to observe that by virtue of a natural inclination characteristic of all reasonable beings,—namely the love of liberty, —most of the Swiss soldiers, when their terms of enlistment shall have expired, will resign and joyfully embrace this opportunity to place themselves at ease: and for two important reasons: first, which is negative, in order that they may, in good time, liberate themselves from the evil pursuit of war,—a calling illy suited to the tastes of all who desire to lead the lives of honest Christians;—and, for a second reason, which I call positive, that they may secure for themselves the sweet and virtuous companionship born of marriage. For it is certain that there are scarcely any Swiss soldiers who would not marry if their Captains would grant them the liberty of doing so; and there is no man in the world, however stupid he may be, who does not long, at least during his old age, for a home which will shelter him from the horrors of poverty and misery.

The public being once fully persuaded of the fertility of Carolina, what joy will fill the hearts of the poor, and with what eagerness will they hasten thither when they are well assured that they will go to end their days in one of the most delightful countries in the universe! We may safely assert that many French refugees, and many from Switzerland, from Wirtemberg, from the Palatinate, from Holland, from Saxony, and from other Protestant countries,—more indeed than the King's ships could carry,—would present themselves, all of whom would prove faithful subjects of Great Britain, and cost absolutely nothing except the expense of transportation. But this expense is so insignificant a charge upon the General Government, that it need not be considered when compared with the fruits, oils, wax, cotton, tobacco, indigo, cocoa, leather, furs, wood for building and other purposes, resin, tar, hemp, wool, silk, brandy, and excellent wines, wheat, rice, and other products,—useful as medicines and dyestuffs,—which will surely be realized, and which will demand nothing in exchange save the merchandize proceeding from the manufactories of Great Britain.

In truth there is matter for surprize at the indifference, not to say contempt, which is evinced, even among the most enlightened nations of Europe, towards individuals who are informed above their fellows, and who could, by their superior knowledge, fortified by large experience, contribute to the re-establishment of the shattered fortunes at least of certain States: while, on the other hand, we see a people, barbarous and fierce, whose territory is for more than half of the year covered with snow, interested in agriculture, commerce, and navigation, cherishing the arts and sciences, and searching with all imaginable eagerness for such as can prove serviceable to them in these departments. Witness the recent Declaration of the Czar, published only a few days since, in favor of strangers who might desire to establish themselves at Petersburg or in other commercial cities of his dominion, and in which her Majesty, the Empress of Russia, promises to defray the expenses of their journey, to have houses built for them, to exempt them from taxes for a period of twenty years, to furnish them with the means requisite for carrying on their trades, to extend free religious toleration and to pay one hundred rubles per annum to the pastor of each colony in case it is unable of its own means to support him.

In view of this, can it be possible that England will look with an indifferent eye upon the new forces which the French are to-day collecting in order that they may go and take possession of the best portion of the fertile country of Carolina,—I mean that which lies between the Mississippi river and the original concession? [For it is quite true that they have actually equipped four half-galleys to transport by that river as many colonists as they can secure.] Can it be possible that the English, on their part, are willing to do nothing, to undertake nothing, and that they will not bestir themselves in an effort to prevent this, especially during a period of peace when the roads are open on every hand by which peoples may be assembled, and when the King's vessels are unemployed? England should at least make Carolina the store-house and granary for the islands of Jamaica, Barbadoes, and Saint Christopher,—which produce neither bread nor wine,—and remember that she can, without wronging any one, reduce it now into possession and make of it a country which, when populated and cultivated properly, may be ranked with the most extensive and richest domains in the Universe.

But here is the principal article upon which I beg you, my Lord, to bestow your particular attention: it is SILK. There is no article of merchandize which furnishes support for so many people, in which so much money is invested, or which commands more general consumption throughout the world. Provence and Languedoc produce some little of an excellent quality, but they are not situated in a degree of heat to yield a great deal, and of the most desirable sort. Italy, Spain, and Sicily succeed much better for the reason I have indicated. But Carolina will undoubtedly far surpass all the countries I have just named, because it is located precisely in the degree of heat and temperature which best befits the nature of the silk-worm, so that in about thirty years, more or less, if it is desired to put into general use certain sure and infallible methods for the cultivation of this article,—which the writer offers to indicate at any time and place,—Great Britain will, in that event, be able to produce on her own lands a quantity of silk sufficient to supply the needs not only of her own subjects, but also, if she found it necessary, of the rest of Europe. This is the reason why the writer is persuaded that there is perhaps nothing in the world more advantageous to the State, nothing having a greater tendency to enhance the wealth of Great Britain in general and of the English in particular, than the consummation of such a project. Consequently it is most worthy of attention.

Should the fine opportunity, presented to-day, unfortunately be allowed to escape, we are very apprehensive that it will never occur again.

> I am, with very profound respect,
> My Lord,
> by your permission,
> Your very humble,
> and very obedient servant,
> JEAN PIERRE PURRY.

At London, the 18th
of July, 1724.—

Some Account of the Designs of the
Trustees for establishing the Colony
of *Georgia* in *America*.

Some Account of the Designs of the Trustees for establishing the Colony of GEORGIA in AMERICA.

 N AMERICA there are fertile Lands sufficient to subsist all the useless Poor in *England*, and distressed Protestants in *Europe*; yet Thousands starve for want of mere Sustenance. The Distance makes it difficult to get thither: The same Want, that renders Men useless here, prevents their paying their Passage; and if others pay it for them, they become Servants, or rather Slaves for Years to those who have defrayed that Charge: Therefore Money for Passage is necessary, but is not the only Want; for if the People were set down in *America*, and the Land before them, they must cut down Trees, build Houses, fortify Towns, dig and sow the Land before they can get in a Harvest, and 'till then they must be provided with Food, and kept together, that they may be assistant to each other for their mutual Support and Protection.

Some Account of the Designs of the Trustees for establishing the Colony of *Georgia* in *America*.

I N America there are fertile Lands sufficient to subsist all the useless Poor in *England*, and distressed Protestants in *Europe*; yet Thousands starve for want of mere Sustenance. The Distance makes it difficult to get thither: The same Want, that renders Men useless here, prevents their paying their Passage; and if others pay it for them, they become Servants, or rather Slaves for Years to those who have defrayed that Charge: Therefore Money for Passage is necessary, but is not the only Want; for if the People were set down in *America*, and the Land before them, they must cut down Trees, build Houses, fortify Towns, dig and sow the Land before they can get in a Harvest, and 'till then they must be provided with Food, and kept together, that they may be assistant to each other for their mutual Support and Protection.

The *Romans* esteemed the sending forth of Colonies amongst their noblest Works; they observed that *Rome*, as she increased in Power and Empire, drew together such a Conflux of People from all Parts, that she found herself overburthened with their Number, and the Government brought under an Incapacity to provide for them, or keep them in Order. Necessity, the Mother of Invention, suggested to them an Expedient which at once gave Ease to the Capital, and increased the Wealth and Number of industrious Citizens, by lessening the useless and unruly Multitude; and by Planting them in Colonies on the Frontiers of their Empire gave a new Strength to the whole; and this they looked upon to be so considerable a Service to the Common Wealth, that they created peculiar Officers for the Establishment of such Colonies, and the Expence was defrayed out of the publick Treasury.

From the Charter.

His Majesty having taken into his Consideration the miserable Circumstances of many of his own poor Subjects, ready to perish for Want; as likewise the Distresses of many Foreigners, who would take Refuge here from Persecution; and having a princely Regard to the great Danger the Southern Frontiers of South-Carolina *are exposed to, by Reason of the small Number of white Inhabitants there, hath out of his fatherly Compassion towards his Subjects been graciously pleased to grant a Charter for incorporating a Number of Gentlemen by the Name of* THE TRUSTEES FOR ESTABLISHING THE COLONY OF *GEORGIA* IN AMERICA. *They are impower'd to collect Benefactions, and lay them out in Cloathing, Arming, Sending over, and supporting Colonies of the Poor, whether Subjects or Foreigners in* GEORGIA: *And his Majesty farther grants all his Lands between the Rivers* Savanah *and* Alatamaha, *which he erects into a Province by the Name of* GEORGIA, *unto the Trustees in Trust for the Poor, and for the better Support of the Colony. At the Desire of the Gentlemen there are Clauses in the Charter restraining them and their Successors from receiving any Salary, Fee, Perquisite, or Profit whatsoever by or from this Undertaking; and also from receiving any Grant of Lands within the said District to themselves, or in Trust for them. There are farther Clauses granting to the Trustees, proper Powers for establishing and governing the Colony, and Liberty of Conscience to all who shall settle there.*

The Trustees intend to relieve such unfortunate Persons as cannot subsist here, and establish them in an orderly Manner, so as to form a well regulated Town. As far as their Fund goes they will defray the Charge of their Passage to *Georgia*; give them Necessaries, Cattle, Land and Subsistance, till such Time as they can build their Houses, and clear some of their Lands. They rely for Success, first upon the Goodness of Providence, next upon the compassionate Disposition of the People of *England*; and they doubt not, that much will be spared from Luxury, and superfluous Expences by generous Tempers, when such an Opportunity is offered them by the giving of Twenty Pounds to provide for a Man or Woman, or ten Pounds a Child for ever.

In Order to prevent the Benefactions given to this Purpose from ever being misapplied, and to keep up as far as human Precaution can, the Spirit of Disinterestedness, the Trustees have established the following Method. That each Benefactor may know that what he has contributed, is safely lodged, and justly accounted for, all Money given will be deposited in the Bank of *England*, and Entries made of every Benefaction, in a Book to be kept for that Purpose, by the Trustees, with the Benefactors Names, or, if conceal'd, the Names of those by whose Hands they sent their Money. There are to be annual Accounts of all the Money receiv'd, and how the same has been disposed of, laid before the Lord High Chancellor, the Lord Chief Justice of the *King's-Bench*, the Master of the Rolls, the Lord Chief Justice of the *Common-Pleas*, and the Lord Chief Baron of the *Exchequer*, or two of them, and printed Copies of the said Accounts will be transmitted to every considerable Benefactor.

By such a Colony many Families who would otherwise starve, will be provided for, and made Masters of Houses and Lands; the People in *Great-Britain* to whom these necessitous Families were a Burthen, will be relieved; Numbers of Manufacturers will be here employed for supplying them with Cloaths, working Tools, and other Necessaries; and by giving Refuge to the distressed *Saltz-burghers* and other persecuted *Protestants*, the Power of *Britain*, as a Reward for its Hospitality, will be encreased by the Addition of so many religious and industrious Subjects.

The Colony of *Georgia*, lying about the same Latitude with Part of *China*, *Persia*, *Palestine*, and the *Maderas*, it is highly probable, that when hereafter it shall be well peopled, and rightly cultivated, *England* may be supplied from thence with *raw Silk*, *Wine*, *Oil*,

Dies, *Drugs*, and many other Materials for Manufactures, which she is obliged to purchase from Southern Countries. As Towns are established, and grow populous along the Rivers *Savanah* and *Altamaha*, they will make such a Barrier as will render the Southern Frontier of the *British Colonies* on the Continent of *America*, safe from *Indian* and other Enemies.

All human Affairs are so subject to Chance that there is no answering for Events; yet from Reason and the Nature of Things it may be concluded, that the Riches, and also the Number of Inhabitants in *Great-Britain* will be increased by importing at a cheap Rate from this new Colony the Materials requisite for carrying on in *Britain* several Manufactures: For our Manufacturers will be encouraged to marry and multiply, when they find themselves in Circumstances to provide for their Families, which must necessarily be the happy Effect of the Increase and Cheapness of the Materials of those Manufactures, which at present we purchase with our Money from Foreign Countries at dear Rates; and also many People will find Employment here, on Account of such farther Demands by the People of this Colony for those Manufactures, which are made from the Produce of our own Country, and, as has been justly observ'd, the People will always abound, where there is full Employment for them.

Christianity will be extended by the Execution of this Design; since the good Discipline established by the Society will reform the Manners of those miserable Objects, who shall be by them subsisted; and the Example of a whole Colony, who shall behave in a just, moral, and religious Manner, will contribute greatly towards the Conversion of the *Indians*, and taking off the Prejudices received from the profligate Lives of such, who have scarce any thing of Christian but the Name.

The Trustees in their general Meetings will consider of the most prudent Methods for effectually establishing a regular Colony; and that it may be done is demonstrable. Under what Difficulties was *Virginia* planted? The Coast and Climate then unknown, the *Indians* numerous, and at Enmity with the first Planters, who were forced to fetch all Provisions from *England*; yet is it grown a mighty

Province, and the Revenue receives 100,000 Pounds for Duties upon the Goods, that they send yearly Home. Within these fifty Years *Pensilvania* was as much a Forest as *Georgia* is now, and in those few Years, by the wise Oeconomy of WILLIAM PENN, and those who assisted him, it now gives Food to 80,000 Inhabitants, and can boast of as fine a City as most in *Europe*.

This new Colony is more likely to succeed than either of the former were, since *Carolina* abounds with Provisions, the Climate is known, and there are Men to instruct in the Seasons and the Nature of cultivating that Soil. There are but few *Indian* Families within four hundred Miles, and those in perfect Amity with the *English*; *Port-Royal*, the Station of his Majesty's Ships is within thirty, and *Charles-Town*, a great Mart, is within one hundred and twenty Miles. If the Colony is attacked, it may be relieved by Sea from *Port-Royal*, or the *Bahamas*; and the *Militia* of *South-Carolina*, is ready to support it by Land.

For the continuing the Relief which is now given, there will be Lands reserved in the Colony, and the Benefits arising from them is to go to the carrying on of the Trust. So that at the same Time the Money by being laid out preserves the Lives of the Poor, and makes a comfortable Provision for those, whose Expences are by it defray'd; their Labour in improving their own Lands will make the adjoining reserved Lands valuable, and the Rents of those reserved Lands will be a perpetual Fund for the relieving more poor People. So that instead of laying out the Money upon Lands, with the Income thereof to support the Poor, this is laying out the Money upon the Poor, and by the relieving those who are now unfortunate, raises a Fund for the perpetual Relief of those who shall be so hereafter.

There is an Occasion now offered for every one to help forward this Design, the smallest Benefaction will be received and applied with the utmost Care; every little will do something, and a great Number of small Benefactions will amount to a Sum capable of doing a great deal of good.

Select Tracts

Relating to Colonies

SELECT
TRACTS
RELATING TO
COLONIES.

CONSISTING OF

I. An Effay on Plantati-
ons. By Sir Francis
Bacon Lord Chan-
cellor of *England*.

II. Some Paffages taken
out of the *Hiftory of
Florence*, &c.

III. A Treatife. By John

De Witt Penfioner
of *Holland*.

IV. The Benefit of Plan-
tations or Colonies.
By William Penn.

V. A Difcourfe concer-
ning Plantations. By
Sir Josiah Child.

LONDON,

Printed for J. Roberts at the *Oxford-Arms* in
Warwick-Lane.

Price Six-pence.]

Select Tracts

Relating to Colonies

THE INTRODUCTION.

 *OTHING so much improves the Mind, and directs the Judgment to right Determinations as Experience and the Opinions of wise Men. As new Colonies are now so much talked of, it may be agreeable to the Publick, to see what has been writ upon that Subject by Philosophers, Statesmen, and Merchants, Men of different Professions, living in different Ages and Countreys, who could have no common View in deceiving. To save the Reader therefore the Trouble of hunting their Opinions out in many Books, the following Tracts are collected and published.*

The first is by one whose great Genius was not only an Ornament to the Nation and Age he lived in, but an Honour to Mankind. It is by Tradition deliver'd down, that he writ his Treatise on Plantations upon the following Occasion.

Sir Walter Raleigh *the excellent Historian, Soldier, Statesman, and Philosopher, made many Attempts to settle in* America, *went twice in Person to* Guiana *and once to* Virginia, *the latter of these was granted to him by Queen* Elizabeth, *who loved great Designs, carried her Views far, and studied the Welfare of* England *in future Generations as well as in her own Age. Under her Countenance he settled the first Colony in* Virginia, *so nam'd in Compliment to her Majesty. The Queen died,* and with her expired all Encouragement to noble Undertakings. Raleigh *not fit for a weak Mixture of timorous and arbitrary Measures was disgraced, condemned, imprisoned; the Plantation neglected, and all Thoughts of* America *given over by the Court.*

But tho' Sir *Walter was destroyed, his Spirit survived*, and* "many worthy Patriots, Lords, Knights, Gentlemen, Merchants, and others held Consultation and procured a Patent establishing a Council and Company, whereby *Colonies* to *Virginia* should be deduced, and the Affairs of that Plantation should be governed." *The Earl of* Southampton *and Sir* Edwin Sandys, *among many other very considerable Men, were of that Council, and they being intimate Friends of Sir* Francis Bacon, *prevailed with him to write Instructions concerning the new Colony. This was afterwards printed amongst his Essays, and is here annexed.*

The next consists of Passages taken out of different Parts of the Florentine *Historian. He treats of* Colonies *as a Politician, and therefore mentions them as they may be useful or prejudicial towards the preserving or increasing the Power of the Prince or State. Being thoroughly conversant with the Ancients, he from the* Roman *Maxims chalks the Outlines of a Plan for peopling a whole Countrey in a regular Manner, and by that Means remedying the Inconveniencies of Climate, Air, and Soil. He shews the Difference between supporting Conquests by Garrisons of* Colonies, *and supporting them by mercenary Troops, and just sketches out the only Plan upon which he seems to think they can be successfully founded, viz. Religion, Liberty, good Laws, the Exercise of Arms, and Encouragement of Arts. It is much to be lamented, that he did not write upon this Subject professedly, but only took it up cursorily; this makes him very short, but yet he who reads with Attention will find great Depth in what he writes, and many excellent Things to be learnt.*

The third Tract was writ by John De Witt *the famous Pensionary of* Holland, *who being both a Statesman and a Merchant mixes political with trading Considerations. This Piece was first published single,*

---

* See a short Collection of the most remarkable Passages from the Beginning to the Dissolution of the *Virginia* Company, *p.* 2. printed 1651.

but afterwards some small *Additions made and printed in his political Maxims.*

The fourth Tract is writ by William Penn *Proprietary of* Pensilvania. *It was printed in the Year* 1680, *about the Time that he began to settle that* Colony, *and given amongst his Friends, but never sold; so that the Copies of it are exceeding scarce. These were the Maxims upon which he acted, and which he so successfully pursued, that he peopled the Province of* Pensilvania, *where he laid out the City of* Philadelphia. "Foreseeing the Effects of Justice, Liberty, and wise Regulations, he formed the Plan to admit of great Increase; he chose a Situation between two navigable Rivers, and designed a Town in Form of an oblong Square, extending two Miles in Length from one River to the other. The long Streets eight in Number, and two Miles in Length, he cut at right Angles by others of one Mile in Length and sixteen in Number, all strait and spacious; he left proper Spaces for Markets, Parades, Keys, Wharfs, Meeting-houses, Schools, Hospitals, and other future publick Buildings. In the Province there is now eighty Thousand Inhabitants and in the Town of *Philadelphia,* a great Number of Houses. It increases every Day in Buildings, which are all carried on regularly according to the first Plan."

The fifth Tract is a Discourse by Sir Josiah Child. *He writ with an excellent Intention, that of undeceiving the People, by exposing several vulgar Errors; the twelfth of which vulgar Errors, and which in this Discourse he labours to confute is,* "That our Plantations depopulate, and consequently impoverish *England.*" *He did this so effectually, that whereas before he wrote, the generality of the World believed that Plantations depopulated the Kingdom, and consequently strove to hinder them; all wise Men have since the publishing of his Book been undeceived, and the Plantations have been continually encouraged by Parliament, to the great Increase of the Wealth, Trade, and People of the Kingdom.*

An Essay on Plantations by Sir Francis Bacon
Ld. *Verulam.*

PLANTATIONS are amongst Ancient, Primitive, and Heroical Works. When the World was young, it begat more Children; but now it is old it begets fewer: For I may justly account new Plantations to be the Children of former Kingdoms. I like a Plantation in a pure Soil, that is, where People are not displanted, to the end, to plant others; for else it is rather an Extirpation, than a Plantation. Planting of Countries is like planting of Woods; for you must make account to lose almost twenty Years profit, and expect your Recompence in the End. For the principal Thing that hath been the Destruction of most Plantations, hath been the base and hasty drawing of Profit in the first Years. It is true, speedy Profit is not to be neglected, as far as may stand with the good of the Plantation, but no farther. It is a shameful and unblessed Thing, to take the Scum of People, and wicked condemned Men, to be the People with whom you plant: And not only so, but it spoileth the Plantation; for they will ever live like Rogues, and not fall to work, but be lazy, and do mischief, and spend Victuals, and be quickly weary; and then certify over to their Countrey to the Discredit of the Plantation. The People wherewith you plant, ought to be Gard'ners, Plowmen, Labourers, Smiths, Carpenters, Joiners, Fishermen, Fowlers, with some few Apothecaries, Surgeons, Cooks, and Bakers. In a Countrey of Plantation, first look about what kind of Victual the Countrey yields of it self to hand; as Chesnuts, Wallnuts, Pine-Apples, Olives, Dates, Plumbs, Cherries, Wild-honey, and the like, and make use of them. Then consider what Victual, or esculent Things there are, which grow speedily, and within the Year; as Parsnips, Carrots, Turnips, Onions, Radish, Artichoaks of *Jerusalem*, Maiz and the like. For Wheat, Barley and Oats, they ask too much labour: But with Pease and Beans you may begin, both because they ask less labour, and because they serve for Meat as well as for Bread. And of Rice likewise cometh a great Increase, and it is a Kind of Meat. Above all, there ought to be brought store of Bisket, Oat-meal, Flour, Meal, and the like in the Beginning, till Bread may be had. For Beasts and Birds, take such as are least subject to Diseases, and multiply fastest; as Swine, Goats, Cocks, Hens, Turkeys, Geese, House-Doves, and the like. The Victual in Plantations ought to be expended almost as in a besieged Town, that is, with a certain Allowance; and let the main Part of the Ground employed to Gardens or Corn, be to a common Stock, and to be laid in, and stored up, and then delivered out in Proportion, besides some Spots of Ground that any particular Person will manure for his own private Use. Consider likewise what Commodities the Soil, where the Plantation is, doth naturally yield, that they may some way help to defray the Charge of the Plantation: So it be not, as was said, to the untimely Prejudice of the main Business; as it hath fared with Tobacco in *Virginia.* Wood commonly aboundeth but too much, and therefore Timber is fit to be one. If there be Iron-Ore, and Streams whereupon to set the Mills, Iron is a brave Commodity where Wood aboundeth. Making of Bay-Salt, if the Climate be proper for it, should be put in Experience. Growing Silk likewise, if any be, is a likely Commodity. Pitch and Tar, where Store of Firs and Pines are, will not fail. So Drugs and Sweet-Woods, where they are, cannot but yield great Profit. Soap-Ashes likewise, and other Things thay may be thought of. But moil not too much under Ground; for the Hope of Mines is very uncertain, and useth to make the Planters lazy in other Things. For Government, let it be in the Hands of one assisted with some Counsel; and let them have Commission to exercise martial Laws with some Limitation. And above all, let Men make that Profit of being in the Wilderness, as to have God always, and his Service before their Eyes. Let not the Government of the Plantation depend upon too many Counsellors and Undertakers in the Countrey that planteth, but upon a temperate Number; and let those be rather Noblemen and Gentlemen, than Merchants; for they look ever to the present Gain. Let there be Freedoms from Customs, till the Plantation be of Strength; and not only Freedom from Customs but Freedom to carry their Commodities, where they may make the best of them, except there be some special Cause of Caution. Cram not in People, by sending too fast, Company after Company, but rather hearken how they waste, and send Supplies proportionably; but so, as the Number may live well in the Plantation, and not by Surcharge be in Penury. It hath been a great endangering to the Health of some Plantations, that they have built along the Sea and Rivers in marshy and unwholesome Grounds. Therefore, tho' you begin there to avoid Carriage and other like Discommodities, yet still build rather upwards from the Streams, than along. It concerneth likewise the Health of the Plantation, that they have good Store of Salt with them, that they may use it with their Victuals, when it shall be necessary. *If you plant where Savages are, do not only entertain them with Trifles and Gingles, but use them* JUSTLY *and graciously*, with sufficient Guard nevertheless; and do not win their Favour by helping them to invade their Enemies, but for their Defence it is not amiss. And send oft of them over to the Countrey that plant, that they may see a better Condition than their own, and commend it when they return. When the Plantation grows to Strength, then it is time to plant with Women as well as with Men, that the Plantation may spread into Generations, and not be ever pieced from without. It is the sinfullest Thing in the World to forsake or destitute a Plantation once in forwardness; for besides the Dishonour, it is Guiltiness of Blood of many commiserable Persons.

Some Passages taken out of the History of Florence,
Book II.

AMONGST the great and admirable Orders of former Kingdoms and Common-wealths (tho' in our Times it is discon-
tinued and lost) it was the Custom upon every Occasion to establish Colonies and build new Towns and Cities; and indeed nothing
is more worthy and becoming an excellent Prince, a well dispos'd
Common-wealth, nor more for the Interest and Advantage of a
Province, than to erect new Towns, where Men may cohabit with
more Convenience both for Agriculture and Defence. For besides
the Beauty and Ornament which followed upon that Custom, it
render'd such Provinces as were conquer'd more dutiful and secure
to the Conqueror, planted the void Places, and made a commodious
Distribution of the People; upon which living regularly and in Order, they did not only multiply faster, but were more ready to invade, and more able for Defence. But by the Negligence and Omis-
sion of Common-wealths and Principalities this Method of establishing Colonies being at present disused, the Provinces are become
weaker and some of them ruined. For (as I said before) it is this
Order alone that secures a Countrey and supply's it with People.
The Security consists in this, that in a new Countrey a Colony
placed by Authority, is a Fortress and Guard to keep the Natives
in Obedience; neither without this can a Province continue inhabited, or preserve a just Distribution of the People, because all
Places being not equally fertile or healthful, where it is barren they
desert; where unwholesome they die; and unless there be some Way
to invite or dispose new Men to the one as well as the other, that
Province must fail; the abandoning some Places leaving them desolate and weak, and the thronging to others, making them indigent
and poor. And forasmuch as these inconveniencies are not to be
remedied by Nature, Art and Industry is to be applied; and we see
many Countries which are naturally unhealthful, much better'd
by the Multitude of Inhabitants; the Earth being purifi'd by their
Tillage, and the Air by their Fires, which Nature alone could never

have effected. Of this *Venice* is an Instance sufficient; for tho' seated in a sickly and watrish Place, the Concourse of so many People at one Time made it healthful enough. *Pisa* by reason of the Malignity of the Air was very ill inhabited till the Inhabitants of *Genoa* and its Territories, being defeated and dispossessed by the *Saracens*, it followed that being supplanted all of them at once, and repairing thither in such Numbers, that Town in a short Time became populous and potent. But the Custom of sending Colonies being laid aside, new Conquests are not so easily kept, void Places not so easily supplied; nor full and exurberant Places so easily evacuated. Whereupon many Places in the World, and particularly in *Italy*, are become desolate and deserted in respect of what in former Ages they have been, which is imputable to nothing but that Princes do not retain their ancient Appetite of true Glory, nor Commonwealths the laudable Customs of the Ancients.

The PRINCE.

CHAPTER III. *Speaking of the Methods by which distant Provinces may be kept in Subjection, he says,*

THERE is another Remedy rather better than worse, and that is to plant *Colonies* in one or two Places, which may be as it were the Keys of that State, and either that must be done, or of Necessity an Army of Horse and Foot be maintain'd in those Parts, which is much worse; for Colonies are of no great Expence; the Prince sends and maintains them at a very little Charge, and intrenches only upon such as he is constrained to dispossess of their Houses and Land for the Subsistence and Accommodation of the new Inhabitants, who are but few, and a small Part of the State; they also who are injured and offended, living dispersed and in Poverty, cannot do any Mischief, and the rest being quiet and undisturbed, will not stir, lest they should mistake, and run themselves into the same Condition with their Neighbours.

I conclude likewise, that those Colonies which are least chargeable, are most faithful and inoffensive, and those few who are of-

fended are too poor and dispersed, to do any hurt, as I said before.
——But if instead of Colonies an Army be kept on foot it will be much more expensive, and the whole Revenue of that Province being consumed in the keeping it, the Acquisition will be a Loss, and rather a Prejudice than otherwise.——In all Respects therefore, this Kind of Guard is unprofitable, whereas on the other Side Colonies are useful.——The *Romans* in their new Conquests observ'd this Course, they planted their Colonies, entertained the inferior Lords into their Protection without increasing their Power, they kept under such as were more potent, and would not suffer any Foreign Prince to have Interest among them.

CHAPTER X. *In the following Paragraph, he gives an Example from the* Germans *how Cities or* COLONIES *may be safe, where the Friendship of the neighbouring Inhabitants is doubtful.*

THE Towns in *Germany* are many of them safe, tho' their Countrey and District be but small.——Because they are all so well fortified, every one looks upon the taking of any one of them as a Work of great Difficulty and Time, their Walls being so strong, their Ditches so deep, their Works so regular, and well provided with Cannon, and their Stores and Magazines always furnished for a Twelvemonth. Besides which, for the Aliment and Sustenance of the People, and that they may be no Burthen to the Publick, they have Workhouses, where for a Year together the Poor may be employed in such Things as are the Nerves and Life of that City, and sustain themselves by their Labour. Military Discipline and Exercises are likewise in much request there, and many Laws and good Customs they have to maintain them.

DISCOURSES *upon* TITUS LIVIUS.

BOOK I. CHAPTER I.

A L L Cities are built either by Natives born in the Countrey where they were erected, or by Strangers. The first happens when, to the Inhabitants dispersed in many and little Parties, it appears their Habitation is insecure, not being able apart (by Reason of their Distance or Smallness of their Numbers) to resist an Invasion (if any Enemy should fall upon them) or to unite suddenly for their Defence without leaving their Houses and Families exposed, which by Consequence would be certain Prey to the Enemy. Whereupon to evade those Dangers, moved either by their own Impulse, or the Suggestions of some Person among them of more than ordinary Authority, they oblige themselves to live together in some Place to be chosen by them for Convenience of Provision and Easiness of Defence.——The second Case, when a City is raised by Strangers, it is done either by People that are free, or by those who are depending (as Colonies) or else by some Prince or Republick to ease and disburthen themselves of their Exuberance, or to defend some Territory, which being newly acquired, they desire with more Safety and less Expence to maintain of which Sort of Colonies several were built by the People of *Rome* all over their Empire——And because Men build as often by Necessity as Choice, the Judgment and Wisdom of the Builder is greater where there is less Room and Latitude for his Election; it is worthy our Consideration, whether it is more advantageous building in barren and unfruitful Places, to the end that the People being constrain'd to be industrious, and less obnoxious to Idleness might live in more Unity, the Poverty of the Soil giving them less Opportunity of Dissension. Thus it fell out in *Raugia*, and several other Cities built in such Places; and that Kind of Election would doubtless be most prudent and profitable, if Men could be content to live quietly of what they had, without an ambitious Desire of Command. But there being no Security against that, but Power, it is necessary to avoid that Sterility, and build in the fruitfulest Places can be found, where their

Numbers increasing by the Plentifulness of the Soil, they may be able not only to defend themselves against an Assault, but repel any Opposition shall be made to their Grandeur: And as to that Idleness to which the Richness of the Situation disposes, it may be provided against by Laws and convenient Exercise joined, according to the Example of several wise Men, who having inhabited Countreys pleasant, fruitful, and apt to produce such lazy People improper for Service; to prevent the Inconvenience which might follow thereupon, enjoined such a Necessity of Exercise to such as were intended for the Wars, that by Degrees they became better Soldiers than those Countreys which were mountainous and barren could any where produce. Among whom may be reckoned the Kingdom of *Egypt*, which notwithstanding that it was extremely pleasant and plentiful, by the Virtue and Efficacy of its Laws, produced excellent Men, and perhaps such, as had not their Names been extinguished with Time, might have deserved as much Honour as *Alexander* the Great, and many other great Captains whose Memories are so fresh and so venerable among us. And whoever would consider the Government of the *Soldan*, the Discipline of the *Mamalukes*, and the rest of their Militia before they were extirpated by *Selimus* the *Turk*, might find their great Prudence and Caution in exercising their Soldiers, and preventing that Softness and Effeminacy to which the Felicity of their Soil did so naturally incline them.

For these Reasons I conceive best to build in a fruitful Place, if the ill Consequences of that Fertility be averted by convenient Laws. *Alexander* the Great being desirous to build a City to perpetuate his Name, *Dinocrates* an Architect came to him, and undertook to build him one upon the Mountain *Athos*, and to recommend and enforce his Proposal besides the Goodness of the Soil he persuaded him it should be made in the Shape and Figure of a Man a Thing which would be new, wonderful and suitable to his Greatness. But when *Alexander* enquired whence it was to be supplied, the Architect replied he had not consider'd of that; at which *Alexander* laugh'd very heartily, and leaving him and his Mountain to themselves, he built *Alexandria*, where People might be tempted to plant by the Richness of the Soil, the nearness of the Sea, and Convenience of the River *Nile*.

CHAPTER X.

AMONG all excellent and illustrious Men, they are most Praiseworthy who have been the chief Establishers of Religion and of the Worship of the Deity. In the second Place are they who have laid the Foundations of any Kingdom or City; in the third, those who having the Command of great Armies have enlarged their own or the Dominion of their Countrey; in the next Place learned Men of all Sciences, according to their several Studies and Degrees; and last of all (as being infinitely the greatest Number) come the Artificers and Mechanicks; all to be commended as they are ingenious or skilfull in their Professions. On the other Side they are infamous and detestable, who are contemners of Religion, Subverters of Governments, Enemies of Virtue, of Learning, of Art, and in short of every Thing that is useful and honourable to Mankind; and of this Sort are the Prophane, the Seditious, the Ignorant, the Idle, the Debauch'd, and the Vile. And altho' Nature has so order'd it, that there is neither wise Man nor Fool, nor good Man, nor bad, who if it were propos'd to him which he would chuse of these two Sorts of People, wou'd not prefer that which was to be preferr'd, and condemn the other; yet the Generality of Mankind deluded by a false Impression of Good, and vain Notion of Glory, leaving those Ways which are excellent and commendable, either wilfully or ignorantly wander into those Paths which lead them to Dishonour; and whereas to their immortal Honour they might establish a Commonwealth or Kingdom as they please, they run headlong into a Tyranny, not considering what Fame, what Glory, what Affection, what Security, what Quiet and Satisfaction of Mind they part with; nor what Reproach, Scandal, Hate, Danger and Disquiet they incurr. It is impossible but all People (whether of private Condition in the Common-wealth, or such as by their Fortune or Virtue have arriv'd to be Princes) if they have any Knowledge in History, and the Passages of old, would rather chuse (if private Persons) to be *Scipios* than *Cæsars:* and (if Princes) to be *Agesilaus, Timoleon* and

Dion, than *Nabis*, *Phalaris*, or *Dionysius*; because they must find one highly celebrated and admired, and the other as much abhor'd and condemn'd; they must find *Timoleon* and the rest to have as much Interest and Authority in their Countries as *Dionysius* or *Phalaris* had in theirs, and much more Security. Nor let any Man deceive himself in *Cæsar*'s Reputation, finding him so exceedingly eminent in History, for those who have cry'd him up, were either corrupted by his Fortune, or terrified by his Power, for whilst the Empire continued, it was never permitted that any Man should speak any Thing against him, and doubtless had Writers had their Liberty they could have said as much of him as of *Cataline*; and *Cæsar* is so much the worse of the two, by how much it is worse to effect and perpetrate an ill Thing, than to design it;

CHAPTER XI.

HE that would establish a virtuous City at this Day, would find it more easy among the rude People of the Mountains, who have not been acquainted with Civility, than among such as have been educated in Cities, where their Civility was corrupted; like rude unpolish'd Marble, which is more readily carved into a Statue, than what has been mangled already by some bungling Workman. So that all Things consider'd, I conclude that Religion being introduced by *Numa*, was one of the first Causes of that City's Felicity, because Religion produced good Laws, good Laws good Fortune, and good Fortune a good End in whatever they undertook. And as strictness in divine Worship, and Conscience of Oaths, are great Helps to the Advancement of a State, so Contempt of the one and Neglect of the other are great Means of its Destruction. Take away Religion, and take away the Foundation of Government.

CHAPTER XXI. *The Author in the following Passage proves, that any Kind of Men may be made Soldiers; from whence may be drawn, that there is no need of having regular Soldiers, if the Men who form a* COLONY *be disciplin'd.*

THERE is scarce any Body ignorant, that of late Years the *English* invaded *France*, and entertain'd no Soldiers but their own; and yet tho' *England* had had no Wars of thirty Years before, and had neither Officer nor Soldier who had ever seen a Battle, they ventured to attack a Kingdom, where the Officers were excellent, the Soldiers good, having been trained up for several Years together in the *Italian* Wars. This proceeded from the Prudence of the Prince, and the Excellence of the Government, in which (though in Times of Peace) the Exercise of Arms is not intermitted. *Pelopidas* and *Epaminondas* having relieved *Thebes*, and rescued it from the Tyranny of the *Spartans*, finding themselves in the Middle of a servile and effeminate People, they so order'd it by their Virtue and Discipline, that they brought them to the Use of Arms, took the Field with them against the *Spartans*, and overthrew them. From whence that Historian infers, that there are Soldiers not only in *Lacedemon*, but wherever there are Men, if there be any Body to exercise and train them; which *Tullus* perform'd most exquisitely among the *Romans*, as is most excellently express'd by *Virgil*, in these Words;

———*Desidesque movebit*
Tullus *in arma viros.*

BOOK II. CHAPTER VI.

WE shall now speak of the *Roman* Customs,——by which it will appear with what Wisdom they deviated from the common Ways of the World, and by what easy Methods they arriv'd at their Supremacy and Grandeur. He who makes War at his own Choice and is under no Constraint, or else by Ambition has doubtless this End, to get what he is able, and keep it whilst he can, and rather to enrich than impoverish his own Countrey: For such a one it is necessary to have Regard to his Charge, and to see that neither the conquering nor maintaining are more expensive to him than will conflict with his Revenue.——And whoever considers their Wars from the Beginning of *Rome* to the Siege of the *Vei*, will find that they were determined in a very short Time, some in six, some in ten, and some in twenty Days. For their Custom was upon the first Appearance of a War, immediately to draw out their Army, and seeking out the Enemy they did what they could to bring him to a

Battle. Having beaten him by Reason of the Surprize; the Enemy, that his Countrey might not wholly be harrass'd, for the most Part proposed an Agreement, in which the *Romans* were sure to insist upon some Part of their Territory; which either they converted to their particular Profit, or consigned to some *Colony*, which was to be placed there for the Security of their Frontiers; by which means the Wars being ended in a short Time, their Conquests were kept without any considerable Expence; for the *Colony* had that Countrey for their Pay, and the *Romans* had their *Colonies* for their Security. Nor could there be any Way more advantageous and safe; for whilst there was no Enemy in the Field, those Guards were sufficient; and when any Army was set out to disturb them, the *Romans* were always ready with another in their Defence, and having fought them, they commonly prevail'd, forced them to harder Conditions, and return'd when they had done: by which Means they gain'd daily upon the Enemy, and grew more powerful at Home: And in this Manner they proceeded till their Leaguer before *Veij*.——From that Time they maintain'd War at greater Distance, whereby they were obliged to continue longer in the Field, yet they left not their old Custom of dispatching it as soon as they could, with respect to the Circumstances of Place and Time; for which Reason they continued their *Colonies*.——And then for continuing their *Colonies*; the great Advantage and Convenience that resulted from them, was sufficient to prevail. This Practice therefore was observed perpetually among the *Romans* in the Management of their Wars, only they varied something about the Distribution of the Prey.——They thought convenient, that the Publick should have its Share; that upon any new Enterprize they might not be constrain'd to lay new Taxes upon the People; and by this Way their Coffers were fill'd in a short Time. So that by these two Ways, by the Distribution of their Prey, and the Settling of *Colonies Rome* grew rich by its Wars, whereas other Princes and States (without great Discretion) grow poor.

CHAPTER VII. *What Proportion of Land the* Romans *allow'd to every Man in their* Colonies.

I THINK it no easy Matter to set down the exact Proportion of Land which the *Romans* assign'd to every single Person in their *Colonies*; for I believe they gave more or less, according to the Barrenness or Fertility of the Soil; and that in all Places they were sparing enough. And the first Reason that induces me, is, that thereby they might send more Men, and by Consequence their Frontiers be better guarded: Another is, because living at Home indigent themselves, it is not to be supposed they would suffer those whom they sent abroad to grow too opulent and rich: And in this I am much confirm'd by *Livy*, where he tells us that upon the taking of *Veij*, the *Romans* sent a *Colony* thither, and in the Distribution of the Land alotted every Man no more than three Acres, and a little more according to our Measure. They might consider likewise that their Wants would not be supplied by the Quantity so much as the Improvement and Cultivation of their Land. Yet I do not doubt but they had publick Pastures and Woods to sustain their Cattle, and supply themselves with firing, without which a *Colony* could hardly subsist.

CHAPTER XIX.

THESE false Opinions are so rooted in the Minds of Men, and so confirm'd with ill Examples, that no Body thinks of reforming our late Errors, or restoring the old Discipline of the *Romans*.——— Which if Princes and Commonwealths could be persuaded to believe, they would commit fewer Faults, be more strong against the Insults of the Enemy, and those who had the Government of any civil State, would know better how to conduct and manage themselves, either as to the Enlargement, or Conservation of their Dominion, and find, that Leagues and Confederacies, rather than absolute Conquests; sending *Colonies* into what they had conquer'd; making publick Funds of the Spoils of the Enemy; to infest and perplex the Enemy rather with Excursions, and Battles, than Sieges; to keep the Publick rich, and the Private poor, and with all possible Caution to keep up a well Disciplined and orderly Militia are the Ways to make a Commonwealth formidable and great.

A Treatise *proving that it would be very advantageous for the Rulers and People of* Holland, *and for Traffick and Commerce, as well as Navigation, to erect* Dutch Colonies *in Foreign Countries. By* John De Witt, *Pensioner of* Holland.

SUPPOSING all the Expedients which the wisest of Men could invent to attract or allure Foreigners to become Inhabitants of *Holland* were practised, and those Inhabitants made to subsist by due Administration of Justice, yet would there be found in *Holland* many old and new Inhabitants, who for want of Estate and Credit, live very uneasily, and therefore would desire to remove thence. It is evident first as to Persons and Estates, that the Inhabitants here are not only exposed to the ordinary Misfortunes of Mankind, of not foreseeing future Events, Weakness, and Want; but besides, they make very uncertain Profit by Manufactures, Fishing, Trading, and Shipping. And on the other side by Sickness, Wars, Piracies, Rocks, Sands, Storms, and Bankrupts, or by the Unfaithfulness of their own Masters of Ships they may lose the greatest Part of their Estates, whilst in the Interim they continue charged with the natural Burdens of *Holland*, as great House-Rent, Imposts, and Taxes; nor have they any reformed Cloisters to provide creditable Opportunities for discharging themselves by such Losses of maintaining their Children, or according to the Proverb to turn Soldier or Monk; so that by such Accidents falling into extreme Poverty, they consequently lose their Credit and Respect among Men: For to have been Rich is a double Poverty, and nothing is less regarded than a poor Man's Wisdom; In such Cases he would find himself in the most lamentable Condition that can befal a Man in this World.

And secondly, as to Reputation: It is well known that in this Republick the Government consists of very few Men in proportion to the Number of Inhabitants; And that the said Government is not by Law annexed or restrained to any certain Family, but is open to all the Inhabitants; so that they who have been eight or ten Years Burgers, may be chosen to the Government in most Cities, and have the most eminent Employments of *Scheepen* or Burgomaster. Whence we may infer, that many that were of the Offspring of those that were heretofore made use of in the Government, and also many others, who by reason of their ancient Stock, and great Skill in Polity and extraordinary Riches, thro' natural Self-love and Ambition, conceive themselves wronged, when other new Ones of less Fitness and Estate, are chosen to the Government before them; and therefore thinking themselves undervalued, seek a Change, and would be induced to transport themselves to other Countries, where their Qualifications, great Estate, and Ambition, might produce very good Effects. Whereas on the other Side, whilst they continue to dwell in these Lands, they speak ill of the Government and Rulers in particular. And if by this or any other Accident, Tumults should be occasioned against the Rulers in particular, or the Government itself, they, being Persons of Quality, might become the Leaders of the Seditious, who to obtain their End, and to have such Insurrections tend to their Advantage, would not rest till they had displaced and turned out the lawful Rulers, and put themselves in their Places, which is one of the saddest Calamities that can befal the Republick, or Cities: Seeing Rulers who became such by Mutiny, are always the Cause of horrible Enormities before they attain the Government, and must commit many Cruelties e'er they can fix themselves on the Bench of Magistracy.

And seeing we have already made many Conquests of Countries in *India,* and finding how hardly (and that with great Charge of Soldiers) they must be kept; and that *the Politicians of old have taught us, that there is no better Means, especially for a State which depends on Merchandize and Navigation, to preserve Foreign Conquests, than by setling* COLONIES *in them:* We may easily conclude, that the same Method would be very useful and expedient for our State.

Thirdly, it is well known, that the poorest People of all the Countries round about us, come to dwell in *Holland* in Hope of earning their Living by Manufactury, Fisheries, Navigation, and other Trades; or failing that, that they shall have the Benefit of Alms-Houses and Hospitals, where they will be better provided for than in their own Countrey. And altho' in this Manner very many poor People have been maintained; yet in bad Times it could not last long; but thence might easily arise a general Uproar, with the Plunder and Subversion of the whole State: To prevent which, and other the like Mischiefs, and to give discontented Persons and Men in Straits an open Way, the Republicks of *Tyre, Sidon, Carthage, Greece,* and *Rome, &c.* in ancient Times, having special Regard to the true Interest of Republicks, which were perfectly founded on Traffick, or Conquests of Lands, did not neglect to erect many *Colonies:* Yea even the Kings of *Spain, Portugal,* and *England, &c.* have lately very profitably erected divers *Colonies,* and continue so doing in remote and uncultivated Countries; which formerly added an incredible Strength, to those ancient Republicks, and do still to *Spain, Portugal,* and *England, &c.* producing besides their Strength the greatest Traffick and Navigation. So that it is a wonderful Thing that *Holland* having these old and new Examples before their Eyes; and besides by its natural great Wants, and very great Sums of Money given yearly for Charity to poor Inhabitants, and being yearly press'd by so many broken Estates, and want of greater Traffick and Navigation, hath not hitherto made any free *Colonies* for the Inhabitants of *Holland*; tho' we by our Shipping have discovered and navigated many fruitful, uninhabited, and unmanured Countries, where if *Colonies* were erected, they might be free, and yet subject to the Lords the States of *Holland*, as all the open Countries and Cities that have no Votes amongst us are; and it might cause an incredible great and certain Traffick and Navigation with the Inhabitants of *Holland*.

It is well worth Observation, that these Colonies would no less strengthen the Treasure and Power of the States in Peace and War, than they do those of *Spain*, *Portugal*, and *England*, which during the manifold intestine Dissensions and Revolutions of State, have always adhered to their ancient native Countrey against their Enemies. And by this Means also many ambitious and discontented Inhabitants of *Holland* might conveniently *sub Specie honoris*, be gratified, by having some Authority in and about the Government of the said *Colonies*. But some may object, that heretofore the Rulers of *Holland* in the respective Grants or Charters given to the East and *West-India* Companies, have given them alone the Power of navigating their districts, with Exclusion of all other Inhabitants, which extend so far, that out of them the whole World hath now no fruitful uninhabited Lands, where we might erect new *Colonies*; and that those Districts are so far spread, because our Rulers trusted, that the said Companies could, and would propagate and advance such Colonies: Tho' supposing those *Colonies* must indeed in Speculation be acknowledged singularly profitable for this State, yet nevertheless those respective Districts and Limits Bounds of the said Companies, were purposely extended so far by the States General, and especially by the States of *Holland*, effectually to hinder the making of those Colonies, since our Nation is naturally averse to Husbandry, and utterly unfit to plant Colonies, and ever inclined to merchandizing.

To which I answer, that it's likely the first Grants or Charters, both of the East and West, and other copious Districts, were probably made upon mature Deliberation; but that the Rulers perceiving afterwards how very few Countries the said Companies do traffick with, and what a vast many Countries and Sea-Ports in their Districts remain without Traffick or Navigation, they cannot be excused of too great Imprudence in that they have, notwithstanding the Continuance of such Districts to this Day, kept their common trading Inhabitants, consisting of so great Numbers, from those uninhabited Countries by our Companies: So that by Reason of the Want of trafficking Countries or new Colonies in little *Europe* and its Confines, the *Hollanders* are necessitated to overstock all Trade and Navigation, and to spoil and ruin them both, to the great Prejudice of such Merchants and Owners of Ships on whom it falls, altho' *Holland*, during that Time of their Trades being over-stock'd had a greater Commerce, and deterred the Traders of other Countries from that Traffick, which the *Hollanders* with the first Appearance of Gain do, and must reassume, if they will continue to live in *Holland*; where all Manner of Foreign Trade since the erecting the said Companies was necessitated to be driven, not-withstanding the Uncertainty of Gain, and Fear of over-trading our selves.

And that the said Companies neither have nor do endeavour to make new Colonies for the Benefit of the Lands, and the Inhabitants thereof, hath hitherto abundantly appeared, and we must not lightly believe that they will do otherwise for the future; which I suppose will also appear, if we consider, that the Directors from whom this should proceed, are advanced and privately sworn to promote the Benefit of the Subscribers of the respective Companies; so that if the Colonies should not tend to the Benefit of the Subscribers in general, we cannot expect the Companies should promote them. Yea, supposing such Colonies should tend to the greatest Profit of the said Subscribers in general, yet such is the common Corruption of Man, that those Plantations should not be erected unless such Directors or Governors can make their own Advantage by them.

And seeing all new Colonies in unmanured Countries, must for some Years together have Necessaries carried to them, till such Plantations can maintain themselves out of their own Product, begin to trade and go to Sea, and then there is some small Duty imposed on the Planters and their Traffick, or Navigation, whereby the Undertakers may be reimbursed: Yet the Partners having expended so much, are not assured, that their Grant or Lease of Years shall be prolonged and continued to them on the same Terms. Moreover, in regard of these new Colonies, the Directors ought therefore to have less Salary, seeing by this free Trade of the Planters and Inhabitants, they may be eased of the great Pains they take about their general Traffick and Equipage of Ships, which concerns them much in particular for many considerable Reasons not here to be mention'd.

And as concerning our People in the East and West, they being hitherto of so loose a Life, are so wasteful, expensive, and lazy, that it may thence seem to be concluded, that the Nation of *Holland* is naturally and wholly unfit for new Colonies; yet I dare venture to say it is not so: But certain it is, that the Directors of the said Companies their Mariners and Soldiers, and likewise their other Servants are hired on such strait-laced and severe Terms, and they require of them such multitude of Oaths, importing the Penalty of the Loss of all their Wages and Estate, that very few Inhabitants of *Holland*, unless out of mere Necessity, or some poor ignorant slavish-minded and debauched Foreigners, will offer themselves to that heard Servitude. It is also true that all such as are in the *Indies*, especially the *East-Indies*, do find that not only while they serve, but after they have served their Time for which they are bound, they are under an intollerable compulsive Slavery; insomuch, that none can thrive there but their great Officers, who being placed over them, to exact the Oaths of the Mercenaries or Hirelings, and to put in Execution the Companies Commands, and being without Controul, to accuse or check them, they commonly favour one another, and afterwards coming Home with great Treasures are in Fear that they will be seized and confiscated by the Directors. So that it is no Wonder that so few good, and so many ignorant, lazy, prodigal, and vicious People take Service of the *East-India* Company. But it is doubly to be admired, that any intelligent, frugal, diligent, and virtuous People, especially *Hollanders*, unless driven by extreme Necessity, should give up themselves to that slavish Servitude.

All of which being true, let none think it strange, that the Scum of *Holland* and of most other Nations having by their Service become Freemen there, and yet not permitted to drive any Trade by Sea, or with Foreign People, are very unfit, and have no Inclination at all to those forced Colonies, do always thirst after their own sweet and free native Countries of *Holland:* Whereas notwithstanding on the contrary, the ingenious, frugal, industrious *Hollanders,* by those

Virtues which are almost peculiar to them, are more fit than any Nation in the World to erect Colonies and to live on them, when they have the Liberty given them to manure them for their own Livelihoods. And those that doubt thereof, let them please to observe, that the *Hollanders* before and since these two licens'd Companies, even under Foreign Princes, have made very many new Colonies; namely, in *Lysland, Prussia, Brandenburgh, Pomerania, Denmark, Sleswick, France, England, Flanders, &c.* and moreover have not only manured unfruitful unplanted Lands, but also undertaken the chargeable and hazardous Task of draining of Fenlands. And it is observable that in all the said Places their Butter, Cheese, Fruits, and Product of the Earth, are more desired, and esteemed than those of their Neighbours. And if we farther observe, that no Countries in the World, whether the Land be for Breeding, or Feeding, are so well order'd as those of our plain Lands in *Holland*; and that no others, Boors or Husbandmen, do travel so many Countries as ours do; we shall be convinced, that no Nation under Heaven is so fit for setting up of new Colonies, and manuring of Ground as our People are. And if in our Nation there is also to be found (which however is unjustly and unwisely denied by the Opposers of these new *Holland* Colonies) a very great Aptness and Inclination to Merchandising and Navigation, then we may in all Respects believe, that we under our own free Government might erect very excellent Colonies when it shall please the State to begin and encourage the same on good Foundations, and to indulge them for a short Time with their Favour and Defence.

The Benefit of Plantations, or Colonies.
By William Penn.

COLONIES are the Seeds of Nations, begun and nourish'd by the Care of wise and populous Countries; as conceiving them best for the Increase of humane Stock, and beneficial for Commerce.

Some of the wisest Men in History, have justly taken their Fame from this Design and Service: We read of the Reputation given on this Account to *Moses*, *Joshua*, and *Caleb*, in Scripture Records; and what Renown the *Greek* Story yields to *Lycurgus*, *Theseus*, and those *Greeks* that planted many Parts of *Asia*. Nor is the *Roman* Account wanting of Instances to the Credit of that People; they had a *Romulus*, a *Numa Pompilius*; and not only reduc'd, but moraliz'd the Manners of the Nations they subjected; so that they may have been rather said to conquer their Barbarity than them.

Nor did any of these ever dream it was the Way of decreasing their People or Wealth: For the Cause of the Decay of any of those States or Empires was not their Plantations, but their Luxury and Corruption of Manners: For when they grew to neglect their ancient Discipline that maintain'd and rewarded Virtue and Industry, and addicted themselves to Pleasure and Effeminacy, they debased their Spirits and debauch'd their Morals, from whence Ruin did never fail to follow to any People. With Justice therefore I deny the vulgar Opinion against Plantations, that they weaken *England*; they have manifestly inrich'd, and so strengthen'd her, which I briefly evidence thus.

First, Those that go into a Foreign Plantation, their Industry there is worth more than if they stay'd at Home, the Product of their Labour being in Commodities of a superiour Nature to those of this Countrey. For Instance, what is an improv'd Acre in *Jamaica* or *Barbadoes* worth to an improv'd Acre in *England*? We know 'tis three times the Value, and the Product of it comes for *England*, and is usually paid for in *English* Growth and Manufacture. Nay, *Virginia* shews, that an ordinary Industry in one Man produces three

Thousand Pound Weight of Tobacco, and twenty Barrels of Corn yearly: He feeds himself, and brings as much of Commodity into *England* besides, as being return'd in the Growth and Workmanship of this Countrey, is much more than he could have spent here: Let it also be remembred, that the three Thousand Weight of Tobacco brings in two Thousand Two-pences by Way of Custom to the King, which makes twenty-five Pounds; an extraordinary Profit.

Secondly, More being produc'd and imported than we can spend here, we export it to other Countries in *Europe*, which brings in Money, or the Growth of those Countries, which is the same Thing; and this is the Advantage of the *English* Merchants and Seamen.

Thirdly, Such as could not only not marry here, but hardly live and allow themselves Cloaths, do marry there and bestow thrice more in all Necessaries and Conveniences (and not a little in ornamental Things too) for themselves, their Wives and Children, both as to apparel and houshold Stuff; which coming out of *England*, I say 'tis impossible that *England* should not be a considerable Gainer.

Fourthly, But let it be consider'd, that the Plantations imploy many Hundreds of Shipping, and many Thousands of Seamen; which must be in divers Respects an Advantage to *England*, being an Island, and by Nature fitted for Navigation above any Countrey in *Europe*. This is follow'd by other depending Trades, as Shipwrights, Carpenters, Sawyers, Hewers, Trunnel-makers, Joyners, Slop-sellers, Dry-salters, Iron-workers, the East-land Merchants, Timber-sellers, and Victuallers, with many more Trades which hang upon Navigation: So that we may easily see the Objection (that the *Colonies* or Plantations hurt *England*) is at least of no Strength, especially if we consider how many Thousand *Blacks* and *Indians* are also accommodated with Cloaths and many Sorts of Tools and Utensils from *England*, and that their Labour is mostly brought hither, which adds Wealth and People to the *English* Dominions. But 'tis further said, they injure *England*, in that they draw away too many of the People; for we are not so populous in the Countries as formerly. I say there are other Reasons for that.

First, Countrey People are so extremely addicted to put their Children into Gentlemens Service, or send them to Towns to learn Trades, that Husbandry is neglected; and after a soft and delicate Usage there, they are for ever unfitted for the Labour of a farming Life.

Secondly, The Pride of the Age in its Attendance and Retinue is so gross and universal, that where a Man of a Thousand Pounds a Year formerly kept but four or five Servants, he now keeps more than twice the Number; he must have a Gentleman to wait upon him in his Chambers, a Coachman, a Groom or two, a Butler, a Man Cook, a Gardner, two or three Lacques, it may be an Huntsman, and a Faulkner; the Wife a Gentlewoman and Maids accordingly: This was not known by our Ancestors of like Quality. This hinders the Plough and the Dairy from whence they are taken, and instead of keeping People to manly Labour, they are effeminated by a lazy and luxurious Living; but which is worse, these People rarely marry, tho' many of them do worse; but if they do, it is when they are in Age; and the Reason is clear, because their usual keeping at their Masters is too great and costly for them with a Family at their own Charge, and they scarcely know how to live lower; so that too many of them chuse rather to vend their Lusts at an evil Ordinary than honestly marry and work. The Excess and Sloth of the Age not allowing of Marriage, and the Charge that follows; all which hinders the Increase of our People. If Men, they often turn Soldiers, or Gamesters, or Highwaymen; if Women, they too frequently dress themselves for a bad Market, rather than know the Dairy again, or honestly return to Labour; whereby it happens that both the Stock of the Nation decays, and the Issue is corrupted.

Thirdly, Of old Time the Nobility and Gentry spent their Estates in the Countrey, and that kept the People in it: And their Servants married and sat at easy Rents under their Masters Favour, which peopled the Place: Now the great Men (too much loving the Town and resorting to *London*) draw many People thither to attend them, who either don't marry, or if they do, they pine away their small Gains in some petty Shop; for there are so many, they prey upon one another.

Fourthly, The Countrey thus neglected, and no due Ballance kept between Trade and Husbandry, City and Countrey, the poor Countrey man takes double Toil, and cannot (for Want of Hands) dress and manure his Land to the Advantage it formerly yielded him; yet must he pay the old Rents, which occasions Servants, and such Children as go to Trades, to continue single, at least all their youthful Time, which also obstructs the Increase of our People.

Fifthly, The Decay of some Countrey Manufactures (where no Provision is made to supply the People with a new Way of Living) causes the more Industrious to go abroad to seek their Bread in other Countries, and gives the lazy an Occasion to loiter and beg, or do worse; by which Means the Land swarms with Beggars. Formerly 'twas rare to find any asking Alms but the Maim'd or Blind, or very aged; now Thousands of both Sexes run up and down, both City and Countrey, that are sound and youthful, and able to work, with false *Pretences* and *Certificates*; nor is there any Care taken to employ or deter such *Vagrants*, which weakens the Countrey as to People and Labour.

To which let me add, that the great Debauchery in this Kingdom has not only render'd many unfruitful when married, but they live not out half their Time, through Excesses, which might be prevented by a vigorous Execution of our good Laws against Corruption of Manners. These and the like Evils are the true Grounds of the Decay of our People in the Countrey, to say nothing of Plague and Wars. Towns and Cities cannot complain of the Decay of People, being more replenish'd than ever, especially *London*, which with Reason helps the Countrey-Man to this Objection. And tho' some do go to the Plantations, yet numbering the Parishes in *England*, and computing how many live more than die, and are born than buried, there goes not over to all the Plantations a fourth Part of the yearly Increase of the People; and when they are there, they are not (as I said before) lost to *England*, since they furnish them with much Cloaths, Household-stuff, Tools, and the like Necessaries, and that in greater Quantities than here their Condition could have needed; or they could have bought; being there well to pass, that were but low here, if not poor; and now Masters of Families too, when here they had none, and could hardly keep themselves; and very often it happens that some of them after their Industry and Success there have made them wealthy, they return and empty their Riches into *England*, one in this Capacity being able to buy out twenty of what he was when he went over.

A Discourse concerning Plantations. By Sir Josiah Child, *Published* 1692.

THE Trade of our *English* Plantations in *America* being now of as great Bulk, and employing as much Shipping as most of the Trades of this Kingdom, it seems not unnecessary to discourse more at large concerning the Nature of Plantations, and the good or evil Consequences of them, in Relation to this and other Kingdoms; and the rather because some Gentlemen of no mean Capacities, are of Opinion, that his Majesty's Plantations abroad have very much prejudic'd this Kingdom, by draining us of our People; for the Confirmation of which Opinion they urge the Example of *Spain*, which they say is almost ruin'd by the Depopulation which the *West-Indies* hath occasion'd. To the End therefore a more particular Scrutiny may be made in this Matter, I shall humbly offer my Opinion in the following Propositions, and then give those Reasons of Probability which presently occur to my Memory, in Confirmation of each Proposition.

First, I agree that Land (tho' excellent) without Hands proportionable, will not enrich any Kingdom.

Secondly, That whatever tends to the depopulating of a Kingdom, tends to the Impoverishment of it.

Thirdly, That most Nations in the civiliz'd Parts of the World, are more or less rich or poor proportionably to the Paucity or

Plenty of their People, and not to the Sterility or Fruitfulness of their Lands.

Fourthly, I do NOT *agree that our People in* England *are in any considerable Measure abated by Reason of our* FOREIGN PLANTA-TIONS, *but propose to prove the* CONTRARY.

Fifthly, I am of Opinion, that we had immediately before the Plague, many more People in *England,* than we had before the inhabiting of *Virginia, New-England, Barbadoes,* and the rest of our *American* Plantations.

The first PROPOSITION, That Lands, tho' in their nature excellently good, without Hands proportionable, will not enrich any Kingdom.

This first Proposition I suppose will readily be assented to by all judicious Persons, and therefore for the Proof of it, I shall only alledge a Matter of Fact.

The Land of *Palestine,* once the richest Countrey in the Universe, since it came under the *Turk's* Dominion, and consequently unpeopled, is now become the poorest.

Andaluzia and *Granada,* formerly wonderful rich, and full of good Towns, since dispeopled by the *Spaniard* by Expulsion of the Moors, many of their Towns and brave Countrey-Houses are fallen into Rubbish, and their whole Countrey into miserable Poverty, though their Lands naturally are prodigiously fertile.

A Hundred other Instances of Fact might be given to the like Purpose.

The Second PROPOSITION, Whatever tends to the populating of a Kingdom, tends to the Improvement of it.

The former Proposition being granted, I suppose this will not be denied, and the Means is good Laws, whereby any Kingdom may be populated and consequently enriched.

The third PROPOSITION, That most Nations in the civiliz'd Parts of the World, are more or less rich or poor, proportionable to the Paucity of Plenty of their People.

This third is a Consequent of the two former Propositions: And the whole World is a Witness to the Truth of it. The seven united Provinces are certainly the most populous Tract of Land in Christendom, and for their Bigness undoubtedly the richest. *England* for its Bigness, except our Forests, Wastes, and Commons, which by our Laws and Customs are barred from Improvement, I hope it yet a more populous Countrey than *France*, and consequently richer; I say in Proportion to its bigness: *Italy* in like Proportion more populous than *France*, and richer, and *France* more populous and richer than *Spain*, *&c.*

The fourth PROPOSITION, *I do* not *agree that our People in* England *are in any considerable Measure abated, by Reason of our Foreign Plantations,* but *propose to prove the* contrary.

This I know is a controverted Point, and do believe where there is one Man of my Mind there may be a Thousand of the contrary; but I hope when the following Grounds of my Opinion have been thoroughly examin'd, there will not be so many Dissenters.

That very many People now go, and have gone from this Kingdom almost every Year for these sixty Years past, and have and do settle in our Foreign Plantations, is most certain. But the first Question will be, whether if *England* had no Foreign Plantations for those People to be transported unto, they could or would have stay'd and liv'd at Home with us?

I am of opinion they never would nor could.

To resolve this Question we must consider what Kind of People they were, and are, that have and do transport themselves to our Foreign Plantations.

New-England (as every one knows) was originally inhabited, and hath since successively been replenish'd, by a Sort of People call'd *Puritans*, which could not conform to the Ecclesiastical Laws of *England*; but being wearied with Church Censures and Persecutions, were forc'd to quit their Father's Land, to find out new Habitations, as many of them did in *Germany* and *Holland*, as well as *New-England*; and had there not been a *New-England* found for some of them, *Germany* and *Holland* probably had receiv'd the rest: But old *England* to be sure had lost them all.

Virginia and *Barbadoes* were first peopled by a Sort of loose vagrant People, vicious and destitute of Means to live at Home (being either unfit for Labour, or such as could find none to employ themselves about, or had so misbehav'd themselves by Whoring, Thieving, or other Debauchery, that none would set them on work) which Merchants and Masters of Ships by their Agents (or Spirits as they were call'd) gather'd up about the Streets of *London* and other Places, cloath'd and transported to be employ'd upon Plantations; and these, I say, were such as, had there been no *English* Foreign Plantation in the World, could probably never have liv'd at Home to do Service for their Countrey, but must have come to be hang'd or starv'd, or died untimely of some of those miserable Diseases, that proceed from Want and Vice; or else have sold themselves for Soldiers, to be knock'd on the Head, or starv'd, in the Quarrels of our Neighbours, as many Thousands of brave *Englishmen* were in the low Countries, as also in the Wars of *Germany*, *France*, and *Sweden*, &c. or else if they could by begging, or otherwise, arrive to the Stock of half a Crown to waft them over to *Holland*, become Servants to the *Dutch*, who refuse none.

But the principal Growth and Increase of the aforesaid Plantations of *Virginia* and *Barbadoes* happen'd in, or immediately after, our late Civil Wars, when the worsted Party by the Fate of War being depriv'd of their Estates, and having some of them never been bred to Labour, and others made unfit for it by the lazy Habit of a Soldier's Life, there wanting Means to maintain them all abroad with his Majesty, many of them betook themselves to the aforesaid Plantations, and great Numbers of *Scotch* Soldiers of his Majesty's Army, after *Worcester* Fight, were by the then prevailing Powers voluntarily sent thither.

Another great Swarm, or Accession of new Inhabitants to the aforesaid Plantations, as also to *New-England*, *Jamaica*, and all other his Majesty's Plantations in the *West-Indies*, ensued upon his Majesty's Restauration; when the former prevailing Party being by a divine Hand of Providence brought under, the Army disbanded, many Officers displac'd, and all the new Purchasers of publick Titles dispossest of their pretended Lands, Estates, &c. many became impoverish'd, destitute of Employment; and therefore such as could find no Way of living at Home, and some which fear'd the Re-istablishment of the Ecclesiastical Laws, under which they could not live, were forc'd to transport themselves or sell themselves for a few Years, to be transported by others to the Foreign *English* Plantations: The constant Supply that the said Plantations have since had, hath been such vagrant loose People, as I have before mention'd, pick'd up, especially about the Streets and Suburbs of *London* and *Westminster*, and Malefactors condemn'd for Crimes, for which by the Law they deserv'd to die; and some of those People call'd Quakers, banish'd for meeting on Pretences of religious Worship.

Now if from the Premises it be duly consider'd what Kind of Persons those have been, by which our Plantations have at all Times been replenish'd: I suppose it will appear that such they have been, and under such Circumstances, that if his Majesty had had no Foreign Plantations, to which they might have resorted, *England* however must have lost them.

To illustrate the Truth whereof a little further, let us consider what Captain *Graunt* the ingenious Author of the Observations upon the Bills of Mortality faith, *p.* 76. and in other Places of his Book concerning the City of *London*; and it is not only said, but undeniably prov'd, *viz.* that the City of *London*, let the Mortality be what it will, by Plague or otherwise, repairs its Inhabitants once in two Years. And *p.* 101. again, if there be encouragement for a hundred Persons in *London* (that is, a way how a hundred may live better than in the Countrey) the evacuating of a fourth or third Part of that Number must soon be supplied out of the Countrey, who in a short Time remove themselves from thence hither so long, until the City, for want of Receipt and Encouragement, refuses them.

First, What he hath prov'd concerning *London*, I say of *England* in general; and the same may be said of any Kingdom or Countrey in the World.

Such as our Employment is for People, so many will our People be; and if we should imagin we have in *England* Employment but for one Hundred People, and we have born and bred amongst us a Hundred and fifty People; I say the fifty must away from us, or starve or be hang'd to prevent it, whether we had any Foreign Plantations or not.

Secondly, If by Reason of the Accommodation of living in our Foreign Plantations, we have evacuated more of our People than we should have done if we had no such Plantations, I say with the aforesaid Author in the Case of *London*; and if that Evacuation be grown to an Excess (which I believe it never did barely on the Account of the Plantations) that Decrease would procure its own Remedy; for much Want of People, if our Laws gave Encouragement, would procure us a Supply of People without the Charge of breeding them, as the *Dutch* are, and always have been supplied in their greatest Extremities.

Object. I. But it may be said, Is not the Facility of being transported into the Plantations, together with the enticing Methods customarily us'd to persuade People to go thither, and the Encouragement of living there with a People that speak our Language, strong Motives to draw our People from us; and do they not draw more from us than otherwise would leave us, to go into Foreign Plantations where they understand not the Language?

I answer first, it is not much more difficult to get a Passage to *Holland*, than it is to our Plantations.

Secondly, Many of those that go to our Plantations, if they could not go thither, would and must go into Foreign Countries, tho' it were ten times more difficult to get thither than it is; or else, which is worse (as hath been said) would adventure to be hang'd, to prevent begging or starving, as too many have done.

Thirdly, I do acknowledge that the Facility of getting to the Plantations, may cause some more to leave us, than would do if they had none but Foreign Countries for Refuge: But then if it be consider'd, that our Plantations spending mostly our *English* Manufactures, and those of all Sorts almost imaginable, in egregious Quantities, and employing near two Thirds of all our *English* Shipping, do therein give a constant Sustenance to, it may be, two Hundred Thousand Persons here at Home; then *I must needs conclude upon the whole Matter, that we have not the fewer, but the more People in* England *by Reason of our* English *Plantations in* America.

Object. II. But it may be said, is not this inferring and arguing against Sense and Experience? Doth not all the World see that the many noble Kingdoms of *Spain*, in *Europe*, are almost depopulated and ruinated, by Reason of their Peoples flocking over to the *West-Indies?* And do not all other Nations diminish in People after they become possess'd of Foreign Plantations.

Answ. I. I answer with Submission to better Judgments, that in my Opinion contending for Uniformity in Religion hath contributed ten Times more to the depopulating of *Spain* than all the *American* Plantations: What was it but that, which caused the Expulsion of so many Thousand *Moors*, who had built and inhabited most of the chief Cities and Towns of *Andaluzia*, *Granada*, *Aragon*, and other Parts? What was it but that and the Inquisition, that hath and doth daily expel such vast Numbers of rich *Jews* with their Families and Estates into *Germany*, *Italy*, *Turky*, *Holland*, and *England?* What was it but that, which caus'd those vast and long Wars between that King and the low Countries, and the Effusion of so much *Spanish* Blood and Treasure, and the final Loss of the seven Provinces; which we now see so prodigious rich, and full of People, while *Spain* is empty and poor, and *Flanders* thin and weak, in continual Fear of being made a Prey to their Neighbours?

Secondly, I answer, we must warily distinguish between Countrey and Countrey; for tho' Plantations may have drain'd *Spain* of People, it does not follow that they have or will drain *England* or *Holland*; because where Liberty and Property are not so well preserv'd, and where Interest of Money is permitted to go at twelve *per Cent.* there can be no considerable Manufactures, and no more of Tillage and Grazing, than, as we proverbially say, will keep Life and Soul together; and where there is little Manufacturing, and as little Husbandry of Lands, the Profit of Plantations, *viz.* the greatest Part thereof, will not redound to the Mother Kingdom, but to other Countries, wherein there are more Manufactures and Productions from the Earth; from hence it follows, Plantations thus manag'd, prove Drains of the People from their Mother Kingdom; whereas Plantations belonging to Mother-Kingdoms or Countries, where Liberty and Property is better preserv'd, and Interest of Money restrain'd to a low Rate, the Consequence is, that every Person sent abroad with the Utensils he is constrain'd to employ, or that are employ'd with him; I say in this Case we may reckon, that for Provisions, Cloaths, and Houshold-goods, Seamen, and all others employ'd about Materials for Building, Fitting, and Victualling of Ships, every *Englishman* in *Barbadoes* or *Jamaica* creates Employment for four Men at Home.

Thirdly, I answer, That *Holland* now sends as many, and more People, to reside yearly in their Plantations, Fortresses, and Ships in the *East-Indies* (besides many into the *West-Indies*) than *Spain*; and yet is so far from declining in the Number of their People at Home, that it is evident they do monstrously increase: And so, I hope, under the next Head to prove that *England* hath constantly increas'd in People at Home, since our Settlement upon Plantations in *America*, altho' not in so great a Proportion as the *Dutch*.

The fifth PROPOSITION, *I am of Opinion, that we had immediately before the late Plague, more People in* England, *than we had before the inhabiting of* NEW-ENGLAND, VIRGINIA, BARBADOES, *&c.*

The Proof of this at best, I know, can but be conjectural; but in Confirmation of my Opinion, I have, I think, of my Mind, the most industrious *English* Calculator this Age hath produc'd in publick, *viz.* Captain *Graunt* in the foremention'd Treatise, *p.* 88. his Words are "Upon the whole Matter we may therefore conclude, that the People of the whole Nation do increase, and consequently the Decrease of *Winchester, Lincoln*, and other like Places, must be attributed to other Reasons than that of refurnishing *London* only."

Secondly, It is manifest by the aforesaid worthy Author's Calculations, that the Inhabitants of *London*, and Parts adjacent, have increas'd to almost double within these sixty Years; and that City hath usually been taken for an Index of the whole.

I know it will be said, that altho' *London* have so increas'd, other Parts have so much diminish'd, whereof some are named before; but if to answer the Diminution of the Inhabitants in some particular Places, it be consider'd how others are increas'd, *viz. Yarmouth, Hull, Scarborough*, and other Ports in the North; as also *Liverpool, Westchester* and *Bristol, Portsmouth, Lime*, and *Plimouth*; and withal, if it be consider'd what great Improvements have been made these last sixty Years upon breaking up and inclosing of Wastes,

Forrests, and Parks, and draining of the Fens, and all those Places inhabited and furnish'd with Husbandry &c. then I think it will appear probable, that we have in *England* now, at least had before the late Plague, more People than we had before we first enter'd upon Foreign Plantations, notwithstanding likewise the great Numbers of Men which have issued from us into *Ireland*; which Countrey, as our Laws now are, I reckon not among the Number of Plantations profitable to *England*, nor within the Limits of this Discourse, tho' peradventure something may be picked out of these Papers, which may deserve Consideration in Relation to that Countrey.

But it may be said, if we have more People now than in former Ages, how came it to pass that in the Times of King *Henry* IVth and Vth, and other Times formerly, we could raise such great Armies, and employ them in Foreign Wars, and yet retain a sufficient Number to defend the Kingdom, and cultivate our Lands at Home.

I answer, First the Bigness of Armies is not always a certain Indication of the Numerousness of a Nation, but sometimes rather of the Nature of the Government, and Distribution of the Lands: As for Instance: Where the Prince and Lords are Owners of the whole Territory, altho' the People be thin, the Armies upon Occasion may be very great, as in *East-India*, *Turky*, and the Kingdoms of *Fesse* and *Morocco*, where *Falselet* was lately said to have an Army of one Hundred and Fifty or two Hundred Thousand Men, altho' every Body knows that Countrey hath as great a scarcity of People as any in the World: But since Freeholders are so much increas'd in *England* and the servile Tenures alter'd, doubtless it is more difficult, as well as more chargeable, to draw great Numbers of Men into Foreign Wars.

Since the Introduction of the new Artillery of Powder, Shot, and Fire-Arms into the World, all War is become rather an Expence of Money than Men; and Success attends those that can most and longest spend Money, rather than Men; and consequently Princes Armies in *Europe* are become more proportionable to their Purses than to the Number of their People.

Finis.

The Provinces of

South-Carolina and *Georgia*

A

New and Accurate ACCOUNT

OF THE

PROVINCES

OF

SOUTH-CAROLINA

AND

GEORGIA:

With many curious and useful Observations on the Trade, Navigation and Plantations of *Great-Britain*, compared with her
most powerful maritime Neighbours in antient and modern Times.

LONDON:

Printed for J. WORRALL at the *Bible* and
Dove in *Bell-Yard* near *Lincoln's-Inn* ; and Sold
by J. ROBERTS near the *Oxford-Arms* in
Warwick-Lane. 1732.

(Price One Shilling.)

The Provinces of

South-Carolina and *Georgia*

THE PREFACE.

THERE *have been several Accounts of the Provinces of* Carolina *publish'd formerly; among which, Mr.* Archdale's *Description of* South-Carolina *is of most undoubted Credit. Another Account in the Form of a Letter, (first printed in the Year* 1710*) was lately re-printed by Mr.* Clarke *near the* Royal-Exchange. *I could shew many Faults in this Piece, both as to Facts and Reasoning, but shall only mention a few that are obvious to almost every Reader who has ever heard any Thing of that Province. The Author is fawningly Partial to the then Administration of Government there. He praises its great Blemishes. He finds a Beauty in their Attack upon St.* Augustino; *an Expedition improvidently projected, and unsuccessfully attempted. He applauds their Paper Currency, which was a wretched Expedient to salve up the Wounds their little Republick had received in that unhappy War: A Remedy like those which our profligate young Fellows frequently meet with at the Hands of Quack-Doctors, who have just Skill enough in Drugs to remove a Clap by establishing a Pox in the Room of it. If that Writer had any Knowledge of Commerce, or History, he must have known that a* forced Paper Credit *is* incompatible with Trade, *and never held up to* Par *in any Age or Country in the World; much less could it suit the Commerce of an Infant-Colony,* *whose very Existence (in the Notion of People at a Distance) was at that Time precarious. I shall no farther pursue the Crudities of that Author, it is sufficient to observe, That if his Account had been as just and accurate as Mr.* Archdale's, *it could not answer the Expectations of the Publick at this Time. Those Treatises tell us of Twenty Sail of Shipping, but now we can truly say that there are yearly Two Hundred freighted at* Charles-Town. *The wide Extent of their Rice Trade; the amazing Encrease of their Stock of Negroes and of Cattle; and the encouraging Essays they have made in Wine and Silk, render* South-Carolina *a new Country to the Geographers. Neither of these Writers is copious enough on the Topick of the Benefits which may arise to* Great-Britain *by Peopling this fruitful Continent: That Argument is therefore handled the more largely in the following Pages. About Two Years ago,* Captain Purry, *a* Swiss *Gentleman, wrote* * *an authentick Account of that Country in* French, *which was printed at* Neufchattel *in* Switzerland: *And to shew that he believ'd himself when he gave a beautiful Description of* South-Carolina, *he is gone to settle there with Six Hundred of his Countrymen.*

> And he that hangs, or beats out's Brains
> The Devil's in him if he feigns.   *Hud.*

Mr. Archdale's *Veracity will hardly be question'd by any but Bigots, when the Publick shall be inform'd of his remarkable Integrity in his own Principles. He, being a Quaker, was chosen into Parliament by the Town of* Colchester *in* Essex, *but chose to relinquish his Seat rather than violate his Conscience with regard to Oaths and the Testact. He governed* South-Carolina *with that Moderation, that the Colony blesses his Memory; and their latest Posterity will have cause to bless it; for, under Providence, they owe to him their very Being.*

An Anonymous Author ought to have Vouchers for his Facts. I make an impartial Judgment of the Incorrectness of my Style, and therefore can't resolve to prefix my Name to this Piece: But by proper References to Mr. Archdale *and Mr.* Purry, *I shew that they concur*

* This is entitled, *Description Abregee de l' Etat presest de la Caroline meridionale.*

with me in the Geography and natural History of the Country. The Reasonings and Observations are the Result of various Reading and Conversation in many Years: Let these therefore stand, or fall by themselves.

Since the following Chapters were prepared for the Press, I have read a curious Pamphlet, entitled, Select Tracts relating to Colonies, *&c. Sold by Mr.* Roberts, *the Publisher of this Essay. Those Tracts were written by the most knowing Men of their Respective Generations, and the Style and Matter of the Introduction to them sufficiently evince the eminent Abilities of the Person (whoever he was) that collected them. Had I seen them earlier, they would have been of singular Use to me in many of my Observations and Arguments in the following Sheets: I now must be content to pride my self in having accidentally fallen into the same Way of Reasoning with the great Authors of those Tracts.*

I designed to have added a Chapter, containing the Scheme for settling the new Colony of Georgia: *But, upon a Revisal of an Elegant Piece which was published in the* Craftsman *to that effect, I thought proper to desist, for my own Sake. I shall only take Leave here to mention a Precedent of our own for planting Colonies, which, perhaps, in Part, or in the Whole, may be worthy our Imitation.*

England *was more than four Hundred Years in Possession of a great Part of* Ireland *before the Whole was compleatly conquer'd: The Wars there, and Loss of* English *Blood were infinite, the Invaders mixed and intermarried with the Natives throughout the Provinces, and degenerated in Habit, Language, Customs and Affections. In the Days of K* James *the First, the* Londoners *were at the Charge of sending into the most dangerous Part of that Kingdom more than four Hundred poor Families. There were a City, and a Town built, as had been agreed on: The City of* London-derry *contained three Hundred, the Town of* Colerain *a Hundred Houses; these were fortified with Walls and Ditches, and established with most ample Privileges. They send two Members each to the Parliament of that Kingdom, and the Mayor of* London-derry *is always the First in the Commissions of Oyer and Terminer and Assise. That City chooses two Sheriffs as our* London *does, and they are of Course Sheriffs of the County at large, as the Sheriffs of*

London *are Sheriffs of the County of Middlesex. The Salmon Fish-eries were given to the City of* London *who generally receive more than a Thousand Pounds* per Ann. *from them. What the present House-Rents of their City and Town amounts to, I shall not pretend to say, but believe they make a considerable Yearly Sum, because the Tenants have lately been too brisk Bidders for each others Bargains. The City of* London-derry, *and its Liberties, (which I think are three Miles round it) the Town of* Colerain *and the Fisheries, belong to the Twelve Companies of* London *consider'd as one aggregate Body. There are two Men chosen out of each Company to make up this Corporation, and, I think, they are called the* London Society *for the Plantation of* Ulster. *Besides this great Estate belonging to them in one Body, each Company, in its own Right, and by itself, has, or lately had, a large and rich Manor belonging to it. One of them was lately sold for Twenty Thousand Pounds, and I think a Quit Rent of a Hundred a Year re-served upon it to the Company for ever. The* Londoners *have drawn above a Hundred Thousand Pounds from that Colony within Ten Years last past, and 'tis not probable that the first Settlement ever cost them Eight Thousand Pounds, which made Four Hundred Families of their poor Freemen happy, at the same Time that it purchased so good an Estate and strengthened the* English *Interest in that Kingdom. No other Part of* Ireland *is now so perfectly free from the native* Irish *as are those two Towns and their Districts. The Populace of* London-derry *and of the adjoyning Country were so vigorous at the Revolution as to endure a Siege which has made that* English *Colony memorable to latest Posterity.*

'Tis needless to expatiate in the just Commendation *of the* Trustees *for establishing the* Colony *in* Georgia. *They have, for the Benefit of Mankind, given up that Ease and Indolence to which they were en-titled by their Fortunes and the too prevalent* Custom *of their* Native Country. *They, in some Degree, imitate their Redeemer in Sympa-thizing with the Miserable, and in Labouring to Relieve them. They take not for their* Pattern *an* Epicurean Deity: *They set before their Eyes the Giver of all good Gifts, who has put it into their Hearts, (and may he daily more and more enable their Hands) to save Multitudes of his living Images from Perdition.*

CHAPTER I.

The Situation of Carolina, *the Historical Account of it; how far the Right to a new Country is acquir'd by the first Discovery; by Occupancy; lost by Dereliction.*

THE Great and Beautiful Country of *Carolina* is bounded on the *North* between 35 and 36 Deg. of *N.* Latitude with *Virginia* and the *Apalatian* Mountains, on the *East* with the *Atlantick* Ocean, on the *South* about 30 Deg. *N.* Latitude, with Part of the *Atlantick*, or *Gulph* of *Florida*, and with * *Florida*, and on the *West* its Extent is unknown. All the Charters, or Patents of our Kings that describe its Bounds, have carried it *Westward* in a direct Line as far as the *South* Seas.

The *Spaniards* formerly included it all under the general Name of *Florida*, and pretended a Right to it by Virtue of the Pope's Donation, as indeed they did to all *America*. The *French*, in the Days of their *Charles* the IXth, made a little Settlement there by the Countenance and Encouragement of Admiral *Coligny*; but the civil Wars in *France* prevented him from taking due Care of it, and it came to nothing. He made a Second, but almost all his Men were murdered by the *Spaniards* after Quarter given; and the *French* King did not resent it, probably because they were Protestants. 'Tis not unlikely that the Admiral's View in sending these Colonies was to secure a Retreat for himself and the rest of the Reformed in case they were conquered in *France*.

The *Spaniards* by Injustice and Cruelty provoked the *Indians*, and prepared them for the Arrival of a Third Body of *French*, who put all the *Spaniards* to the Sword. The Commander of this Third Expedition contented himself with making a Tour in the Country; he made no Settlement there, nor did the *Spaniards* seek to recover

---

* *Florida* is a Country to the *South* of *Carolina*, claim'd by the *Spaniards*, who have a little Fort there call'd St. *Augustino*, about 150 Miles from the Borders of *Carolina*, or rather of the new Province of *Georgia*.

it; so that from the Year 1567 it lay deserted by all *European* Nations, 'till the Days of our King *Charles* the IId, when the *English* effectually settled there, by Virtue of His Majesty's Grant to certain Lords Proprietors, and compleated that Right, which his Predecessor, K. *Henry* the VIIth, had acquired by the first Discovery of this Part of the Continent. 'Tis true, indeed, the *Spaniards* were acquainted with this Country so early as the Year 1512, under the Conduct of *John Ponce de Leon*, but Sir *Sebastian Cabot*, or *Cabota*, born at *Bristol*, of *Venetian* Parents, had first discover'd it in the Year 1497, under the Commission, at the Costs, and in the name of our K. *Henry* the VII, as appears by foreign Writers of that Age of great Repute in the learned World, and some of them are *Spanish* Authors.

I think the *Civilians* are not all agreed upon sure Canons, or Maxims concerning the best Method of acquiring the Dominion of Countries, nor how far the first Discovery can vest, or establish a Right. Some *Romish* and *Spanish* Lawyers have been so fond as to fancy that the Pope's Donation is the best Title imaginable; yet (I know not how it happens) not only the Hereticks of *England*, but even the most Christian King, the eldest Son of the Church, has contravened that Title, has taken Possession of large Countries in *America* and grasps at more.

I believe the Doctrine most generally received is this: That Occupancy is the most unquestionable Title by the Law of Nature; and that touching at a Coast for Fuel and Water; erecting a Cross, or the Arms of a Prince, or State, and trapanning away two or three of the Savage Natives into Captivity, are not such an Occupancy as can reasonably acquire the Dominion of a Country; for at that rate *Cain*, who was a Vagabond on Earth, might have claimed universal Monarchy, and have left no Room for the Children of *Seth*. The common Sense of Mankind could not fail to establish a Rule, that Dereliction should be as certain a Method of waving, or giving up Property, as the true and genuine Occupancy is of acquiring it; and for a like Reason; for if I am entitled to take a Thing out of the Common of Nature, and make it my separate Property by using it, my not using it any longer is the most natural

Waiver and Abdication of that Property, and justly throws that Thing into the Common again, to be possess'd by the next Occupant. This Occupancy then consists in a Settlement of People, dwelling in fixed Habitations and tilling the Earth; and this is what Princes and States would prefer to all other Rights, let Declarations and Manifestoes swell with never so many historical Claims of the earliest Discovery, when Sovereigns are disposed to quarrel. And this Right, like all other Rights, must at all Times be accompanied with a sufficient Force to defend it from Invaders, for Reasons too obvious here to be enlarg'd on.

Under this rational Notion of acquiring Dominion, an Extent of the antient *Florida* of Three Hundred Miles in Length by the Ocean Coast, became the Property of *England* more than Sixty Years ago. For King *Charles* the IId having by His * Letters Patents granted the same to several Lords Proprietors by the Name of *Carolina*, they Peopled it with a Colony which has ever since subsisted, tho' frequently check'd in its Growth by heavy Difficulties and Discouragements.

This Colony had a very promising Beginning; there were a great Number of Laws, or Constitutions agreed to by the Lords Proprietors, which gave a general Toleration for tender Consciences, and contain'd many other wholesome Regulations. These had been drawn up by the great Lawyer and famous Politician the Earl of *Shaftsbury*, with the Assistance of Mr. *Lock* the Philosopher, but were not duly observ'd when the Lords Proprietors came to exercise their Jurisdiction over Numbers of People: There was a natural Infirmity in the Policy of their Charter, which was the Source of many of the Misfortunes of the Colony, without any Imputation on the noble Families concern'd. For the Grantees, being Eight in Number, and not incorporated, and no Provision being made to conclude the whole Number by the Voices of the Majority, there could not be the timely Measures always agreed on which were proper, or necessary for the Safety and good Government of the

---

* The Letters Patents to the Earl of *Clarendon*, &c. bore Date the 29th Day of *March*, 1663.

Plantation. In the mean Time the Inhabitants grew unruly and quarrelled about Religion and Politicks, and while there was a meer Anarchy among them, they were expos'd to the Attacks and Insults of their *Spanish* and *Indian* Neighbours, whom they had imprudently provok'd and injur'd; and to discharge the Debts contracted by their unsuccessful Attempts, they unskilfully forced a Paper-Currency upon the Subject, by an Act of their Parliament, which naturally put an End to Credit and suspended their Commerce; and as if they had conspir'd against the Growth of the Colony, they repealed their Laws for Liberty of Conscience, tho' the Majority of the People were Dissenters, and had resorted thither under the publick Faith for a compleat Indulgence, which they considered as Part of their *Magna Charta*. Their strict Conformity-Law was indeed repealed long before the Lords Proprietors surrendered their Patent, but it was long enough in Force to do abundance of Mischief.

And yet such are the natural Advantages of this happy Climate, that even under these Discouragements, the Colony grew so considerably, that *Charles-Town* has now near * Six Hundred good Houses, and the whole Plantation has above Forty Thousand Negroe Slaves, worth at least a Million of Pounds *Sterling*, besides an infinite Number of Cattle. Tho' it was only within these Four Years that an End was put to their Sorrows; for about that Time, the Lords Proprietors and Planters (who long had been heartily tired of each other) were, by the Interposition of the Legislature, fairly divorced forever, and the Property of the Whole vested in the Crown.

CHAPTER II.

Of the Air, Soil, Climate, and Produce of South-Carolina *and* Georgia. *Reasons why this Country is not well-peopled with* Indians. *The Natives describ'd.*

FROM what was said in the foregoing Chapter it can't be a Matter of Wonder, That a great Part of *Carolina* should have hitherto remain'd uninhabited. The Whole is divided into Two distinct Governments, by the Names of *North-Carolina* and *South-Carolina*. I shall confine my self to treat of the Latter. The new Province of *Georgia* is taken out of it, and divided from it on the *North* by the River *Savannah*, equal to the *Rhine*; its *Southern* Boundary is the River *Alatamaha*; it lies about the 30th and 31st Degree, North-Latitude, in the same Climate with *Barbary*, the *North* Part of *Ægypt*, the *South* Part of *Natolia*, or *Asia-Minor*, and the most temperate Parts of *Persia* and *China*.

* The Air is healthy, being always serene, pleasant and temperate, never subject to excessive Heat or Cold, nor to sudden Changes; the Winter is regular and short, and the Summer cool'd with refreshing Breezes; and tho' this Country is within Three Hundred Miles of *Virginia*, it never feels the cutting *North-West-Wind* in that uneasy and dangerous Degree that the *Virginians* complain of. This Wind is generally attributed to those great Seas of fresh Water which lie to the *Northwest* beyond the *Apalachean* Mountains. It seems a Journey of an Hundred Leagues in that warm Climate, blunts the Edge which the Wind gets in its Passage over those prodigious Lakes. Nor on the other Hand doth this Country ever feel the intense Heats of *Spain, Barbary, Italy,* and *Ægypt*; probably because, instead of the scorching Sands of *Africk* and *Arabia*, it has to the *Southward*, the spacious Bay of *Mexico*, which is much more temperate in its effect upon the Winds, than are those burning sandy Desarts.

* *Archdale's* Descrip. p. 7, 8, and Descrip. Abreg. p. 16.

* The Soil of this Country is generally Sandy, especially near the Sea; but 'tis impregnated with such a fertile Mixture that they use no Manure, even in their most antient Settlements, which have been under tillage these Sixty Years. It will produce almost every Thing in wonderful Quantities with very little Culture. Farther up the Country the Land is more mixed with a blackish Mould, and its Foundation generally Clay good for Bricks. They make their Lime of Oystershells, of which there are great Quantities on Banks near the Shore. All Things will undoubtedly thrive in this Country that are to be found in the happiest Places under the same Latitude. Their Rice, the only considerable Staple which requires many of their Hands at present, is known to be incomparably better than that of the *East Indies*; their Pitch, Tar and Turpentine (of which they export great Quantities) are the Rewards of their Industry in clearing the Land of superfluous Timber. † Mulberries both Black and White, are Natives of this Soil, and are found in the Woods as are many other Sorts of Fruit-Trees of excellent Kinds, and the Growth of them is surprizingly swift; for a Peach, Apricot, or Nectarine, will, from the Stone, grow to be a bearing Tree in four or five Years Time. All Sorts of Corn yield an amazing Increase, an Hundred Fold is the common Estimate, tho' their Husbandry is so slight, that they can only be said to scratch the Earth and meerly to cover the Seed. ‡ All the best Sorts of Cattle and Fowls are multiplied without Number, and therefore almost without a Price; you may see there more than a Thousand Calves in the same Inclosure belonging to one Person. § The Vine is also a wild Native here, Five or Six Sorts grow wild in the Woods; it has been said that the Stone of the Grape is too large, and the Skin too thick, but several who have tried, find all imaginable Encouragement to propagate the different Kinds from *Europe*; nor is it doubted that by proper Culture this wild Grape may be meliorated, so as well to reward the Care of the Planter.

* Descr. Abreg. p. 6. *Archd.* Descr. p. 8.
† Descr. Abreg. p. 13.
‡ Descr. Abreg. p. 11, 12, 13.
§ Ib. 10.

The wild Beasts are Deer, Elks, Bears, Wolves, Buffaloes, Wild-Boars, and abundance of Hares and Rabbits: They have also the Cata-mountain, or small Leopard; but this is not the dangerous Species of the *East Indies*. Their Fowls are no less various; they have all the Sorts that we have in *England*, both wild and tame, and many others either useful or beautiful. It would be endless to enumerate their Fishes, the River *Savannah* is plentifully stock'd with them of many excellent Kinds: No Part in the World affords more Variety or greater Plenty. They have Oak, Cedar, Cypress, Fir, Walnut and Ash, besides the Sassafras. They have Oranges, Lemons, Apples and Pears, besides the Peach and Apricot mention'd before; some of * these are so delicious, that whoever tastes them will despise the insipid watry Taste of those we have in *England*; and yet such is the Plenty of them, that they are given to the Hogs in great Quantities. *Sarsaparilla*, *Cassia*, and other Sorts of Trees grow in the Woods, yielding Gums and Rosin, and also some Oyl excellent for curing Wounds.

† The Woods near the *Savannah* are not hard to be clear'd, many of them have no Underwood, and the Trees do not stand generally thick on the Ground, but at considerable Distances asunder. When you fell the Timber for Use, or to make Tar, the Root will rot in Four or Five Years, and in the mean Time you may pasture the Ground. But if you would only destroy the Timber, 'tis done by half a Dozen Strokes of an Ax surrounding each Tree a little above the Root; in a Year or two, the Water getting into the Wounds, rots the Timber, and a brisk Gust of Wind fells many Acres for you in an Hour, of which you may then make one bright Bonfire. Such will be frequently here the Fate of the Pine, the Walnut, the Cypress, the Oak, and the Cedar. Such an Air and Soil can only be fitly describ'd by a Poetical Pen, because there's but little Danger of exceeding the Truth. Take therefore Part of Mr. *Waller*'s Description of an Island in the Neighbourhood of *Carolina* to give you an Idea of this happy Climate.

* *Archd*. Descr. p. 7.
† Descr. Abreg. p. 7.

The lofty Cedar which to Heav'n aspires,
The Prince of Trees is fuel for their Fires.
The sweet Palmettaes a new Bacchus *yield,*
With Leaves as ample as the broadest Shield.
Under the Shadow of whose friendly Boughs
They sit carousing where their Liquor grows.
Figs there unplanted thro' the Fields do grow,
Such as fierce Cato *did the* Romans *show:*
With the rare Fruit inviting them to spoil
Carthage, *the Mistress of so rich a Soil.*
With candid Plantines and the juicy Pine,
On choicest Melons and sweet Grapes they dine,
And with Potatoes fat their lusty Swine.
———*The kind Spring, which but salutes us*
    here,
Inhabits there and courts them all the Year.
Ripe Fruits and Blossoms on the same Trees live,
At once they promise, what at once they give.
So sweet the Air, so moderate the Clime,
None sickly lives, or dies before his Time.
Heav'n sure has kept this Spot of Earth uncurst,
To shew how all Things were created first.

The Thought of the Poet in the last Couplet is adopted by the
Ingenious Dr. *Burnet* in his Theory of the Earth, with fine Improvements of it. The Dr. seems fully convinced that the Temper-
ament of the Climate of *Bermudas* approaches very near to that of
the Antediluvian World, in which he fancies that Spring and Autumn were continual and universal over the Face of the Earth, 'till
the Almighty (as *Milton* has it) turned the Poles askance: And by
physical Reasoning he deduces the Longævity of the Antediluvi-
ans from this happy Equality of Seasons, uninterrupted by the
shocking Vicissitude of Heat and Cold, which tear the human
Frame asunder. He thinks that a Person born in *Bermudas*, and
continuing there all his Life-Time, has a moral Probability of living
Three Hundred Years. This Conjecture seems to be supported by
what we are told in *Purchas* his Pilgrimage of one of the *Indian*

Kings of *Florida*, who was Three Hundred Years old, and his Father was Fifty Years older, and then living. The Father is describ'd as a Skeleton cover'd with Skin; his Sinews, Veins and Arteries, and other Parts appear'd so clearly through his Skin, that a Man might easily tell and discern them the one from the other. His Son shewed five Generations descended from himself. 'Twas such a Figure as this *Indian* King, which induc'd the Antients to feign that *Tithonus* being very old was chang'd into a Grasshopper.

Longa Tithonum *minuit senectus*. (Hor.) Now *Georgia* is just about the Middle of *Purchas* his *Florida*. But not to go too far with the Poet, *Theorist*, and Old Historian; 'tis probable those *Indians* divided the solar Year into two Years as the *Virginian Indians* did. Let us rely upon what we know at this Day; it must not be concealed, that in this Country, as almost in every new Climate, Strangers are apt to have a Seasoning; an Ague, or Sort of a Fever; but then 'tis very slight: And for the rest, People very seldom want Health here but by Intemperance, (which indeed is too common) And notwithstanding their several Skirmishes with the *Spaniards* and *Indians*, and that the Plague was imported thither in the Year One Thousand Seven Hundred and Six; yet there are now several aged Persons living at *Charles-Town*, who were of that little Number that first settled there and hewed down Timber above Sixty Years ago.

By the Healthiness of this Climate, and some Accounts of *Spanish* Expeditions hither in early Times, which were vigorously repulsed by great Armies of the Natives, one would expect to find the Country by this Time fully peopled with *Indians*. It is indeed probable that they were much more numerous in those Days than they are at present, or else they could not have defended themselves against the *Spaniards* as they did. But if their Numbers were formerly considerable they have since greatly decreased; and that might easily happen in a Century, even tho' the Country be naturally fertile and healthy, for the *Indians* in all the Continent of North *America*, near the *Atlantick* Ocean, have been discovered to have this Resemblance in common: They are small Tribes of Huntsmen, exceedingly apt to make War upon each other, as our 5 Nations of *Iroquois* beyond New-*England* and New-*York*, have within these Forty Years driven many other Nations from fertile inland Countries, of the extent of many Millions of Acres, and that not without incredible Slaughter. Add to which, that these poor Creatures, living with hardly any Husbandry, or Stores of Provisions, must perish in Heaps if the Fruits of the Woods, or their Hunting should once fail them; one scanty Season would infallibly famish whole Nations of them. Another great Cause of their Destruction was the Small-pox, the *Europeans* brought this Distemper among them: Now their common Cure in all Fevers is to sweat plentifully, and then to stop that Evacuation at once by plunging instantly into a River. They can't be persuaded to alter this Method in the Case of the Small-pox, and it certainly kills them. Rum also has been a fatal Liquor to them, many of them have been inclined to drink it to such an Excess as we sometimes hear of at Home in the Abuse of Geneva, and sometimes they are so little Masters of their Reason, when intoxicated, as to be too apt to commit Murders; but there are many sober Men among them who abhor the Abuse of this Liquor. Thus Mr. *Archdale* relates, that, when he was Governour, he order'd an *Indian* to be executed, who being drunk with Rum had murder'd an *Indian* of another Tribe. The King of his Tribe came to him and reminded him how often he had warned him of the Dangers attending Excesses in that Liquor, but exhorted him (since Death was unavoidable) to die like a Man, which the unhappy Man performed with Firmness and Gallantry. I have mentioned this Story because a vulgar Error prevails, as if the *Indians* were all addicted to this Vice. But to return to the Opposition against the *Spaniards*. 'Tis also probable that many Tribes were leagued together in the Common Cause, and that the *Spaniards* were thence induced to think the People of this Part of the Continent much more numerous than in Truth they were. 'Tis most certain that the Nations of *Carolina* in our Days have exactly answer'd in all Respects the Descriptions we have of the Inhabitants of *Virginia*, when we first got footing there in the Beginning of the last Century. Captain *Smith* (next to Sir *Walter Rawleigh*) the most indust'rous and resolute Planter of *Virginia* in those Days, computed that all the Tribes in a Country much more fertile and little less in Extent than *England*, could not draw into the Field above Five Thousand fighting Men, tho' the Tract of Land is sufficient to maintain more than Ten Millions of People.

———— *Sane populus numerabilis, utpote parvus.* Hor.

This is confirmed and illustrated by the well-attested Story that one of their little Kings instructed his Minister, who was coming hither, to number our Tribe; the Minister, at his Arrival, attempted to execute his Commission by making Notches on a Stick, but soon grew tir'd of his Arithmetick, and at his Return express'd the Multitude of our Fore-Fathers by pointing to the Stars, and to the fallen Leaves of a Wood in Autumn. And here I can't omit saying, that it is a Policy of considerable Benefit to our Colonies, and an Expence well laid out, at proper Distances of Time to persuade some of the chiefest Savages, both for Authority and Understanding, to visit *Great Britain*. That awed with the high Idea which our Metropolis gives them of the Grandeur of this Empire, and propagating that Idea among their Tribes, our Planters in their several Neighbourhoods may enjoy uninterrupted Peace and Commerce with them, and even Assistance from them, for at least one Generation. Such was the Journey of the *Irroquois* Chiefs in the Reign of Queen *Anne*, and such was lately the Visit from our *Indian* Neighbours of *Carolina*. The good Effects of these Visits are well known to the Planters of those Colonies respectively, and probably will be felt with Pleasure for an Age to come.

The Description of the *Carolina-Indians* in their present State of Nature, is as follows, * They are somewhat tawny, occasioned chiefly by oyling their Skins, and by exposing themselves naked to the Rays of the Sun. They are generally streight-body'd, comely in Person, quick of Apprehension, and great Hunters, by which they are not only serviceable by killing Deer to procure Skins for Trade with us, but our People that live in Country Plantations procure of them the whole Deer's Flesh, and they bring it many Miles for the Value of Six Pence Sterling, and a wild Turkey of Forty Pound Weight for the Value of Two Pence.

* *Archd.* Descr. p. 7.

CHAPTER III.

Persons reduc'd to Poverty are not Wealth to the Nation, may be happy in Georgia, *and profitable to* England; *they are within the Design of the Patent.*

SINCE the Time that the Lords Proprietors sold their Rights in *Carolina* to the Crown, the Governour there, has been ordered and instructed to assign liberally Portions of Land to every new Planter according to his Ability to occupy it; to erect Towns and Parishes of Twenty Thousand Acres of Land in each District; and to grant to each Parish the Privilege of sending two Members to the Assembly of the Province, as soon as One Hundred Masters of Families shall be settled in it. Neither will the Planters be confin'd to the Ground first allotted them, their Lots are to be augmented as they become able to cultivate a larger Quantity. These Lands are to be granted in Fee-simple under the Yearly Rent of Four-pence for every Hundred Acres: But this Rent is not to be charged for the first Ten Years; during that Time the Lands shall be entirely Free.

But all this Encouragement was not sufficient to People this Country, they who can make Life tolerable here are willing to stay at Home, as 'tis indeed best for the Kingdom that they should, and they who are oppress'd by Poverty and Misfortunes are unable to be at the Charges of removing from their Miseries. These were the People intended to be relieved, but they were not able to reach the friendly Arm extended for their Relief, something else must be done, of which more shall be said in a proper Place. Let us in the mean Time cast our Eyes on the Multitude of unfortunate People in the Kingdom of reputable Families, and of liberal, or at least, easy Education: Some undone by Guardians, some by Law-Suits, some by Accidents in Commerce, some by Stocks and Bubbles, and some by Suretyship. But all agree in this one Circumstance, that they must either be Burthensome to their Relations, or betake themselves to little Shifts for Sustenance, which ('tis ten to one) do not answer their Purposes, and to which a well-educated Mind descends with the utmost Constraint. What various Misfortunes may reduce the Rich, the Industrious, to the Danger of a Prison, to a moral Certainty of Starving! These are the People that may relieve themselves and strengthen *Georgia*, by resorting thither, and Great *Britain* by their Departure.

I appeal to the Recollection of the Reader (tho' he be Opulent, tho' he be Noble) does not his own Sphere of Acquaintance? (I may venture to ask) Does not even his own Blood, his Set of near Relations furnish him with some Instances of such Persons as have been here describ'd? Must they Starve? What honest Mind can bear to think it? Must they be fed by the Contributions of Others? Certainly they must, rather than be suffered to perish. Are these Wealth to the Nation? Are they not a Burthen to themselves, a Burthen to their Kindred and Acquaintance? A Burthen to the whole Community?

I have heard it said (and 'tis easy to say so) let them learn to work; let them subdue their Pride and descend to mean Employments, keep Ale-houses, or Coffee-houses, even sell Fruit, or clean Shoes for an honest Lively-hood. But alas! These Occupations, and many more like them, are overstock'd already by People who know better how to follow them, than do they whom we have been talking of. Half of those who are bred in low Life, and well versed in such Shifts and Expedients, find but a very narrow Maintenance by them. As for Labouring, I cou'd almost wish that the Gentleman, or Merchant, who thinks that another Gentleman, or Merchant in want, can thresh, or dig, to the Value of Subsistence for his Family, or even for himself; I say I could wish the Person who thinks so, were obliged to make trial of it for a Week, or (not to be too severe) for only a Day: He would find himself to be less than the Fourth Part of a Labourer, and that the Fourth Part of a Labourer's Wages could not maintain him. I have heard it said, that a Man may learn to labour by Practice; 'tis admitted: But it must also be admitted that before he can learn, he may starve. Suppose a Gentleman were this Day to begin, and with grievous toil found himself able to earn Three Pence, how many Days, or Months, are necessary to form him that he may deserve a Shilling *per diem?*

Men, whose Wants are importunate, must try such Expedients as will give immediate Relief. 'Tis too late for them to begin to learn a Trade when their pressing Necessities call for the Exercise of it.

Having thus described (I fear, too truly) the pityable Condition of the better Sort of the Indigent, an Objection rises against their Removal upon what is stated of their Imbecility for Drudgery. It may be asked, if they can't get Bread here for their Labour, how will their Condition be mended in *Georgia?* The Answer is easy; Part of it is well attested, and Part self-evident. They have Land there for nothing, and that * Land is so fertile that (as is said before) they receive an Hundred Fold increase for taking very little Pains. Give here in *England* Ten Acres of good Land to One of these helpless Persons, and I doubt not his Ability to make it sustain him, and this by his own Culture, without letting it to another: But the Difference between no Rent, and Rack-Rent, is the Difference between eating and starving. If I make but Twenty Pound of the Produce of a Field, and am to pay Twenty Pound Rent for it; 'tis plain I must perish if I have not another Fund to support me: But if I pay no Rent, the Produce of that Field will supply the mere Necessities of Life.

With a View to the Relief of People in the Condition I have described, His Majesty has this present Year incorporated a considerable Number of Persons of Quality and Distinction, and vested a large Tract of *South-Carolina* in them, by the Name of *Georgia*, in Trust to be distributed among the Necessitous. These Trustees not only give Land to the Unhappy who go thither, but are also impower'd to receive the voluntary Contributions of charitable Persons to enable them to furnish the poor Adventurers with all Necessaries for the Expence of the Voyage, occupying the Land, and supporting them 'till they find themselves comfortably settled. So that now the Unfortunate will not be obliged to bind themselves to a long Servitude, to pay for their Passage, for they may be carried *gratis* into a Land of Liberty and Plenty; where they immediately find themselves in Possession of a competent Estate, in an happier Climate than they knew before, and they are Unfortunate indeed if here they can't forget their Sorrows.

* Descr. Abreg. p. 13.

CHAPTER IV.

England *will grow* Rich *by sending her* Poor Abroad. *Of Refugees,* Conversion *of* Indians, *small Offenders,* Roman Colonies.

BESIDES the Persons described in the preceding Chapter, there are others whom it may be proper to send Abroad for the Reasons hereafter given, which Reasons will also shew at whose Expence these other Sorts of indigent People ought to be removed. I think it may be laid down for a Rule, that *we may well spare all those, who having neither Income, nor Industry, equal to their Necessities, are forced to live upon the Fortunes, or Labours of others*; and that they who now are an heavy *Rent-charge* upon the Publick, may be made an immense *Revenue* to it, and this by an happy Exchange of their Poverty for an Affluence.

Believing it will be granted that the People described in the last Chapter ought in Prudence to go Abroad; and that we are bound in Humanity and Charity to send them: There arises a Question, whether our aiding their Departure be consistent with good Policy? I raise this Objection on purpose to answer it, because some who mean very well to the Publick have fancy'd that our Numbers *absolutely taken*, without a Distinction, are real Wealth to a Nation. Upon a little Examination, this will appear to be a mistaken Notion. It arises from a Mis-Application of Sir *William Petty*'s Political Arithmetick, and of Sir *William Temple*'s Observations on the united *Netherlands*. But when these great Men esteem People as the Wealth of a Nation, surely they can only mean such as labour, and by their Industry add yearly to the Capital Stock of their Country, at the same Time, that they provide the Necessaries or Comforts of Life for themselves. Perhaps the Rasp-houses may be reckoned Part of the Riches of *Holland*, because the Drones are made to work in them: But is an Infirmary of Incurables Wealth to a Community? Or (which is worse, because 'tis remediable and is not remedied) are Hundreds of Prisons filled with Thousands of

English Debtors, are they a Glory, or a Reproach, a Benefit, or a Burthen, to the Nation? Who can be so absurd as to say that we should be enriched by the Importation of a Multitude of Cripples, who might be able perhaps to earn a Fourth Part of what is necessary to sustain them? If Ten Thousand of these would be an Addition to our Wealth, Ten Millions of them must add a Thousand Times as much to it. Did the Fire of *London* add to the Wealth of the Nation? I am sure it gave abundance of Employment to the Poor, just as People are employed in Trade to feed and cloath the Inhabitants of Prisons. But these are also a slow Fire, an Hectick Fever to consume the Vitals of the State. The true State of National Wealth is like that of private Wealth, 'tis comparative. The Nation, as well as Individuals, must work to save and not to spend. If I work hard all Day and at Night give my Wages to the next Cripple I see, it may be profitable to my Soul, but my worldly Fortune is in the same Condition as if I had stood idle. If the Produce of the Nation be in Moveables Land and Labour Fifty Millions in a Year, and only Forty Eight Millions are expended to maintain the People: Now has the Nation added Two Millions to its Capital, but if it spends Fifty One Millions, then is that to be made good by sinking Part of the Personal Estate, or Mortgaging the real. And upon a *par, plus* a Million, and *minus* a Million in Earnings and Expences will operate nothing towards encreasing the National Wealth, if you proceed in *infinitum*, 'tis only impoverishing the Rich to maintain the Poor; it seems indeed to have something of Levelling in it; to prevent which, I think our Men of Fortune would act wisely once for all; to put these poor People on a Footing of their own, and shake off the perpetual Incumbrance by a single Act of prudent Beneficence.

One of the Gentlemen would have *Scotland, Ireland* and *Wales* sunk under Water, but all the People saved and settled in *England.* He certainly deceived himself with a View of the * artificial Strength of the *Dutch,* when their Fishery was at the highest Pitch, and when they were Carriers for Mankind. But they have not been able to preserve these Branches of Trade entire, and their Numbers

* See the 6th Chapter.

must decrease as do the Means of maintaining them. * Therefore instead of taking it for granted, that Numbers of People necessarily create a Traffick; we may invert the Proposition, and safely hold, that an extensive Traffick will infallibly be attended with sufficient Numbers of People.

And yet these unhappy People, who are not able to earn above a Fourth Part of their Sustenance at Home, and as we have shewn are a Load on the Fortunes and Industry of others, may in the new Province of *Georgia* well provide by their Labour a decent Maintenance, and at the same Time enrich their Mother Country.

Upon what has been said, the Reader may be desirous to see a State of the Difference (with respect to the Interests of the Industrious and Wealthy Part of the Nation,) between a poor Person here, earning but Half his Sustenance, and the same Person settled in a Freehold, of a fertile Soil without Tithes or Taxes: And in this Computation let us remember that of the many Thousands of poor

* To illustrate the Doctrine laid down in this Sentence, take the following Part of a Description of a neighbouring Country by a celebrated Author.

"I met in my Days Journey, nine Cars loaden with old musty shrivel'd Hides, one Car-load of Butter, one Cow and Calf driven by a Man and his Wife. A Colony of one Hundred and Fifty Beggars, all repairing to People our Metropolis, and by encreasing the Number of Hands, to encrease its Wealth; upon the old Maxim, that People are the Riches of a Nation. And therefore one Thousand Mouths with hardly Ten Pair of Hands, or any Work to employ them, will infallibly make us a rich and flourishing People. Secondly, Travellers enough, but Seven in Ten wanting Shirts and Cravats; Nine in Ten going barefoot and carrying their Broagues and Stockings in their Hands. One Woman in Twenty having a Pillion, the rest Riding bare back'd. Above Two Hundred Horsemen, with Four Pair of Boots amongst them all, Seventeen Saddles of Leather, (the rest being made of Straw,) and most of their Garranes only shod before. I went into one of the Principal Farmers Houses out of Curiosity, and his whole Furniture consisted of Two Blocks for Stools, a Bench on each side the Fire-Place made of Turf, six Trenchers, one Bowl, a Pot, six Horn-spoons, three Noggins, three Blankets (one of which served the Man and Maid-Servant; the other Two, the Master of the Family, his Wife and five Children,) a small Churn, a wooden Candlestick, a broken Stick for a pair of Tongs. In the publick Towns, one third of the Inhabitants walking the Streets barefoot, &c."

Debtors, who fill our Prisons, few earn any Thing at present; and this Colony is chiefly intended for the Unfortunate, there being no Danger of the Departure of such as are able to maintain themselves here.

A Man who is equal in Ability, only to the Fourth Part of a Labourer, (and many such there are,) we will suppose to earn Four Pence *per Diem*, or Five Pounds *per Annum*, in *London*; his Wife and a Child of above Seven Years Old Four Pence *per Diem* more: Upon a fair Supposition (because 'tis the common Case) he has another Child too Young to earn any Thing. These live but wretchedly at an Expence of Twenty Pounds *per Ann.* to defray which they earn Ten Pounds; so that they are a Loss to the Rich and Industrious Part of the Nation of Ten Pounds *per Ann.* for there are but three general Methods of supplying the Defect of their Ability. Whatever they consume more than they earn, must be furnished, First, either by the Bounty, or Charity of others; or Secondly, by Frauds, as by running in Debt to the Ruin of the Industrious, *&c.* Or, Thirdly by what our Law calls Force and Felony, as Theft and Robbery, *&c.* They must be supplied at some of these Rates, therefore (as I said before,) this Family is a Loss to the Rich and Industrious of Ten Pounds *per Ann.* and if the Particulars of their Consumption, or an Equivalent for them could have brought Ten Pounds from any Foreign Market, then has the whole Community lost Ten Pounds by this Family.

Now this very Family in *Georgia*, by raising Rice and Corn sufficient for its Occasions, and by attending the Care of their Cattle and Land (which almost every one is able to do for himself in some tolerable Degree) will easily produce in the gross Value, the Sum of Sixty Pounds *per Ann.* nor is this to be wonder'd at, because of the valuable Assistance it has from a fertile Soil and a Stock given *gratis*, which must always be remembred in this Calculation.

The Lots to be assigned to each Family, as 'tis said, will be about Fifty Acres. The usual * Wages of a common Labourer in *Carolina*

* Descr. Abreg. p. 9.

is Three Shill. *per Diem*, *English* value, or Twenty Shillings of their Money. Therefore our poor Man, (who is only equal to the Fourth Part of a Man,) at about Nine Pence *per Diem*, earns about Twelve Pounds *per Ann*. his Care of his Stock on his Land in his Hours of Resting from Labour, (amounting to one Half of each Day) is worth also Twelve Pounds *per Ann*. his Wife and eldest Child may easily between them earn as much as the Man; So that the Sum remaining to be raised by the Wealth of the Soil and the Stock thereon (abstracted from the Care and Labour of the Husband-man) is only Twelve Pounds *per Ann*. it must be observed that tho' this Family, when in *London*, was dieted but meanly, yet it could afford very little for Cloaths out of the Twenty Pounds it then expended, but now it will fare much better in *Georgia*, at the same Expence, because Provisions will be cheap, and it will also pay Forty Pounds a Year to *England* for Apparel, Furniture and Uten-sils of the Manufacture of this Kingdom. Behold then the Benefit the Common Weal receives by relieving her famishing Sons. Take it stated only upon One Hundred such Families as follows,

In *London* an Hundred Men earn	500 *l*.
An Hundred Women and an Hundred Children	500 *l*.
	Total 1000 *l*.
In *Georgia* an Hundred Families earn	
An Hundred Men for Labour	1200 *l*.
Ditto for Care	1200 *l*.
An Hundred Women and an Hundred Children	2400 *l*.
Land and Stock in themselves	1200 *l*.
	Total 6000 *l*.
In *London* an Hundred Families consume	2000 *l*.
Supplied by their Labour	1000 *l*.
By the Wealth of others	1000 *l*.
In *Georgia* an Hundred Families	
consume of their own Produce	2000 *l*.
Of *English* Produce	4000 *l*.

Thus taking it that we gained One Thousand Pounds *per Ann*. (which was the Value of their Labour) before their Removal, that we now gain Four Thousand Pounds, and we have got an Addition of Three Thousand Pounds *per Ann.* to our Income; but if, (as the Truth is) we formerly lost One Thousand Pounds *per Ann.* and the Nation now gains Four Thousand Pounds *per Ann.* the Rich and Industrious are now profited to the Value of Five Thousand Pounds *per Ann.* I might also shew other great Advantages in the Encrease of our Customs, our Shipping, and our Seamen. It is plain that these Hundred Families, thus removed, employ near Two Hundred Families here to work for them, and thus by their Absence they encrease the People of *Great Britain*, for Hands will not be long wanting where Employment is to be had: If we can find Business that will feed them, what between the Encouragement and Encrease of Propagation on the one Hand, and the Preservation of those who now perish for Want on the other: We should quickly find we had strengthened our Hive by sending a Swarm away to provide for themselves.

It is also highly for the Honour and Advancement of our holy Religion to assign a new Country to the poor *Germans*, who have left their own for the Sake of Truth. It will be a powerful Encouragement to Martyrs and Confessors of this Kind to hold fast their Integrity, when they know their Case not to be desperate in this World. Nor need we fear that the King of *Prussia* will be able to engross them all, we shall have a Share of them if we contribute chearfully to their Removal. The Society for the Propagation of the Gospel in foreign Parts have gloriously exerted themselves on this Occasion: They have resolv'd to advance such a Sum of Money to the Trustees for the Colony of *Georgia*, as will enable them to provide for Seven Hundred poor *Salzburghers*. This is laying a Foundation for the Conversion of the Heathen, at the same Time, that they snatch a great Number of poor Christians out of the Danger of Apostacy. 'Tis to be hoped this laudable Example will be followed by private Persons, who may thus at once do much for the Glory of God, and for the Wealth and Trade of *Great Britain*. Subjects thus acquir'd by the impolitick Persecutions, by the superstitious Barbarities of neighbouring Princes, are a noble Addition to the capital Stock of the *British* Empire. If our People be

Ten Millions, and we were to have an Access of Ten Thousand *use-ful* Refugees, every Stock-jobber in *Exchange-Alley* must allow that this would encrease our Wealth and Figure in the World, as one added to a Thousand, or, as $\frac{1}{10}$ *per Cent.* This would be the Proportion of our Growth compar'd with our Neighbours, who have not been the Persecutors; but as against the Persecutor, the Increase of our Strength would be in a double Ratio, compounded as well of negative as of positive Quantity. Thus if *A* and *B* are worth One Thousand Pounds each, and a Third Person gives Twenty Shillings to *A*, now *A* is become richer than *B* by $\frac{1}{10}$ *per Cent.* but if *A* gains Twenty Shillings from *B*, then *A* is become richer than *B* by $\frac{2}{10}$ or $\frac{1}{5}$ *per Cent.* for *A* is worth One Thousand and One Pounds, and *B* is worth only Nine Hundred and Ninety Nine Pounds.

The Encrease of our People, on this fruitful Continent, will probably, in due Time, have a good Effect on the Natives, if we do not shamefully neglect their Conversion: If we were moderately attentive to our Duty on this Head, we have no Reason to doubt of Success. The *Spaniard* has at this Day as many Christians, as he has Subjects in *America*, Negroes excepted. We may more reasonably hope to make Converts and good Subjects of the *Indians* in Amity with us, by using them well, when we grow numerous in their Neighbourhood, than the *Spaniards* could have expected to have done by their inexpressible Cruelties, which raised the utmost Aversion in the Minds of the poor *Indians* against them and their Religion together. One of their own Friers who had not relinquish'd his Humanity, tells us of an *Indian* Prince, who just as the *Spaniards* were about to murder him, was importuned by one of their Religious to become a Christian; the Priest told him much of Heaven and Hell, of Joy and Misery eternal; the Prince desired to be informed which of the two Places was allotted for the *Spaniards?* Heaven, quoth the Priest; says the Prince, I'm resolved not to go there. How different from this was the Reflection of an *Indian* Chief in *Pensilvania:* * *What is the Matter, says he, with us that we*

* *Brit. Emp.* Fol. 1. p. 162.

are thus sick in our own Air, and these Strangers well? 'Tis as if they were sent hither to inherit our Land in our steads; but the Reason is plain, they love the Great God and we do not. Was not this *Indian* almost become a Christian? *New-England* has many Convert-*Indians*, who are very good Subjects, tho' no other Colony had such long and cruel Wars with its *Indian* Neighbours.

The pious Benefactions of the People of *England* have in all Ages equall'd, if not surpassed, all Instances of the Kind in other Countries. The mistaken Piety of our Ancestors gave a third Part of the Kingdom to the Church: Their Intentions were right, tho' they erred in the Object. Since the Statutes against *mort-main* and superstitious Uses, our great and numerous Foundations of Hospitals and Alms-houses are the Wonder of Foreigners. Some of these, especially of the largest, are doubtless of great Use, and excellently administered. And yet, if the Numbers in this Nation, who feel the Woes of others and would contribute to relieve them, did but consider the Cases of the People describ'd in the last Chapter, of the *German* Emigrants, and even of the poor *Indians*; they would be apt to conclude that there ought to be a Blessing in Store for these also. About Eight Pounds allowed to an indigent Person here, may poorly support him, and this must be repeated yearly; but a little more, than double that Sum, relieves him for Life, sends him to our new World, gives Plenty there to him and his Posterity; putting them in Possession of a good Estate, of which, they may be their own Stewards.

But this is not all, that Sum which settles one poor Family in the Colony does not end there; it in Truth purchases an Estate to be applied to like Uses, in all future Times. The Author of these Pages is credibly inform'd that the Trustees will reserve to themselves square Lots of Ground interspers'd at proper Distances among the Lands, which shall be given away: As the Country fills with People, these Lots will become valuable, and at moderate Rents will be a growing Fund to provide for those whose melancholy Cases may require Assistance hereafter: Thus the Settlement of Five Hundred Persons will open the Way to settle a Thousand more afterwards with equal Facility. Nor is this Advance of the Value of these Lots of Land a chimerical Notion; it will happen certainly and suddenly. All the Lands within Fifty Miles of *Charlestown* have within these Seven Years encreas'd near Four-Fold in their * Value, so that you must pay Three or Four Hundred Pounds for a Plantation, which Seven Years ago you could have bought for a Hundred Pounds, and 'tis certain that Fifty Years ago you might have purchas'd at *Charlestown* for Five Shillings a Spot of Land which the Owner would not sell at this Day for Two Hundred Pounds Sterling.

The Legislature is only able to take a proper Course for the Transportation of small Offenders, if it shall seem best, when the Wisdom of the Nation is assembled; I mean only those who are but Novices in Iniquity. Prevention is better than the Punishment of Crimes, it may reform such to make them Servants to such Planters were reduc'd from a good Condition. The Manners and Habits of very young Offenders would meliorate in a Country not populous enough to encourage a profligate Course of Life, but a Country where Discipline will easily be preserv'd. These might supply the Place of Negroes, and yet (because their Servitude is only to be temporary) they might upon Occasion be found useful against the *French*, or *Spaniards*; indeed, as the Proportion of Negroes now stands, that Country would be in great Danger of being lost, in Case of a War with either of those Powers. The present Wealth of the Planters in their Slaves too probably threatens their future Ruin, if proper Measures be not taken to strengthen their Neighbourhood with large Supplies of Free-men. I would not here be understood to advance that our common Run of *Old-Baily* Transports wou'd be a proper Beginning in the Infancy of *Georgia*. No, they would be too hard for our young Planters, they ought never to be sent any where but to the Sugar Islands, unless we had Mines to employ them.

The Poverty of the Publick, with regard to its immense Debt, and the Anticipation of Taxes attending that Debt, will probably be a Reason to many worthy Patriots, not to afford a large *pecuniary* Assistance in Parliament, tho' they give all other furtherance

* Descr. Abreg. p. 9.

to this Settlement, and yet powerful Reasons might be offer'd, why the Commons of *Great Britain*, with Justice to those that sent them, might apply a large Sum of publick Money to this Occasion. Let us suppose that Twenty Five Thousand of the most helpless People in *Great Britain* were settled there at an Expence of half a Million of Money; the Easiness of the Labour in winding off the Silk and tending the Silk Worm would agree with the most of those who throughout the Kingdom are chargeable to the Parishes. That Labour with the Benefit of Land stock'd for them *gratis*, would well subsist them, and save our Parishes near Two Hundred Thousand Pounds a Year directly in their annual Payments; not to compute would also be saved indirectly, by the Unwillingness of many pretended Invalids to go the Voyage, who would then betake themselves to industrous Courses to gain a Livelyhood.

I shall consider the Benefit of employing them in raising Silk when I come in the Fifth Chapter, to treat of the Commerce of *Carolina*. I shall only here observe that the Number of Poor, last mention'd, being thus dispos'd of, would send us Goods, at least to the Value of Five Hundred Thousand Pounds annually, to pay for their *English* Necessaries; and that would be somewhat better than our being oblig'd to maintain them at the Rate of Two Hundred Thousand Pounds a Year here at Home.

I can't dismiss this Enquiry concerning the proper Persons to plant this Colony, without observing that the Wisdom of the *Roman* State discharged not only its ungovernable distressed Multitude, but also its Emeriti, its Soldiers, which had served long and well in War, into Colonies upon the Frontiers of their Empire. 'Twas by this Policy that they elbow'd all the Nations round them. Their Military Hospital went a Progress, we can trace its Stages *Northward* from the *Tiber* to the *Po*, to the *Rhone*, to the *Rhine*, to the *Thames:* The like Advances they made on all Sides round them, and their Soldiers were at least as fond of the Estates thus settled on them as ours can be of their Pensions.

What I said before in this Chapter, with regard to the encreasing Fund, to arise by reserved Lots of Ground interspersed among the Lands that will be distributed to the Planters, will hold good in the same Manner in such Settlements as might be made at a national Expence, so that Twenty Thousand People, well settled, will raise the Value of the reserved Lands, in such Measure as will bring *Great Britain* to resemble the present *Carolina* in one happy Instance, *viz.* That there is not a * Beggar, or very poor Person in the whole Country. Then should we have no going to Decay, no complaining in our Streets.

CHAPTER V.

Of the present and (probable) future Trade of South-Carolina *and* Georgia. *Rice, Silk, Cotton, Wine,* &c.

THE present State of *South-Carolina* and its Commerce may give us an Idea of the Condition of the early Settlements in the new Colony of *Georgia.* Their first Essays in Trade and Husbandry will doubtless be in Imitation of their nearest Neighbours. We shall therefore consider these Colonies together, the Difference in their Air and Soil being hardly discernable, and the same Traffick being proper for them both.

We are not to imagine that either the present Branches of Trade in that Country, will be perpetual, or that there is not room to introduce others of more Importance than any they have hitherto been acquainted with. Thus it will necessarily fall out that their present Exports of Lumber and of Deer Skins will decrease, or rather wholly cease when the Country grows populous: And this for an obvious Reason, the Land will be better employ'd, it will be dis-afforrested, and no longer left vacant to the Growth of great

* Descr. Abreg. p. 6.

Woods, and the Sustenance of wild Herds of Deer. But the very Reason why these Branches of Trade will cease will also be the Cause of their taking up others, or improving them to such a Degree, as must put these Colonies in a Condition to vie with the most flourishing Countries of *Europe* and *Asia:* And that without Prejudice to their Dependance on *Great Britain.* We shall *by their Growth* in People and Commerce have the Navigation and Dominion of the Ocean *establish'd* in us more firmly than ever. We shall be their Market for great Quantities of * Raw-silk, and perhaps for Wine, Oyl, Cotton, Drugs, Dying-Stuffs, and many other lesser Commodities. They have already tried the Vine and the Silk-Worm, and have all imaginable Encouragement to expect that these will prove most valuable Staple-Commodities to them. And I have been credibly inform'd, That the Trustees for *Georgia* furnish proper Expences for a skilful *Botanist* to collect the Seeds of Drugs and Dying-Stuffs in other Countries in the same Climate, in order to cultivate such of them as shall be found to thrive well in *Georgia.* This Gentleman could not be expected to proceed at his own Charges, but he's the only Person belonging to the Management of that Trust who does not serve *Gratis.*

The Raw-silk, which *Great Britain* and *Ireland* are able to consume, will employ Forty or Fifty Thousand Persons in that Country, nor need they be the strongest, or most industrious Part of Mankind; It must be † a weak Hand indeed that cannot earn Bread where Silk-worms and White Mulberry-trees are so plenty. Most of the Poor in *Great Britain,* who are maintain'd by Charity, are capable of this, tho' not of harder Labour: And the Planters may be certain of selling their Raw-silk to the utmost Extent of the *British* Demand for that Commodity; because a *British* Parliament will not fail to encourage the Importation of it from thence, rather than from *Aliens,* that the Planters may be able to make large Demands upon us for our Home Commodities: For this will be the Consequence of their employing all their People in produc-

* Descr. Abreg. p. 13. *Archd.* Descr. p. 30.
† *Arch.* Descr. p. 30.

ing a Commodity, which is so far from rivalling, that it will supply a rich Manufacture to their Mother-Country.

The present Medium of our Importation of Silk will not be the Measure hereafter of that Branch of Trade when the *Georgians* shall enter into the Management of the Silk-worm. *Great Britain* will then be able to sell Silk-Manufactures cheaper than all *Europe* besides, because the *Georgians* may grow rich, and yet afford their Raw-silk for less than half the Price that we now pay for that of *Piedmont:* The Peasant of *Piedmont*, after he has tended the Worm, and wound off the Silk, pays half of it for the Rent of the Mulberry-trees, and the Eggs of the Silk-worm; but in *Georgia* the working Hand will have the Benefit of all his Labour. This is Fifty in a Hundred, or *Cent per Cent* difference in favour of the *Georgians*, which receives a great Addition from another Consideration, *viz.* the *Georgian* will have his Provisions incomparably cheaper than the *Piemontese*, because he pays no Rent for the Land that produces them; he lives upon his own Estate. But there is still another Reason why *Great Britain* should quickly and effectually encourage the Production of Silk in *Georgia*; for, in effect, it will cost us nothing; it will be purchased by the several Manufactures of *Great Britain*, and this, I fear, is not our present Case with respect to *Piedmont*: Especially (if as we have been lately told) they have prohibited the Importation of Woollen Goods into that Principality.

That this little Treatise may be the more Satisfactory to the Reader, I could wish I had been minutely informed of the present State of our Silk Trade; of the medium Value of Silk *per* Pound; to what Amount it is imported; of its Duty, Freight, Commission and Insurance; and Lastly, by what returns in Commerce it is purchased. I'm persuaded, these Estimates would afford plentiful Matter for Observations in favour of this Position, *viz.* that *Great Britain* ought vigorously to attempt to get this Trade into her own Hands. I shall however aim at a Computation, upon my Memory of Facts, which I have heard from those who understand that Commerce.

1. *Great Britain* imports Silk from *Piedmont*, near the Yearly Value of Three Hundred Thousand Pounds.

2. The medium Price is about Twelve Shillings *per* Pound in *Piedmont*.

3. The Duty here is about Four Shillings *per* Pound.

4. The Price of Raw-Silk in *London*, is generally more than Half of the Price of the wrought Goods in their fullest Perfection.

1*st Observ.* If the *Piemontese* paid no Rent for the Mulberry-Tree and Silk-worm, he might afford Silk at Six Shillings *per* Pound.

2*d Observ.* If Silk were bought in *Piedmont* at Six Shillings *per* Pound, and imported Duty free, it might be sold in *London* at Seven Shillings *per* Pound. For, the Commission, Insurance and Exchange, or Interest of Money would be but Half what they are at present, and there must be some Allowance for the Interest of the Money that was usually applied to pay the Duty.

3*d Observ.* Therefore *Great-Britain*, by encouraging the Growth of Silk in *Georgia*, may save above a Hundred Thousand Pound *per Ann.* of what she lays out in *Piedmont*.

4*th Observ.* The *Georgian* (without taking the Cheapness of his Provisions into Question) may enable *Great-Britain* to under-sell all her Rivals in *Europe* in the Silk-Manufacture in a Proportion resembling what follows.

			l.	*s.*	*d.*
France,	Raw-silk, One Pound Weight		0	14	0
	Workmanship		0	16	0
		Total	1	10	0
Great Britain	Raw-silk, One Pound Weight		0	7	0
	Workmanship		0	16	0
		Total	1	3	0

The Difference of these is Seven Pence in Thirty, which is near Twenty Five Pounds in an Hundred, and is above Thirty *per Cent.* The Reader is desired to consider these Computations as stated by guess. But the same Reasoning will hold in a considerable Degree upon the exact State of the several Values.

* Rice is another Growth of this Province that doth not interfere with *Great Britain*. But we reap their Harvests; for when they have sold the Rice in a foreign Market, they lay out the Money in our Manufactures to carry Home with them. They have already made an handsome Progress in *Carolina*, in cultivating this Grain. They have exported above † Ten Thousand Tuns of it by Weight in a Year already, all produced in a few Years from so small a Quantity as was carried thither in a Bag, fit to hold only a Hundred Pound Sterling in Silver; they have sold Cargoes of it in *Turkey*. They have all the World for their Market. A Market not easily glutted.

The Indulgence of the *British* Legislature to *Carolina* in this Branch of their Trade, shews our new *Georgians* what Encouragement they may expect from that *August* Body, as soon as they shall learn the Management of the Silk-worm. The Law for the Ease of the Rice-Trade, is alone sufficient to enrich whole Provinces: They are now at Liberty to proceed in their Voyages directly to any Part of *Europe*, *South* of *Cape Fenesterre*, or to *Asia* and *Africk* before they touch at *Great Britain*. The Difference of the Charge of Freight is not Half the Benefit they receive from this Act of Parliament; they arrive at the desired Ports time enough to forestall the Markets of *Spain*, *Portugal*, and the *Levant*. It now frequently happens that Cargoes arrive safe, which, as the Law stood formerly, would have been lost at Sea, by Means of the Deviation. This new Law, in a Manner, forces them into the *Spanish*, *Portuguese*, and *Levant* Trades, and gives them Two Returns of Commerce instead of One. They may now dispose of their *American* Grain in the first Place, and then come loaden to *Great Britain* with the most profitable Wares of the Countries where they traded; and lastly, buy for ready Money such *British* Manufactures as they have Occasion to carry Home.

When I speak of the future Trade of these happy Provinces, I might expatiate upon many valuable Branches of it besides the Silk and Rice: Branches which it must ‡ enjoy as certainly as Na-

* Descr. Abreg. p. 13.
† Descr. Abreg. p. 7.
‡ Descr. Abreg. p. 25, 26.

ture shall hold her Course in the Production of Vegetables, and the Revolution of Seasons. But because I would not swell this Treatise to too expensive a Bulk, I shall content my self with acquainting the Reader that they have no Doubt of the kindly Growth of Cotton, Almonds, Olives, &c. And in short, of every Vegetable that can be found in the best Countries under the same Latitude.

I foresee an Objection against what is here laid down: It may be said that all the Countries under the same Latitude do not produce the same Commodities; that some of them are incapable of raising choice Vegetables, which others of them nourish with the utmost Facility. For Answer to this Objection, what was said in the second Chapter shou'd be consider'd: The intemperate Heats of *Barbary*, *Ægypt*, and *Arabia* are there accounted for, from the Vicinity of boundless sandy Deserts; on the other Hand, near Mount *Caucasus* in *Asia*, and particularly in the Kingdom of *Kaschmere*, or *Kasimere*, (which is entirely surrounded by prodigious Mountains) their Seasons are almost as Cold as ours in *England*, tho' they lie in the same Latitude with *Tangier*, or *Gibraltar*.

These Instances of the Temperature in Countries equidistant from the *Æquator*, are very opposite to each other, the Medium between them is the happy Portion of *Georgia*; which therefore must be productive of most of the valuable Commodities in the Vegetable World.

CHAPTER VI.

Observations on the Commerce, Navigation, and Plantations of Great Britain, *compared with those of some of her Neighbours.*

WHOEVER would be fully informed concerning the Figure which *England* has made in all Ages, in Maritime Affairs, may find abundance of curious Matter in *Selden's Mare Clausum*, and from his Time to ours may learn Facts from the *Gazettes*, or read a faithful Transcript of both in *Burchet's* Naval History. I shall take notice of Two remarkable Periods of our antient Maritime Story, because some useful Observations may be made in comparing them, both with other Nations, and with ourselves in our present Situation.

We are told that *Edgar*, King of this Island, had Four Thousand Ships, by the Terrour of which he subdued *Norway*, *Denmark*, all the Islands of the Ocean, and the greatest Part of *Ireland*. These Instances of his Power are specified in a * Record cited by that great Lawyer, Sir *Edward Coke*, in the Preface to his Fourth Report. This Monarch made a Naval Progress yearly round this Island, and once took it in his Head to cause eight conquer'd Kings to row his Barge on the River *Dee*. But it seems that some of his

---

* *Alitonantis Dei largiflua Clementia, qui est Rex Regum & Dominus ominantium, ego* Edgarus Anglorum Basileus, *omniumque Insularum Oceani quae* Britanniam *circumjacent, cunctarumque Nationum quae infra eum includuntur. Imperator & Dominus, gratias ego ipsi Deo omnipotenti Regi meo, qui meum imperium sic ampliavit & exaltavit super Regnum patrum meorum qui licet Monarchiam totius* Angliae *adepti sunt a tempore* Athelstani *qui primus regum* Anglorum *omnes Nationes quae* Britanniam *incolunt sibi armis subegit, nullus tamen eorum ultra fines imperium suum dilatare agressus est, mihi tamen concessit propitia Divinitas cum* Anglorum *Imperio, omnia Regna Insularum Oceani cum suis ferocissimis Regibus usque* Norvegiam, *maximamque partem* Hiberniae *cum sua noblissima civitate de* Dublina Anglorum *regio Subjugare.* Pref. to 4th Co. See also *Rapins* History of *England*, in the Life of *Edgar*.

Successors have had such *pacifick Ministers*, as either neglected to keep our Fleets in repair, or were *afraid* to make use of them: For, at several Periods of Time, since the Days of King *Edgar*, we find that this Kingdom has been *miserably insulted* on the Seas, and even successfully invaded by other Nations.

The *British Neptune* slept, or slumbered, most Part of the Time, from the Reign of King *Edgar* to that of Queen *Elizabeth:* In her Days he sprung up with Vigour, being rous'd by *Spain*, which was then the greatest maritime Power on Earth. From Queen *Elizabeth* to our Time, our naval Strength has gradually encreased, insomuch that at this Day, the *Spanish* Fleets opposed to ours, would make a very contemptible Figure on the Ocean: We now have it in our Power to Lord it over the watry World. It may be worth our Enquiry to know how these Fluctuations have happened in the Dominion of the Seas? And in the Issue, that Enquiry will be found pertinent to the Project now on Foot for planting a new Colony in *Georgia*.

The Tasks and Course of Life of Sea-faring Men are not to be learned in an Instant; their Employment is a laborious Trade: To be acquired only by Application and Industry. Money will buy all naval Stores except Mariners, but unless a Succession of them be preserv'd, no Wealth will be able to purchase them. The surest, the cheapest, I may justly call it, the only *profitable* Method of supporting such a Succession, is to have perpetual Occasion for a Multitude of Seamen in a Course of Trade. 'Tis indeed probable that *Edgar*'s amazing Power at Sea was, for the most Part, owing to his own great Genius, attended with indefatigable Industry in training up, and Year by Year augmenting the Number of his Mariners; for in those Days, *England* had no great Share of foreign Traffick, People generally contenting themselves with the Produce of their native Country. This great Prince must therefore have grieviously oppress'd his Vassals to enable him to keep up so great an Armament; and 'tis no Wonder that it dwindled in succeeding Reigns because it had not that *solid* Aliment, *Trade*, to nourish it.

The *Spanish* Successes in *America* caus'd their Shipping to encrease beyond all their Neighbours; they had Occasion in their Be-

ginnings there, for great Numbers of Transports, to carry not only
Men, but also Horses and other Cattle, and Stores, to their new
Conquests. Add to which, that *Sicily* and a great Part of *Italy* belonged to them at that Time. The Communication with these Places
last mentioned, was by Sea, so that they had a considerable Part in
the Encrease of the *Spanish* naval Power. In this flourishing Condition they continued for a great Part of the long Reigns of their
Philip the 2d, and of our *Elizabeth*. She had not a Fleet able to give
their *Armada* Battle: Her Ships indeed were light and nimble, the
Spanish, tho' larger and more numerous, were unwieldy; therefore
the lighter Vessels being in no Danger of a Chace, fought, or stood
off, as they saw Occasion. But this Advantage would not have been
sufficient, if *Providence* had not interposed a *Tempest*, for the Protection of *England*.

The Queen knew to what Causes she ow'd her *Danger* and her
Deliverance, and became more attentive than ever to plant *Colonies
in* America. Death prevented her from executing her great Designs; but some of her *best* and *wisest* Subjects, and boldest Seamen,
had enter'd so deeply into the Plan, and laid it so nearly to their
Hearts, that what she had intended in the Settlement of *Virginia*
was in a good Measure effected in the Reign of King *James* the 1st,
tho' the Undertaking was a great * Difficulty upon his *timerous*
Councils, because the *Spaniards*, of whom he stood in *servile* Awe,
did not approve of it. But his Shame, *with much Debate*, barely got
the better of his Fears, and that Mine of Treasure was opened to
Great Britain.

This, with what else has since been executed in favour of *England*, both on the Continent, and in the Islands of that new World,
has added such a Weight of maritime Force to the natural Strength
which we owe to our Situation, that we are able to give Law to the
Ocean. *Spain*, indeed, has greater Countries and more Subjects in
America than we have, and yet does not navigate in that Trade a
Tenth Part of the *Shipping* that we do. By a *lucky Kind of Poverty*

* See a short Collection of the most remarkable Passages from the Original
to the Dissolution of the *Virginia* Company.

our Dominions there have no Mines of Gold, or Silver: We must be, and ought to be contented to deal in Rum, Sugar, Rice, Tobacco, Horses, Beef, Corn, Fish, Lumber, and other Commodities that require great Stowage; the Carriage of these employs Millions of Tuns of Shipping. The Value of Five Thousand Pounds in these Wares loads a Vessel, which in the *Spanish* Trade would be freighted Homeward with Half a Million of Pounds Sterling. Thus has the Almighty placed the true Riches of this Earth on the Surface of it; our Rice and Tobacco are more *real* and *permanent Wealth* than their richest Minerals. They are *Wealth* which create a *Power* to defend our Possession of them: And without a sufficient *Force* to defend it, the Possession of all *Wealth is precarious.* Should not *Great Britain* therefore be attentive to the new Settlement of *Georgia?* What an Addition will it quickly make to the Tunnage of our Shipping? And what a seasonable Support will it prove to our *Island Colonies,* who stand in need of so near a Neighbourhood of their Brethren.

The *Dutch* were esteemed all the last Century the only Match for *England* on the Seas; but as a great Part of their Strength was meerly *Artificial,* it subsides like the Vivacity of a Wretch who has raised his Spirits with a Dose of *Opium.* Commerce and that Wealth and Power which attend it may be either *absolutely* in the Power of a State, or Empire, consider'd *in* and by *itself,* without Regard to it's Neighbours, which I call *natural* Wealth, Power and Commerce; or they may depend upon Treaties with other States, or be owing to their Connivance, which *pro tempore* amount to a *tacit* Agreement; these latter Species I call *Technical* Wealth, *&c.* Such was the Fishery of the *Dutch,* which they enjoyed by the *Inactivity* of some of our *English* Kings: And this must decline of Course, because of our superiour Treasures of this Kind on the Banks of *Newfoundland.* Another Branch of their artificial Strength was, that by the Indolence of all Nations they were for a Time the *Carriers of the Universe:* But the World is grown *wiser,* other Nations begin to *work* for themselves, and the *Netherlands* will sadly find that this *temporary Fund* of Strength must also fail them. Their only natural foreign Wealth and Strength is their *East-India* Trade; Part of this is truly their own, because the Land that produces Spices is in their *Possession:* But when the two former Branches shall be cut off, they will find *that Possession* every Day more and more *precarious.*

Thus The *British* Empire has a *natural* Wealth in itself and in its dependent Members; but it has also for many Years past enjoy'd an *adventisious*, or *artificial* Traffick. We have been employ'd by all the World in the *Woollen Manufacture*, but other Nations have begun of late to cloath themselves and their Neighbours too. 'Tis a fond Fancy in us to imagine that there are no fleecy Sheep in the World but our own, or that the Rest of Mankind will not learn the Mystery of Working in Wool. We feel this Trade decreasing Daily, and yet there are those among us who wou'd argue against Demonstration. But when they hope, by any Laws of *Great Britain* to hinder *foreign Nations* from falling into the *Woollen-Manufacture*, they may as well sollicit an Act of Parliament to prevent their *Grass to grow*, and to *intercept* their *Sun-shine.* I will consider one Objection before I leave this Point, because some imagine that we are secure in this Trade, against the Endeavours of all Foreigners; say they, we make *better* Goods than can be made with any foreign *Wool*, unless it be mixed with ours. Be it so. But then, does our great Wealth and Income by that Trade consist only in our *finest* Goods? Do not our Merchants complain that *Ireland* under-sells us in *coarse* goods at *Lisbon*; that because their Wares are *coarse*, they can be afforded *cheap*, therefore they have a *ready Market*, while ours that are *finer*, but *dearer*, may rot in the Ware-house? What says our *Russia-Company?* Has not *Prussia* supplanted us in the Cloathing of the *Muscovite Army?* Who is ignorant of the Extensiveness of the Undertaking at *Abbeville* in *Picardy?* We are sending some armed Sloops to check the *Irish*, but *who will restrain the French and Germans?* The Multitude don't much value the *Fineness* of their Garments, they only desire to be *warm*; 'tis the Cloathing of the Millions that produces Millions of Money*; and this is what other Countries will certainly have their Share in.

Is not this a Time to cast our Eyes upon our *natural Wealth*, and to augment it as fast as possible? If *Muscovy* supplies its own woollen Goods, or is supplied by any other *Foreigner*, it ought to make us resolve to bring our Naval Stores from *North America*; if *Spain* and *Italy* refuse our Drapery, we may reject their Silk, their Raisins, Oyl, Wine, Olives, and Divers other Merchandizes, and be supplied from *Carolina* and *Georgia*. I have been credibly informed that a Gentleman, now living in this Kingdom, was the *first* Person who made *Pitch* in *America*, about Thirty Years ago; the People whom he conversed with then, look'd on his Experiment as a Chimæra, but it has prov'd so real as to reduce that Commodity, I think, four Fifths in its Value: So that we now buy for Twenty Pounds what was formerly worth a Hundred Pound.

France has not the same Advantage as *Great Britain* in its Situation, for maritime Affairs: That Country is extended wide within Land, and has not the Benefit of being penetrated by many deep Creeks, or navigable Rivers; on Half its Borders 'tis bounded with the Continent; and the good Harbours of *France* are but few, compared with the Numbers of ours. These Reasons of our Superiority over them in maritime Affairs in General, served to prevent their encreasing in *North-America* as fast as we did, and there is another special Reason, *viz.* We have had the *Navigation* of *North-America* in us by the *large Traffick* of our early Settlements, and even of the *French Sugar-Colonies*, which we supply with Lumber, Horses and Provisions. We have five Souls on the Continent for one of theirs; their principal Settlement is in a Climate too cold and not very fruitful: And yet they contrive all imaginable Methods of augmenting their Numbers. They *intermarry* with the Natives and convert them; and the *French* King supplies Two Thousand *Persons* Yearly with Money to enable them to go thither, without being afraid that he shall *drain his Country* of People.

'Tis easy to demonstrate that we can afford to send People Abroad better than *France* and *Spain*. They have in each of those Kingdoms more than One Hundred Thousand *Cloyster'd Females*, not permitted to *propagate* their Species, and the Number of Males in a State of *Celibacy* is still abundantly greater as it comprehends their *Secular* and *Regular* Clergy, and a considerable Part of their great Armies who resolve against Marriage, because of the uncomfortable Prospects they have, with regard to their Progeny. It may be said indeed, that these don't marry, yet many of them get Children: But it must be admitted that the usual Fate of that Kind of Propagation is to be destroyed secretly, either before, or after the Birth; and the Former of these Crimes frequently procures Barrenness in the Woman. I have entered into the Consideration of the Loss by the Celibacy of their Males, that no Body may imagine the Computation of their Deficiencies should be made upon their cloyster'd Females only.

And yet let us take a short View of their Losses upon that Calculation, allowing a Monk, or a Priest, for an Husband to each immur'd Woman. The most exact Rules in this Kind of Arithmetick are as follows,

1st. The People who go on in an ordinary Course of Propagation and Mortality, and are not visited with some extraordinary destructive Calamity, grow *double* in their Number in One Hundred *Years*.

2d. Thirty Three *Years*, are a sufficient Allowance for a Generation, or Three Generations to an Hundred Years. Now,

Since the Reformation, near Two Hundred Years are elapsed, at which Time Celibacy was abolish'd in *England*.

Therefore, in that Time *France* has lost more than Five Generations, *Principal* of its Inhabitants, at the Rate of Two Hundred Thousand in each Generation, besides the accumulated Numbers of *Cent per Cent*, for each Hundred Years, which Loss must be reckon'd upon the Second Century as *Interest* upon *Interest*; so that the Two Hundred Thousand individual Persons who were under the Vow in *France*, an Hundred and Eighty Years ago will Twenty Years hence be a *Negative* upon their Numbers to the Value of Eight Hundred Thousand People.

They who understand a little Arithmetick, may divert themselves by computing the Amount of all the Parts of this Loss of People in the Five Generations: To those who do not relish Numbers, I fear, I have here and elsewhere been too tedious.

My aim in this Chapter is to rectify the Notions of some of my Countrymen, upon an Affair so important as our Commerce; to point out the Differences between a *natural* and an *artificial* Trade; to instance them in our Neighbours compared with ourselves; to shew the Industry of the *French* to rival us in *America*, in spite of their Geography and their Religion; and to inculcate that our Strength depends on our *Shipping*, and our *Shipping* on our wide extended *Colonies*, which have neither Gold nor Silver, and *for that very Reason*, confirm us the more Powerfully in the *Dominion of the Seas*.

If what has been offer'd to the Publick in the foregoing Sheets meets a favourable Reception, the Author will add some farther Observations hereafter on the same Subject. At present he only wishes that any Thing here laid down, whether Fact or Observation, may be of use to *Great Britain*.

Finis.

Reasons for Establishing

the *Colony of Georgia*.

REASONS

For Establishing the

COLONY of GEORGIA,

With Regard to the

TRADE of GREAT BRITAIN,

THE

Increase of our People, and the Employment and
Support it will afford to great Numbers of our own Poor,
as well as foreign persecuted PROTESTANTS.

With some Account of the COUNTRY, and the Design
of the TRUSTEES.

---

*Hoc Natura præscribit, ut homo homini, quicunque sit, ob eam ipsam
Causam tamen, quod is homo sit, consultum velit.*

CICERO De Officiis, Lib. III.

L O N D O N:
Printed for W. MEADOWS, at the *Angel* in *Cornhill*. MDCCXXXIII.

Reasons for Establishing

the *Colony of Georgia*.

I T is undoubtedly a self-evident Maxim, that the Wealth of a Nation consists in the Number of her People. But this holds true so far only, as Employment is, or can be found for them; if there be any Poor, who do not, or cannot add to the Riches of their Country by Labour, they must lie a dead Weight on the Publick; and as every wise Government, like the Bees, should not suffer any Drones in the State, these Poor should be situated in such Places, where they might be easy themselves, and useful to the Commonwealth.

If this can be done by transplanting such as are necessitous and starving here, and consequently unnecessary; it is incumbent on us, at this Time more particularly, to promote and enlarge our Settlements abroad with unusual Industry, when the Attention of almost all the Powers in *Europe* is turn'd towards the Improvement of theirs. The *French* are continually undermining us both in the *East* and *West-Indies*. The Emperor is attempting the same: *Portugal* owes her Riches chiefly to her Plantations: *Sweden*, *Denmark*, and *Germany* find themselves poor, because they have none at present, tho' they abound with laborious Men. The Colonies of *Spain* supply the Want of Industry in her Natives, and Trade in her Towns: If the Scarcity of her People at home is imputed to them, I think it unjust; it is evidently owing to the Nature of her Government, her Religion, and its Inquisition: As may be seen by *Italy*, who has no Colonies, yet is thin of Inhabitants, especially in the *Pope*'s Dominions: And tho' of as rich a Soil as any in the World, yet her People are poor, and the Country in many Places uncultivated, by shutting up those, who would serve their Maker in a better Manner by being industrious, and would be more useful Members of Society as Plowmen than as Monks.

It is at all Times our Interest to naturalize as much as we can the Products of other Countries; especially such as we purchase of Foreigners with ready Money, or otherwise to our Disadvantage; such as are necessary or useful to support, or carry on our Manufactures: Such as we have a geat Demand for: And such as we can raise ourselves as good in Kind as any other Country can furnish us with. Because by so doing we not only gain a new Provision for our Poor, and an Increase of our People by increasing their Employment; but by raising such Materials ourselves, our Manufactures come the cheaper to us, whereby we are enabled to cope with other Nations in foreign Markets, and at the same Time prevent our Home Consumption of them being a Luxury too prejudicial to us.

I hope in the following Tract to make these evidently appear, and shew the Advantages that must accrue to our Trade by establishing the Colony of *Georgia*. I shall give some Account of the Country, and the Proceedings of the Trustees, and with Candor take Notice of the Objections that are made to this Design, and endeavour to answer them in the clearest and fullest Manner I can. I think it may be proved that we have many, who are, and will be useless at home, and that the settling such a Colony with these, and the foreign persecuted *Protestants* is consistent with the Interest and Reputation of *Great-Britain*.

To show the Disadvantage under which we purchase some of the Products of other Countries, I shall begin with the *Italian* Trade, the Balance of which is every Year above 300,000 *l.* against us, as appears by Accounts taken from the Custom-house Books. And this Balance is occasion'd by the large Importation of Silk, bought there with our ready Money, tho' we can raise Raw Silk of equal

Goodness in *Georgia*, and are now enabled to work it up here in as great Perfection as the *Italians* themselves.

That we can raise it, we have sufficient Proof by an Importation of it from *Carolina* for several Years, tho' for want of Hands only to carry it on, the Quantity imported has been too small for any thing more than Trials. With many navigable Rivers for the Convenience of its Trade, the Country is extremely rich and fruitful. It produces white Mulberry-Trees wild, and in great Abundance. The Air, as it is healthy for Man, (the Latitude about 32,) is also proper for the Silk-worms; and as Care is the principal Thing requisite in nourishing and feeding these, every Person from Childhood to old Age can be of Use. But the Goodness of this Silk will appear fully by the following Letter from a Gentleman, whose Name will carry more Weight, than any Thing I can offer in behalf of it. This Letter was written to the Trustees for establishing the Colony. On Application to them, I obtain'd a Copy of it, which is here printed with the Gentleman's Leave.

To the Trustees for establishing the Colony of *Georgia*.

GENTLEMEN,

In writing this Answer to the Letter, which I had the Honour to receive from you, Dated the 29th Instant, wherein you desire to know my Sentiments of an Undertaking to raise Raw Silk in your new Settlement in Georgia: *Of the Probability of succeeding therein; the proper Steps to be taken to bring that Work to Perfection: And my Opinion of the Nature, Quality, and Use of the Raw Silk produced in* Carolina: *It is a great Pleasure to me, that from Experiments which I made some Years ago, I can now, besides my Opinion, give you some Information concerning that Silk, which may be depended on.*

The Value and Usefulness of the Undertaking will appear as soon as we consider, that all the Silk consumed in this Kingdom is now of foreign Growth, and Manufacture, which costs the Nation very great Sums of Money yearly to Purchase, and that the raising our Supply thereof in his Majesty's Dominions in America, *would save us all that Money, afford Employment to many thousands of his Majesty's Subjects, and greatly increase the Trade and Navigation of* Great-Britain. *It appears to me as beneficial to this Kingdom, attended with as little Hazard or Difficulty, as much wanted, and which may as soon be brought to Perfection in a proper Climate, as any Undertaking so considerable in itself, that I ever heard of. I therefore think, there is a very great Probability of its succeeding, if such proper Measures are pursued, and such Assistance afforded to the poor People at their first setting out, as are necessary to settle, instruct, and encourage them.*

The Silk produced in Carolina *has as much natural Strength and Beauty, as the Silk of* Italy, *(which is commonly call'd fine Silk,) and by the several Experiments I have try'd with it, I am satisfied, it may be made to answer the same Purposes as* Italian *Silk now do's, if it be reel'd in short Skains, a fine, clean and even Thread; to effect which if some experienc'd Persons are at first sent to teach the People, the Work will soon be made easy to the meanest Capacity, and the Value of the Silk will be thereby greatly increased.*

As for my own Part, if at any Time you should think I can be of Use to promote so good a Work, I shall be ready to execute your Commands, as far as I am able, and always remain,

Old Jewry,   Gentlemen,
  Jan. 31, 1732.

Your most Obedient,
Humble Servant,
THO. LOMBE.

On Inquiry I have found, that the Trustees have some Time ago taken care of what Sir *Thomas Lombe* so much recommends to them. They have sent to *Italy* for a sufficient Quantity of Silk-worms Eggs: They have engag'd two or three *Piemontese* to go and settle in *Georgia*, and instruct the People: One of these, a Man of Capacity and long Experience in the Business, went with the first Embarkation. They likewise in all their Grants of Land, to those who go at their own Expence, as well as those who are sent on the Charity, oblige the People to keep a sufficient Number of white Mulberry-Trees standing on every Acre, or else to plant them where they are wanted.

If an Objection should arise here, that by raising this Silk our-selves, and reducing the Importation from *Italy*, we may likewise reduce our Exportation thither, by her resolving to take none of our Goods: To this it may be answer'd, She takes none but what she is, and will be oblig'd to take; and even of that little she takes at present, but a very small Part is either sold or consumed in those particular States, from whence we have our Supply of *Italian* Silk, which we buy in the Dominions of the King of *Sardinia*, the *Venetians*, and the *Pope*, and seldom or never any otherwise than for ready Money. As *Italy* consists of several small Governments, whose Interests are independent of each other, no Disadvantages in Trade, arising from the Conduct of *Great Britain* to any one of them, will be either felt or resented by the rest. From whence it is clear, that our not taking the usual Quantity of Organzine (*i.e.* Thrown Silk) from *Piedmont*, will not be attended with any Loss in our Exportation to *Tuscany*, *Genoa*, or any of the other States.

The greatest Part of the Silk imported from *Italy* comes in ready thrown, which is owing to the King of *Sardinia*'s prohibiting the Exportation of any Raw Silk out of his Dominions, since the erecting Sir *Thomas Lombe*'s valuable Engine for throwing it here. This should make us double our Diligence, and without further Loss of Time set about raising Raw Silk for ourselves, and thereby save so great an Expence to the Nation. The Quantity of *Italian* Thrown Silk (exclusive of Raw Silk of all Sorts) imported for many Years past, may be computed at 300,000 *lb*. W^t. *per Ann.* which at 20*s. per lb.* of 16 *Oz.* amounts to *L.* 300,000 in Money. The Cost of the like Pound of *Italian* Raw Silk is from 10 to 15*s.* according to its Goodness and Fineness. If then the aforesaid Quantity could be had, was imported in Raw Silk, and made into Organzine (*i. e.* Thrown Silk) at home, by the said Engines, supposing the Raw Silk to cost 13*s. per lb.* on an Average: In such Case, *L.* 105,000 would be annually saved, and gained to the Nation by the Labour of our own People. But in this we are at present obstructed by the Prohibitions in *Italy*, that would oblige us to take their Silk ready thrown.

Since Sir *Thomas Lombe* has erected, and brought to perfection, his Engines at *Derby* for working fine Raw Silk into Organzine, the Price of that Commodity is greatly reduced abroad, and several of our Manufactures have been thereby much improved at home.

By raising Raw Silk in *Georgia*, and gaining it at so easy a Rate for Manufacturing here, we shall save not only the large Sum paid annually to the *Italians*, but we shall likewise prevent a very large Sum going every Year into *France* for her wrought ones; which are almost all of them clandestinely imported, as may be seen by the following Account of all the Wrought Silk publickly imported directly from *France*, and enter'd at the *Custom-House*.

Imported.	Silk Wrought.	Silk mix'd with Gold and Silver.
In 1724	80 *lb. Weight.*	
1725	75	
1726	75$\frac{9}{16}$	33 *lb. Weight.*
1727	7$\frac{3}{4}$	7
1728	19$\frac{1}{4}$	
1729	29$\frac{3}{4}$	
1730	14$\frac{1}{16}$	
1731	37$\frac{1}{4}$	26$\frac{1}{2}$

As it is notorious how great the Consumption of *French* Silks is in *England*, the little publick Importation of them must be a very great Surprize, and becomes a Matter of publick Consideration to prevent so great a Loss to our Revenue, and so great a Prejudice to our Manufactury.

This may be partly prevented (as I observ'd just now) by making the Manufactury and Sale of our own so much cheaper; for the high Value of our Silks is a great Inducement to the Wearing those of *France*, who can make hers more substantial, and afford them cheaper, as she raises most of her Raw Silk within her own Dominions, and receives the Remainder from *Italy* on easier Terms than we do, *viz.* the Exchange of her Goods, which are admitted by the *Italians*, paying less Duties than the Manufactures of *England*: Besides, the Nearness of her Situation to *Italy*, and Cheapness of Labour, make her too potent a Rival for us to contend with in the Silk Trade, in our present Circumstances.

The *Italian, French, Dutch, Indian* and *China* Silks imported thrown and wrought only (including what are clandestinely run) may, on the most moderate Computation, be reckon'd to cost us L. 500,000 *per Ann.* which may all be saved by raising the Raw Silk in *Georgia*, and afterwards working it up here, now we have attain'd the Arts of making Raw Silk into Organzine, and preparing it for our Weavers, who can weave it into all Sorts of Wrought Silks, in as great Perfection as any Nation of the World: So that we only want the Staple (or Raw Silk) and to have it at a reasonable Rate. With this *Georgia* will abundantly supply us, if we are not wanting to ourselves, and do not neglect the Opportunity, which Providence has thrown into our Hands.

The saving this *L.* 500,000 *per Ann.* is not all; but our supplying ourselves with Raw Silk from *Georgia* carries this further Advantage along with it, that it will provide a new or additional Employment for at least twenty thousand People in *Georgia*, for about four Months in the Year, during the Silk Season; and at least twenty thousand more of our Poor here, all the Year round, in working the Raw Silk, and preparing such Manufactures as we send in return; or to purchase the said Raw Silk in *Georgia*, to which Country our Merchants will trade to much greater Advantage, than they can expect to do to *Italy*, and yet the Exportation to this Place will (as I said before) be in all probability preserv'd.

This great Advantage and Saving will arise by supplying our own Consumption only, which we may carry much farther, and extend to a foreign Exportation, because Raw Silk may be raised much cheaper in *Georgia*, where Land is to be had on easy Terms, and Mulberry-Trees abound, than in *Italy* where both are very dear, where the poor Man gives half the Produce of his Labour for the Mulberry-Leaves, which he gathers on the Gentleman's Grounds. As the Cost then of the Mulberry-Leaves are reckon'd half the Charge of making Raw Silk in *Italy*, the People of *Georgia*, who may have them for nothing but the Trouble of Gathering, will have this vast Advantage above the *Italians*.

The Work of making Raw Silk is easy, the Silk Worms will multiply prodigiously in such a Country as *Georgia*, (every Worm is supposed to lay above 200 Egs, as well as spin 3000 Yards of Silk,) and where there is such a Number of white Mulberry-Trees, a sufficient Quantity of Silk might soon be raised to supply all *Europe*, if there were Hands enough properly instructed to carry on the Work.

If then we consider how cheap, and in what large Quantities

Raw Silk may be raised in *Georgia*; that we are now Masters of all the Arts of Manufacturing it at home, and thereby enabled not only to supply our own Consumption, but that of our Neighbours also; we may soon hope, instead of paying a Tribute of *L.* 500,000 *per Ann.* as we now do to *Italy, France, Holland,* and the *East-Indies,* to see the Silk Manufacture made as useful and profitable to us at home, as the Woollen now is.

It is well known, that with the same Ease with which we can raise Silk in *Georgia,* we can supply ourselves with Flax, Hemp and Potashes. (For this last Trade some are ready to embark to settle there at their own Expences.) These Materials we bring at present not only from the East Country, and other Places, but great Quantities from *Russia,* where the Balance is every Year very strong against us, as will appear by the following Account of Importation from thence for the three Years, which could most conveniently be got. This Account shows the total Value of the Importation of all Goods from *Russia* for each Year; the Value of our Exportation thither, and the Excess of the former, which is so much Money paid by us to *Russia.* It likewise shows the Quantity and Value of the Flax, Hemp and Potashes imported from thence. By charging these Articles to *Georgia,* (where they can be rais'd,) and by subtracting the Importation of them from thence, from the Excess of the Importation from *Russia,* the Reader will see the Balance against us is greatly reduc'd.

Imported from *Russia*. 1724.

	C.	q.	lb.		l.	s.	d.
Flax rough	21783	2	8	—	38121	4	11
Hemp rough	70870	3	16	—	59740	5	1
Potashes	757091	*lb. Wt.*		—	9463	12	9
			Total		107325	2	9

	l.	s.	d.
Total Importation from *Russia*	212229	12	9
Exportation to *Russia*	35563	13	9
Excess Imported	176665	19	0
Importation from *Georgia*	107325	2	9
New Balance on the Importation	69340	16	3

Imported from *Russia*. 1725.

Flax rough	18425	3	3 —	32245	2	1
Hemp rough	82885	2	13 —	70452	16	11
Potashes	1337076 *lb. Wt.* —			16712	19	00

Total	119410	18	00

Total Importation from *Russia*	250315	6	11
Exportation to *Russia*	24847	14	10
Excess Imported	225467	12	1
Importation from *Georgia*	119410	18	00
New Balance on the Importation	106056	14	1

Imported from *Russia*. 1726.

Flax rough	34094	3	3 —	59665	17	1
Hemp rough	102843	1	16 —	87416	17	7
Potashes	1177631 *lb. Wt.* —			14720	7	9

	161803	2	5

Total Importation from *Russia*	235869	2	5
Exportation to *Russia*	29512	1	8
Excess Imported	206357	0	9
Importation from *Georgia*	161803	2	5
New Balance on the Importation	44553	17	4

Besides these great Quantities of Flax and Hemp which are imported rough, great Quantities likewise are brought from thence ready drest, and the Article of Linnen from *Russia* is very considerable: If then sufficient Quantities of rough Flax can be rais'd in *Georgia*, and our Linnen Manufactury at home encourag'd, as it was in King *William*'s Reign, the Balance of Trade with *Russia* will be on our Side, instead of being so much against us, and we shall gain much more Employment for our People here.

Tho' these Articles are so very considerable, and enough to justify the Settling such a Colony as *Georgia*; they are not the only ones in which she will be advantageous to us. She can supply us with Indigo, Cochineal, Olives, Dying Woods, and Drugs of various Kinds, and many others which are needless to enumerate. One Article more I shall mention, *viz.* Wine, of which (as she is about the same Latitude with *Madeira*) she may raise, with proper Application and Care, sufficient Quantities, not only for Part of our Consumption at home, but also for the Supply of our other Plantations, instead of their going to *Madeira* for it. The Country abounds with Variety of Grapes, and the *Madeira* Vines are known to thrive there extreamly well. A Gentleman of great Experience in Botany, who has a Salary from the Trustees, by a particular Contribution of some Nobleman and Gentleman for that Purpose, failed from hence almost five Months ago, to procure the Seeds and Roots of all useful Plants. He has already, I hear, sent from *Madeira* a great Number of Malmsey, and other Vines to *Charles-Town*, for the Use of *Georgia*, with proper Instructions for cultivating the Vines, and making the Wine.

If it is granted then, that great Benefits will arise to our Trade from such a Colony, which is to interfere as little as possible with the Products of our other Plantations; the next Consideration is, whether this can, or should be establish'd by our People, who are useless at home, or whether we have any who are so. And here it will be proper to take Notice of two Objections (the only ones I have heard) that have been started by some People to this Design, and for various Reasons. By some from their Want of Attention to, and Examination of it, and the real State of our Trade: By some, from their constant Diffidence of the Success of any Undertaking, how good soever the Prospect may be: By some, from their natural Disposition to censure every Thing, in which they are not themselves concern'd, and their thinking another Man's Generosity and publick Spirit a tacit Reflection on their Want of them: By some, from their Unwillingness to contribute, and a Desire to cover their Avarice under a Dislike of the Design: And by others, from a sincere Opinion of the Force of the Objections, and the Prejudice this Colony may be to *England*.

To these last I would offer such Arguments as occur to me in

Answer to their Objections, and hope they will be found as satisfactory, as they appear to me convincing.

Obj. 1. *Our Colonies may in Time grow too great for us, and throw off their Dependency.*

Obj. 2. *The Planting such a Colony will take off our People, who are wanted to cultivate our Lands at home.*

These are Objections which stand against all Colonies in general, and the last of them (as appears from the Writings of Sir *Josiah Child* and Mr. *Penn*) has been made to the Settling all our old ones; and yet I will appeal to every Man of Reflection and Knowledge, whether our Trade is not at present chiefly supported by them.

It is well known how indefatigable our Neighbours have been in promoting their foreign Settlements ever since the last War; so that the more they can raise there for their own Supplies, the less Occasion they must have for us. It is notorious likewise, what Footing the *French* have on the Continent in *America*, and with what Industry they have been, and will be extending themselves. Is it reasonable then to let so rich and fertile a Country fall entirely into their Possession? Or at best, let our Part of it lye absolutely useless to us, while they are making so great an Improvement of theirs? No certainly; we should anticipate them, and as we have the most convenient Part of it, we should secure it, and be making our Advantages, at the same Time they are pursuing theirs with such Application and Steadiness.

But to answer these Objections in a more particular Manner.

1. *Our Colonies may in Time grow too great for us, and throw off their Dependency.*

If they are govern'd by such mild and wholesome Laws as the *English* are; if these Laws give them so full a Security of their Properties, is it to be imagin'd they will have recourse to a foreign Power, where all their Possessions must become immediately precarious? But, says the Objector, as they want nothing from us, they may set up for an Independency, and form themselves into a Government of their own. To this it may be said, They do, and always will retain a Love for their native Country: We see every Day, that in most of the Plantations as they raise their Families, they send their Children hither for Education; and as they raise their Estates, they send over the Produce of their Labour to be vested in our Funds, or in the Purchase of our Lands, which are the best Hostages we can have for their Behaviour: While they are free, they will never run the Risque of losing their Possessions, and gaining the Displeasure of their Mother Country; they will always be secure while our Constitution is preserved; till we are oppress'd at home, they will never think of an Independency; and when we are, it will be of little Consequence to us what will become of our Colonies.

But should this Objection have any Force against some of our other Colonies, I think it cannot hold against this of *Georgia*, as *England* must be the Market for the greatest Part of her Produce, as her People must send to *England* for all their Manufactures, and as they will be settled with a stricter Regard to the Interest of their native Country, and a more equal Distribution of Lands, the Want of which has been so prejudicial to the well-settling of *Jamaica*. If there should be any Reason then to apprehend a Danger from any of our other Settlements, it would certainly be prudent to have some absolutely dependent on us, that might be a Balance to the Power of the others.

So short an Answer may perhaps be sufficient to clear up an Objection, in which every Man, who will consider it, may soon satisfy himself.

The other, as it seems at first View of more Consequence, will require an Answer more ample.

2. *The Planting such a Colony will take off our People, who are wanted to cultivate our Lands at home.*

That there is a Want of People for the Tillage of our Lands, in many Parts of the Country, I will readily acknowledge. But to what is this owing? Among other Reasons, apparently to the Management of those Schools, which are in almost every Town for the Education of our Poor; to a Charity, which I am far from thinking ought to be suppress'd, but certainly calls for a Regulation. The Youth, who are sent to these Schools, should, at the same Time they are instructed, be inured to the Labour of the Country, that, as they grow up in Strength, they may improve in the Knowledge of their Business, and get a Habit of Labour, and even a Love of it. Whereas by being kept wholly to their Writing and Reading, till they are thought qualified to maintain themselves in a better Manner, they are sent up to *London* to be Apprentices in our little Trades, or to be Servants in Families. And to this is owing the Number of idle and necessitous People, with which the Town abounds, and of which every man must see too many instances every Day of his Life; to this must be imputed that all our Trades are overstock'd, and the daily Complaints we hear from Tradesmen, that they starve one another. Will these People, when reduced, go to the Plough? Can any Man think they will? Does any one see they do? If one of them goes into the Country, he cannot, by his Inexperience, and Want of Strength, do half the Work of an able Labourer; consequently no Farmer will employ him, or, if he does, will give him more than half the Wages. There may be other Causes of the Ruin of Tradesmen, the Fluctuating of Trade from one Place to another, or the Decay of it; our News Papers tell us, that on a strict and impartial Inquiry, eight thousand Houses in the City and Suburbs are found to be at present uninhabited, and the former Owners of most of them entirely ruin'd. Will a broken Mercer, a Weaver, or Perriwig-Maker, how industrious soever, who has been used to a Life less laborious than that of the Country, go with his Family to an Employment, of which he has no Knowledge, and for which he is not qualified? Where at the best he cannot earn above 5*s. per* Week, and may be some Part of the Year without Work, and in a Place, where as a Stranger the Parish will never give him an Allowance? What then is he to do? He cannot throw himself into another Trade, which has the same Complaint as his own, the being overstock'd. We see what he does, he goes into another Country to give them the Benefit of his Labour, and communicates to them perhaps the Knowledge of some useful Manufactury to our Prejudice, or else he lives sometime upon his Credit, to the absolute Ruin of himself, and the Hurt of his Neighbour, or runs into Villainy of any Kind for his Support. Are not these People useless to the Publick? not only so, but a Burthen? Is it not worth while to transplant them to a Place, where they may be of Service, and a great one?

If it should be ask'd here, How will these People, who cannot work at the Plough at home, be able to go thro' the same Labour abroad? The Answer is obvious. Their Fatigue, unless at first, will not be so great, as the Climate is so much kinder, and the Soil so much more fruitful. Besides, tho' a Man, who has not been inur'd to the Labour of the Country, and has a Family, will not go to the Plough for so poor a Support for them, as a Labourer's Hire, and even this likewise precarious; yet he will not repine at any Fatigue, when it is on an Estate of his own, and his Gains from this Estate will rise in Proportion to his Labour. Add to this, the high Value of the Commodities to be rais'd there, and the low Prices of Provisions will make it easy to conceive, that the Man, who cannot do half the Work of an able Man here, may earn a sufficient Provision for himself and Family in *Georgia*, especially when he pays neither Rent nor Taxes for his Lands.

If these People are of no Benefit to the Community, What are all those who are thrown into Prison for Debt? I believe the Calculation will not be thought immodest, if I estimate these at four Thousand every Year; and that above one third Part of the Debts is never recover'd hereby. If then half of these, or only five hundred of them were to be sent every Year into *Georgia*, to be incorporated with those Foreign *Protestants*, who are expelled their own Countries for Religion, What great Improvements might not be expected in our Trade, when those, as well as the Foreigners, would be so many new Subjects gain'd by *England*? For while they are in Prison, they are absolutely lost, the Publick loses their Labour, and their Knowledge. If they take the Benefit of the Act of Parliament, that allows them Liberty on the Delivery of their All to their Creditors, they come naked into the World again; as they have no Money, and little Credit, they find it almost impossible to get into Business, especially when our Trades are overstock'd; they therefore by contracting new Debts, must return again into Prison, or, how honest soever their Dispositions may be, by Idleness and Necessity will be forced into bad Courses, such as Begging, Cheating, or Robbing. These then likewise are useless to the State, not only so, but dangerous. But these (it will be said) may be serviceable by their Labour in the Country: To force them to it, I am afraid, is impracticable; to suppose they will voluntarily do it, I am sure is unlikely. The Colony of *Georgia* will be a proper Asylum for these. This will make the Act of Parliament of more Effect. Here they will have the best Motive for Industry, a Possession of their own, and no Possibility of subsisting without it.

I have heard it said, that our Prisons are the properest Places for those who are thrown into them, by keeping them from being hurtful to others. Surely this Way of Thinking is something too severe. Are these People with their Liberty to lose our Compassion? Are they to be shut up from our Eyes, and excluded also from our Hearts? Many of very honest Dispositions fall into Decay, nay perhaps because they are so, because they cannot allow themselves that Latitude, which others take to be successful. The Ways that lead to a Man's Ruin are various. Some are undone by Over-trading, others by Want of Trade, many by being responsible for others. Do all these deserve such Hardship? If a Man sees a Friend, a Brother, or a Father going to a Prison, where Felons are to be his Society, Want and Sickness his sure Attendants, and Death in all likelyhood his only, but *quick* Relief. If he stretches out his Hand to save him, if to rescue him from immediate Slavery and Ruin, he runs the Risque of his own Liberty, and at last loses it; is there any one, who will say, this Man is not an Object of Compassion, not only so, but of Esteem, and worth preserving for his Virtue? But supposing, that Idleness and Intemperance are the usual Cause of his Ruin: Are these Crimes adequate to such a Punishment, as Confinement for Life? But even yet granting, that these unhappy People deserve no Indulgence, it is certainly imprudent in any State to lose the Benefit of the Labour of so many thousands.

But the publick Loss by throwing Men into Prison, is not confin'd to them only; they have many of them Wives and Children: These are also involv'd in their Ruin. Being destitute of a Support, they must perish, or else become a Burthen on their Parishes by an Inability to work, or a Nusance by their Thefts. These too are useless to Society. Besides, by the Poverty of the Wives, and the Confinement of the Husbands, the Publick loses the Increase, which might be expected from them, and their Children, which, tho' a distant Consideration, is not a trifling one.

In short all those, who can work, yet are supported in Idleness by any mistaken Charity, or are subsisted by their Parishes, which are at this Time thro' all *England*, overburthen'd by indolent and lazy Poor, who claim, and are indulged that Relief design'd only for the impotent Poor: All those, who add nothing by their Labour to the Welfare of the State, are useless, burthensome, or dangerous to it.

To say, there are no indigent Poor in *London*, is disputing a Thing which every Body allows: To say, these can all get Employment here, or live by their Labour in the Country, is asserting a Fact, which no one can prove, and very few will believe. The Point then to be consider'd, is, not sending these into the Country, which appears impracticable, but preventing others for the future coming from thence, which certainly is reasonable: In the mean time, what is to be done with these Necessitous? No body, I suppose, thinks they should continue useless. It will be then an Act of Charity to these, and of Merit to the Publick, for any one to propose, forward, and perfect a better Expedient for making them useful; if he cannot, it is surely just to acquiesce, 'till a better is found, in the present Design of settling them in *Georgia*.

Those, who are convicted of Crimes, are sent to the Plantations; whether they are of benefit to them or no, I shall not here make a Question; but if they are thought proper to be sent, why should not those likewise, whose Morals are as yet untainted, and who have the same Temptations to Villainy, Idleness, and Want?

But Colonies, so far from draining us of our People, certainly add to the Increase of them. Let us suppose only twenty Men in a Town: Twelve of these have constant Employment: This enables them to marry with Comfort, by affording them Subsistence for the Families they may raise; the other Eight who have but Scarcity of Work, prey on each other, and are all hereby kept in Want and Dejection, which prevent their Marrying. For this they are sen-

sible, a quiet Mind, and Conveniences for Life are absolutely requisite: Few are desirous of increasing their Species only to be miserable; nothing indeed but a Possession, or a sufficient Income can
justify a reasonable Creature's wishing for a Progeny. If then of
these eight, three are transplanted into a Country, where they may
be happy, and enabled to marry; they leave the other five more
Work and Subsistence, and by their Labour in our Plantations,
raise Produces to be manufactured in our Mother-Country, and
thereby furnish more Employment for them; this puts these five
Men also in a Capacity to maintain Families, and induces them
therefore to get them. This is not conjectural, but evident from
natural Consequences, and (if need be) from the Example of *Rome*,
who often sent some of her Citizens abroad into Colonies for the
very Increase of her People (*Stirpis augendae Causa*) if we may
credit such an Authority as *Livy*.

Since I have mention'd *Rome*, I cannot help taking Notice of
the great Advantages these People found by their Colonies. They
began so early with them, that *Romulus* in his Reign sent out seven
Colonies, and they continued them (with but few Interruptions)
quite thro' the Commonwealth. Without these they could never
have raised themselves to such an Height: These paved the Way
for the many Conquests they made, and secured them afterwards:
They were a constant Receptacle for the Needy, a Subsistence for
the Industrious, and a Reward for the Veteran, who had spent the
Vigour of his Life in the Service of his Country. They added likewise (as * an ingenious Author observes) very much to the Publick
Revenue; for *Rome* was at last in Possession of Lands in the several
Cantons of *Italy*, in *Sicily*, and the adjacent Isles, in *Spain*, in *Africa*, in *Greece*, *Macedonia*, and all over *Asia*. An easy Rent was
paid by the Citizens (among whom these Lands were divided,) to
the Revenue of *each* State, and the peculiar Domains of these conquer'd Cities and Kingdoms were incorporated in the publick Do-
main, and the Produce of them lodged at last in the *Roman* Treasury.

* Mr. *Moyle*.

Carthage also (which was the greatest Republick except *Rome* the World ever knew,) pursued this Policy. All her Conquests were for the Sake of her Commerce, as all her Citizens were Merchants. The Riches of all *Africa*, from *Egypt* to the Ocean, were brought to *Carthage* as Tribute or Plunder. She extended her Dominions to the Coasts of *Spain*, and in the Islands of *Sicily*, *Corsica*, and *Sardinia*. But these Places when conquer'd she did not depopulate, or suffer to lye uncultivated, but still gather'd the Fruits of them, and made them a Treasury of new and certain Riches.

And such a Treasury are our Plantations; for sooner or later the Wealth, that is rais'd there, centers in *England*; our rich Planters generally come to settle here with their Estates, which are got without any Expence to us. And tho' the Importation from these Places vastly exceeds our Exportation thither, we are still manifestly the Gainers, as we are not, when it happens so from other Countries.

1. As we have the Benefit of manufacturing the Products which they raise.

2. As this Employment by enlarging their Maintenance adds to the Increase of our People at home.

3. As those in the Plantations are increasing more than they could at home, by having a better Provision, and by the Reception of Foreigners.

4. As they consume great Quantities of our Manufactures, they will raise the Value of our Lands, by adding to the Price of Wool.

5. As the Commodities from thence are Conveniences for Life, or necessary for our Navigation, or Trade with other Countries by a Re-exportation. For wherever it happens that foreign Products are not consum'd here in Luxury, but can be re-exported, (as Tobacco and Sugar for Instance) the Importation of them how great soever is a Gain to *England*.

If what I have said here does not answer the second Objection, the Conduct of the Trustees for Establishing the Colony of *Georgia* will, I hope, and doubt not, satisfy those that make it. They have, and constantly do, (as I am credibly inform'd) use the utmost Care, by a strict Examination of those who desire to go over, and by their Enquiries otherwise, to send none, who are in any Respect useful at home. They admit no Sailors, no Husbandmen, or Labourers from the Country. They confine the Charity to such only, as fall into Misfortunes in Trade, and even admit none of these, who can get a Subsistence, how narrow soever it may be. They suffer none to go, who would leave their Wives and Families without a Support; none, who have the Character of lazy and immoral Men; and none, who are in Debt, and would go without the Consent of their Creditors. To prevent which, they have resolv'd (I see by the News-Papers,) to publish the Names of such as shall be chosen at least a Fortnight before an Embarkation; so that the honest Creditor can suffer nothing hereby, nay he will be a Gainer, as well as the Publick. For the poor Artificer and Tradesman, when he finds a Decay in his Trade, and that he cannot support it much longer, instead of holding it, 'till he encreases his Debts, and is thrown into a Dungeon, by which they usually become irrecoverable: Or, instead of running into a foreign Country, in Dread of a Goal, by which the Debts are lost, and his Labour and Increase are also lost by the Publick, and by which he imparts the Knowledge of some useful Manufactury, to the Detriment of his Country; he may now make a Dividend of what he has among his Creditors, he may go with his Wife and Children, who will all be useful, into an easy, a sufficient and pleasant Support; where he will have no reason to be asham'd of his Fortune, as he will see no Inequality; or the Labour of cultivating his Lands, as they will be his own Possession. Nay to such also, whose Creditors compound with them, the Trustees (as I am inform'd) recommend it as a necessary Part of their Duty, to discharge, whenever they come into Affluence, the Remainder of their Debts. They have likewise made such Regulations, as they conceived would best conduce to the promoting Religion, the Preservation of Peace, the Order of Government, and the Encouragement of Industry and Virtue among them.

If then from the Advantages, which will accrue to our Trade, from the Ease which our Parishes, and the Publick will gain by a right Disposing of the Poor, the Establishing such a Colony as *Georgia*, appears so consistent with Prudence; how much more so, is it, with that Humanity we ought to have for our fellow Creatures? How many never gain a sufficient Settlement in the World? Here they may be sure of one. How many, after they have gain'd it, fail by various Misfortunes? Here they may recover, and forget them. How many may be saved hereby from begging and perishing in our Streets by Want? How many from the Gallows, to which, Necessity and Idleness lead the Way? How many may now live to be useful, who are destroyed by their Parents at their very Birth, lest they should be a Burthen too great for their Support; and whose Light is extinguish'd the very Hour they receive it? How many more would see the Light, by the Marriage of those, who are prevented now by the Fear of Want? And how many may be preserved from languishing out a miserable Life in a Prison, to the Loss of their Families, and the Publick, and the Scandal of a Country of Liberty?

How many too may be preserv'd from Self-murder, into which they inconsiderately plunge themselves, to avoid the Infamy of Begging, or the Horrors of a Dungeon? This appears by a late Example of *Smith*, the Book-Binder, who destroyed his Wife, his Child, and himself, which probably he would not have done, could he have been secure of such a Retreat, and Support, as this Colony will afford.

If a Man gives an Alms to a Beggar in the Street, it is undoubtedly a Proof of a compassionate Temper, but is an ill-judg'd one, as it serves only to encourage and confirm him in a Habit of Idleness.

If a Man bestows a Sum upon those miserable Objects in Prison, it is a temporary Relief in their Misery, but not a sufficient one from it.

Every publick Act of Insolvency is likewise an Act of Benevolence, but does not answer the End propos'd, if it makes no Provision for the Poor who are released. Their Discharge otherwise only giving the wretched Advantage of starving at large.

Such then, and such only are right Benefactions, as procure not only immediate Relief for the Unfortunate, but provide for their future Happiness, and Use.

For this beneficent Design, His Majesty has given a large Tract of Land (call'd *Georgia*) near *Carolina*, in Trust. The Management of it is in the Hands of several Noblemen and Gentlemen, who give up their Time and Assistance to the Improvement of it, without any View to their own Interest: Nay at their own Desire are restrain'd, as well as their Successors, by Clauses in the Charter, from receiving any Salary, Fee, Perquisite, or Profit whatsoever, by, or from this Undertaking; and also from receiving any Grant of Lands within the District of *Georgia* to themselves, or in Trust for them.

That each Benefactor may know, that what he has contributed, is safely lodged, and justly accounted for, all the Money is deposited in the Bank of *England*, who have undertaken to give Receipts for the same. Entries are made of every Benefaction in a Book kept for that Purpose by the Trustees, with the Benefactors Names, or if conceal'd, the Names of those, by whose Hands they sent their Money. Annual Accounts of all the Money receiv'd, and how the same has been disposed, are to be laid before the Lord High Chancellor, the Lord Chief Justice of the King's-Bench, the Master of the Rolls, the Lord Chief Justice of the Common-Pleas, and Lord Chief Baron of the Exchequer, or two of them, and printed Copies of the same Accounts will be transmitted to every considerable Benefactor.

The Prospect of Success is as great, and the Difficulties as little as have attended the Planting any other Colonies; perhaps they are less, since *Carolina* (to which *Georgia* is contiguous,) abounds with Provisions. Vast Numbers of Cattle, as well as Hares, Rabbits, and Deer. Fowls and Fish of various Kinds; Fruits of the best Sort. *Indian* Corn, and *European* Grain of every Kind in vast Abundance. The Climate is known; the Air very clear, healthy, and almost always temperate, and there are Men to instruct in the Seasons, and in the Nature of cultivating that Soil, which is a very rich one. *Georgia* is Southward of the present Settlements in *Carolina*. It is a vast Tract of Land, divided from that Province by the River *Savanah*, and bounded on the South by the River *Alatamaha*, which are both large and navigable. By the best Accounts we have yet had, from one River to the other at the Sea is between sixty and seventy Miles, and the Extent of *Georgia* from the Sea to the *Apalatian* Mountains is about three hundred Miles, widening very much in its Progress from the Sea.

The Charter grants to the Trustees and their Successors all the Lands and Territories from the most Northern Stream of the *Savanah* River, all along the Sea-Coast to the Southward unto the most Southern Stream of the *Alatamaha* River, and Westward from the Heads of the said Rivers, respectively in direct Lines to *the South-Seas*, and all that Space, Circuit, and Precinct of Land lying within the said Boundaries, with the Islands in the Sea lying opposite to the Eastern Coast of the said Lands, within twenty Leagues of the same, which are not already inhabited, or settled by any Authority derived from the Crown of *Great-Britain*, together with all the Soils, Grounds, Havens, Ports, Gulfs, and Bays: Mines, as well Royal Mines of Gold and Silver, as other Minerals, Precious Stones, Quarries, Woods, Rivers, Waters, Fishings, Pearls, Commodities, Jurisdictions, Royalties, Franchises, Priviledges, and Pre-heminences within the said Territories, and the Precincts thereof, and thereunto in any Sort belonging; To HOLD to them and their Successors for ever for the better Support of the Colony.

The Country is at present a Forest of Oaks, Beech, Elm, Cedar, Chesnut, Walnut, Cypress, Myrtle-Trees, and many others, besides the Mulberries, and Vines, which I have mention'd before. That it is capable of great Improvements, is generally agreed by those, who have seen the Place; and there needs no other Proof than this: Many of the People in *South-Carolina*, hearing of this Charter, have gone thither to survey the Lands, and have (as I am inform'd) applied since to the Trustees for Grants. His Majesty has order'd the Governor of *South-Carolina* to give what Assistance he can to the new Settlement; this the Assembly also (I hear) have promis'd. The Governor is very hearty in promoting it, and has generously contributed towards it. He has been engaged likewise to provide several Sawyers in *South-Carolina*, and some of the most friendly among the *Indians* to assist the People in clearing the Lands, *&c.* There are but few *Indian* Families within four hundred Miles, and those in perfect Amity with the *English*. *Port-Royal* the

Station of his Majesty's Ships is within thirty; and *Charles-Town* a great Mart, that freights every Year near two hundred Ships, is within one hundred and twenty Miles. If the Colony is attack'd, it may be reliev'd by Sea from *Port-Royal*, or the *Bahamas*, and the Militia of *South-Carolina* is ready to support it by Land.

As Towns are establish'd, and grow populous along the Rivers *Savanah*, and *Alatamaha*, they will make such a Barrier, as will render the Southern Provinces of the *British* Colonies on the Continent of *America*, safe from *Indian*, and other Enemies.

Under what Difficulties was *Virginia* planted? The Coast and Climate then unknown, the *Indians* numerous, and at Enmity with the first Planters, who were forced to fetch all their Provisions from *England*; yet it is grown so great a Province, that the Revenue is increased 100,000 *l.* for Duties upon Goods that are sent yearly home from thence.

Within these fifty Years *Pensilvania* was as much a Forest as *Georgia* is now, and in those few Years, by the wise Oeconomy of Mr. *Pen*, and those who assisted him, it now gives Food to eighty thousand Inhabitants, and can boast of as fine a City as most in *Europe*.

The Poor, who are sent to *Georgia* on the Charity, have all the Expences of their Passage defrayed, have likewise all Conveniencies allowed them in their Passage: And great Care is, (as I hear) and will be taken not to croud too many of them in a Ship for fear of Illness. When they are set down in *Georgia*, the Trustees supply them with Arms for their Defence, Working-Tools for their Industry, Seeds of all Kinds for their Lands, and Provisions for a Year, or 'till the Land can yield a Support.

As Experience has shown the Inconvenience of private Persons possessing too large Quantities of Land in our Colonies, by which means, the greatest Part of it must lye uncultivated, and they are thrown at such a Distance, that they can neither assist, or defend one another; the Trustees settle the People in Towns, a hundred Families in each: And allot no more Land than what can with Ease be cultivated, and yet will afford a sufficient and handsome Maintenance. They divide each Man's Share into three Lots, *viz.* One

Lot for a House and Yard in the Town, another for a Garden near the Town, and a third for a Farm at a little Distance from the Town. These Lots are all to be laid out, and the Houses built by joint Labour and Assistance; and when finish'd, Chance is to determine, who shall be the Proprietors of each of them; by this Conduct no Man will have reason to complain, since Fortune alone can give the Preference.

As they will not, it seems, be suffer'd to alienate their Lands without Leave of the Trustees, none certainly will go over, but with a Design to be industrious; and as they will be settled in such a Frugality, none, who can live here, will think of going thither, where, tho' they will have a sufficient and plentiful Maintenance, they will have no room for Luxury, or any of its attendant Vices.

For continuing the Relief, which is now given, there will be Lands reserv'd in the Colony, and the Benefit arising from them is to go towards carrying on the Trust. So that at the same Time, the Money by being laid out preserves the Lives of the Poor, and makes a comfortable Provision for those, whose Expences are by it defrayed; their Labour in improving their own Lands will make the adjoining reserved Lands valuable, and the Rents of those reserved Lands will be a perpetual Fund for relieving more poor People.

A Power is granted to the Trustees by the Charter to enjoy Lands, &c. in *Great-Britain*, in Fee, not exceeding one thousand Pounds a Year beyond Reprises; also Estates for Lives and Years, and all Chattels and Things whatsoever, for the better settling, supporting, and maintaining the said Colony, and to demise the same for a Term of Years in Possession, and not in Reversion, not exceeding thirty one Years from the Time of Granting; and if no Fine is taken, the full Value to be reserved, otherwise at least a Moiety of the full Value.

The Corporation and their Successors may import and export their Goods at, and from any Port or Ports in *Georgia*, without being obliged to touch at any other Port in *Carolina*.

The People, who settle there, are declared by the Charter to be free, and not subject to any Laws, but such as are fram'd by the Corporation, and their Successors; these not to be repugnant however to the Laws of *England*, and to be approv'd by the King in Council.

Civil Liberty is to be establish'd there in its full Extent. No Appearance of Slavery, not even in *Negroes*; by which means, the People being oblig'd to labour themselves for their Support, will be, like the old *Romans*, more active and useful for Defence of their Government.

That the People may not be long without publick Worship, the Trustees (as I am inform'd,) have already fix'd on a Clergyman, who is well recommended, is to embark very soon, and is to be allowed by the Society for Propagating the Gospel in foreign Parts, as good a Salary, as they give any of their other Missionaries.

As Liberty of Conscience will be granted, it cannot be doubted, but a well regulated Government in a Country so temperate, so pleasant, and so fruitful, will draw thither many of the distress'd *Saltzburghers*, and other persecuted Protestants; and by giving Refuge to these, the Power and Wealth of *Great-Britain*, as a Reward for her Hospitality, will be encreased by the Addition of so many religious and industrious Subjects.

Since I have mention'd the foreign Protestants, it may not be improper to consider their present Situation, and to show how prudent it is to establish such a Colony as *Georgia*, if only on their Account. As Men, as fellow Christians, and as persecuted Christians, they have, as well as our own Poor a Claim on our Humanity, notwithstanding the narrow Opinions, and mistaken Politicks of some, who think their Charity should begin, continue, and end at home *.

The Protestant Interest in *Europe* hath declin'd very much since the Treaty of *Westphalia*. In *France* there were several flourishing Protestant Churches, which are now entirely destroyed. There were five hundred Churches in *Poland*; but being neither permitted to rebuild or repair the Places of Assembly, they are now reduced

---

* *Qui Civium Rationem dicunt esse habendam, Externorum negant, Hi dirimunt communem Humani Generis Societatem; Qua Sublata, Beneficentia, Liberalitas, Bonitas, Justitia funditus tollitur; Quae qui tollunt, etiam adversus Deos immortales Impii judicandi sunt.* Cicero, De Officiis.

to forty, who are harrass'd on every Pretence, of which *Thorn* has been a bleeding Instance. In *Hungary* they are at this Time depriving the Protestants of their Churches, and it is to be fear'd that a Persecution now rages as openly there, as ever it did in *France*. Every one must know, and there can be few but feel the Miseries which the *Saltzburghers* have lately undergone: Their Hardships could only be equal'd by their Resolution in meeting, and their Patience in bearing them. Many of these have been dragg'd from Prison to Prison 'till they perish'd by Want; the rest, Men, Women, and Children forc'd to renounce their Faith, or drove Vagrants from their Country. There have been above twenty three thousand of these Exiles; and by Advices receiv'd here lately, the Number of Converts among them to the Protestant Religion encreases every Day. In the *Palatinate* a conceal'd Persecution is on Foot; *Deux Ponts*, *Bergues*, *Juliers*, and all the *Palatinate* were formerly under Protestant Princes, and are now subject to a zealous *Roman Catholick*. The Head of the House of *Saxony*, that was formerly the great Support of the Protestant Interest in *Germany*, is firmly attach'd to the *Romish* Religion. The Church of *Rome* hath also gain'd the Chiefs of many other Families in *Germany*. The Preferments in the *Teutonick*, and *Malteze* Orders, the rich Benefices, and great Ecclesiastical Sovereignties, the Elective Crown of *Poland*, and the Imperial Dignity itself, are used by that Court to gain or keep the Nobility, and even the Sovereigns of *Germany* dependent on their Supremacy: And when the Sovereigns are of their Profession, they think they can make more Converts in a Day by Force, than in whole Ages by Preaching; for if the Prince orders his Protestant Subjects to renounce their Religion, they must submit, resist, or fly. Resistance is in vain, unless they are assisted by Protestant Princes, which these cannot do without raising a Religious War thro' *Europe*; which is not to be expected on every Oppression for Religion, since it could not be procured in the flagrant Instances of *Thorn* and *Saltzburgh*. They have no Remedy then but Flight. Whither shall they fly? Not to other *Roman* Countries, and the Protestant ones are not capable of giving Assistance to a great Number. *Sweden*, the great Bulwark of the Protestant Religion in the North, having lost all *Livonia*, and the chief of her Corn-bearing Provinces, is reduced to a weak Condition, and has more Men than she can well support, as have many of the Protestant Dominions in *Germany*. Our King, as Elector of *Hanover*, has indeed wisely and generously given Reception to a thousand *Saltzburghers:* The King of *Prussia* has likewise establish'd some of them in regular Colonies on his Frontiers, but he has declar'd he will take no more. There remain then of the Protestant Powers the *Swiss, Holland*, and *England*, to receive these distress'd Protestants. The *Swiss* increase so in People, that instead of receiving others, they are forced to send out great Numbers every Year to foreign Countries; and at this Time a hundred of them, (who have been used to the dressing of Vines, and raising Hemp and Flax,) are petitioning to be sent with their Families, and settled in *Georgia*. *Holland* tho' swarming with People, yet yearly takes at present a vast Number from *Germany*, and *Switzerland*. As for *England*, she is unable to support any great additional Number of Inhabitants in her present Circumstances. For Husbandry-Work, tho' there is indeed a Demand in Harvest-Time, yet there is not Employment enough in Winter, as is evident by the many thousands that come from *Wales* and the West to assist in getting in the Harvest in the Eastern and Midland Counties, and return again, not finding Work sufficient to support them there. As for Trades and Manufactury, the other Means of Livelihood, they are (as I have before observ'd) so Overstock'd, there is not Employment for the Men bred to them. Indeed the Impossibility of *England*'s using any great Number of foreign Hands has been proved by Experience in Queen *Anne*'s Time. It is well known, that all the Endeavours of the Court could not dispose of ten thousand poor *Palatines*, that then came over; and after they had tried all Methods, were forc'd to send some of them to *Ireland*, and the greater Part to *America*, in the last of which Places they have succeeded very well, and the Kingdom has gain'd great Benefit from their Labour.

At a Time when the Protestants are so persecuted, How much will it be for our Honour, that the Crown of *England*, which in Queen *Elizabeth*'s Reign, and at some Times since has been look'd on as the Head of the Protestant Interest in *Europe*, should still preserve the same Title? And at this Time, when his Majesty as Elector of *Hanover*, when *Holland*, and *Prussia* have offer'd Relief to so many of them, how much is our Honour concern'd, that *England* should not be the last to open her Arms to receive her unhappy Brethren, grant them a Support, and allow them the valuable Priviledge of worshipping their Great Creator, in the Way which they think will best secure their Interests in Eternity? As Men can we refuse them Relief? As Christians can we neglect the offering it? Indeed it is possible to frame but one Objection to it, which is, It will be attended with such Advantages to *England*, that it may seem to be the Effect of Self-Interest, not of Charity; and in that Light, for the Sake of most of my Readers, I will consider it.

If there is any Weight in Sir *Josiah Child*'s Calculation, That every Man by the Produce of his Labour in the Plantations gives Employment, *i. e.* Maintenance to four People at home: If (as the same Author proves) where there is Employment, People will always resort; the People of *England* will be considerably increas'd by settling such a Colony as *Georgia*, which will be (by the Possessions and Priviledges it will grant,) such an Invitation to those foreign Protestants, who are forced to fly from home, and those likewise, who are oblig'd openly to profess the *Romish* Religion, because they have no *Asylum*. This will not seem strange to any one, who considers the Reasons why our own Subjects go from hence. The Want of Employment here has furnish'd *France* and *Spain* with Woolen Manufacturers, and *Russia* from the same Cause is able to show us Artificers of our own Countrymen in almost every Trade. If these People had been sure of Work and Subsistence here, they would never have gone to live under Governments, where Liberty and Property are precarious, and at so great a Distance from their Friends and Acquaintance: If therefore Employment abroad will carry away the Subjects of this Country from the superior Advantages of our Government and Constitution, it cannot be doubted, but by raising more Employment at home, they will readily return to their Native Country, which they know is the Seat of Liberty; and it is as little to be fear'd, but Numbers of Foreigners will from all Parts flock hither, rejoicing to find an *Asylum* from Persecution and Arbitrary Power, if they can be sure of a Support. This Support will be granted them by procuring them Work, and Work will never be wanting, if we will raise the rough Materials in such a Colony as *Georgia* for our Manufactury.

I will consider this Question then very shortly on each Side.

If we have not Employment enough for our People, and some of them are hereby in a starving Condition; it is just to send them where they may live by their Labour, and prudent to secure for ourselves the Benefit of it.

If we have Employment enough for our People, and yet a greater Number would be an Addition to the Riches of our Country; it is surely for the Interest of *England*, to settle as many Foreigners as possible in *Georgia*; when she knows that by every thousand, who will be transplanted thither, she will raise the Means for employing four thousand more at home. Yet if none of our People were useless here, it would be absolutely requisite to settle with the Foreigners some of them in *Georgia*, who might keep up the *English* Language and Government.

Among the Crowns which the *Romans* bestow'd on the Deserving, as an Incitement to Virtue, the most honourable was the *Corona Civica*, which was granted to any Soldier, that preserved the Life of a fellow Citizen in an Engagement; the most remarkable Respect and Immunities were annex'd to it, such a Value did that truly wise and great People set on Acts of Generosity, and the Life of a fellow Citizen. Nay, by a Law, which *Romulus* made, it was criminal to kill, or so much as fell an Enemy in War if he yielded; he judging right the Necessity of a Number of Men to cultivate the Lands which he conquer'd. How meritorious then will it be in us to preserve the Lives of so many fellow Citizens and Subjects, and gain so many new ones as will be by this Colony? Not only preserve their Lives, but procure for them Ease and Affluence? And by this very Act of Humanity, get so much new Wealth for our Country, by opening a new Spring for our Trade?

As the Mind of Man cannot form a more exalted Pleasure, than what arises from the Reflexion of having reliev'd the Distressed;

let the Man of Benevolence, whose Substance enables him to contribute towards this Undertaking, give a Loose for a little to his Imagination, pass over a few Years of his Life, and think himself in a Visit to *Georgia*. Let him see those, who are now a Prey to all the Calamities of Want, who are starving with Hunger, and seeing their Wives and Children in the same Distress; expecting likewise every Moment to be thrown into a Dungeon, with the cutting Anguish, that they leave their Families expos'd to the utmost Necessity and Despair: Let him, I say, see these living under a sober and orderly Government, settled in Towns, which are rising at Distances along navigable Rivers: Flocks and Herds in the neighbouring Pastures, and adjoining to them Plantations of regular Rows of Mulberry-Trees, entwin'd with Vines, the Branches of which are loaded with Grapes; let him see Orchards of Oranges, Pomegranates, and Olives; in other Places extended Fields of Corn, or Flax and Hemp. In short, the whole Face of the Country chang'd by Agriculture, and Plenty in every Part of it. Let him see the People all in Employment of various Kinds, Women and Children feeding and nursing the Silkworms, winding off the Silk, or gathering the Olives; the Men ploughing and planting their Lands, tending their Cattle, or felling the Forest, which they burn for Potashes, or square for the Builder; Let him see these in Content and Affluence, and Masters of little Possessions, which they can leave to their Children; and then let him think if they are not happier than those supported by Charity in Idleness. Let him reflect, that the Produce of their Labour will be so much new Wealth for his Country; and then let him ask himself, Whether he would exchange the Satisfaction of having contributed to this, for all the trifling Pleasures, the Money which he has given would have purchas'd.

Of all publick-spirited Actions, perhaps none can claim a Preference to the Settling of Colonies, as none are in the End more useful. If on this Account only, Queen *Elizabeth*'s Name must be ever dear to *England*, who look'd so far into Futurity for the Good of her Subjects; for this so much Esteem is due to the Memory of Sir *Walter Raleigh*, Sir *Francis Bacon*, and those Patriots, who assisted in settling *Virginia*; and we are indebted to the Lord *Shaftsbury*, and that truly wise Man Mr. *Lock*, for the excellent Laws which they drew up for the first Settlement of *Carolina*.

Common is the Complaint we hear, that Publick Spirit is lost among us, and that no one pursues any Dictates but those of his Interest. I hope this is not true, I do not think it is; but if there is any Foundation for it, it is Time to awaken People to a Love of their Country, to see her Welfare, and to promote it. Virtues may become a Habit in a Nation, as well as in a private Man; but then an Emulation must be rais'd as formerly, that the Fire may catch and spread. Every Man can be Beneficent in some Degree, and surely no one who has read * the Man of *Ross* can be otherwise. He who cannot give, may yet by his Approbation excite others to it, who are more able: He, who does not approve, can however be silent, he can forbear giving an ill-natur'd Turn to an Action that has the Appearance of Virtue, 'till he has tried, and found it only an Appearance. If an Instance of Publick Spirit is seen, it becomes a common Interest to support it, and the more singular it is, the greater Encouragement it deserves. Of this I am sure, no one has a Right to censure others for the Want of Publick Spirit, 'till he has shown he is not liable to the same Censure himself.

Whoever then is a Lover of Liberty, will be pleas'd with an Attempt to recover his fellow Subjects from a State of Misery and Oppression, and state them in Happiness and Freedom.

Whoever is a Lover of his Country, will approve of a Method for the Employment of her Poor, and the Increase of her People, and her Trade.

Whoever is a Lover of Mankind, will join his Wishes to the Success of a Design, so plainly calculated for their Good: Undertaken, and conducted, with so much Disinterestedness.

Few Arguments surely are requisite to incite the Generous to exert themselves on this Occasion. To consult the Welfare of Mankind, regardless of any private Views, is the Perfection of Virtue; as the Accomplishing and Consciousness of it is the Perfection of Happiness.

Finis.

* A Character in Mr. *Pope*'s Poem of the Use of Riches.

Postscript.

SINCE this Book first came from the Press, the Author has been inform'd, that the Regulations in the Country Charity Schools, which he has pointed out as necessary, have been some Time since set on Foot, and Rules for that Purpose were publish'd by the Bishop of *London* in the Year 1724, and others since approv'd of by all the Bishops, and lately dispers'd thro' their several Dioceses; and that no Persons have been sent to Town directly by the Trustees for those Schools.

The Common-Council of the TRUSTEES
for Establishing the Colony of *Georgia* in *America*.

Since the Publishing this Book, a Letter from Mr. *Oglethorpe* has been receiv'd by the Trustees, an Extract of which, with a

Copy of the Governor and Council's Letter to Mr. *Oglethorpe*, and the Resolutions of the Assembly of *South-Carolina*, are here added as a Confirmation of several Things alledg'd in the Book.

To the TRUSTEES for Establishing the Colony of *Georgia* in *America*.

From the Camp near *Savanah*, *Feb*. 10, 173$\frac{2}{3}$.

GENTLEMEN,

I Gave You an Account in my last, of our Arrival at Charles-Town. *The Governor and Assembly have given us all possible Encouragement. Our People arrived at* Beaufort *on the* 20th *of* January, *where I lodged them in some new Barracks built for the Soldiers, while I went myself to view the* Savanah *River. I fix'd upon a healthy Situation about ten Miles from the Sea. The River here forms a Half-Moon, along the South-Side of which the Banks are about forty Foot high, and on the Top a Flat, which they call a Bluff. The plain high Ground extends into the Country five or six Miles, and along the River-Side about a Mile. Ships that draw twelve Foot Water can ride within ten Yards of the Bank. Upon the River-Side in the Center of this Plain I have laid out the Town. Opposite to it is an Island of very rich Pasturage, which I think should be kept for the Trustees Cattle. The River is pretty wide, the Water fresh, and from the Key of the Town you see its whole Course to the Sea, with the Island of* Tybe, *which forms the Mouth of the River; and the other Way, you see the River for about six Miles up into the Country. The Landskip is very agreeable, the Stream being wide, and border'd with high Woods on both Sides. The whole People arrived here on the first of* February. *At Night their Tents were got up. 'Till the seventh we were taken up in unloading, and making a Crane, which I then could not get finish'd, so took off the Hands, and set some to the Fortification, and began to fell the Woods. I mark'd out the Town and Common; Half of the former is already cleared, and the first House was begun Yesterday in the Afternoon. Not being able to get* Negroes, *I have taken ten of the Independent Company to work for us, for which I make them an Allowance. I send you a Copy of the Resolutions of the Assembly, and the Governor and Council's Letter to me. Mr.* Whitaker *has given us one hundred Head of Cattle. Col.* Bull, *Mr.* Barlow, *Mr.* St. Julian, *and Mr.* Woodward *are come up to assist us with some of their own Servants. I am so taken up in looking after a hundred necessary Things, that I write now short, but shall give you a more particular Account hereafter. A little* Indian *Nation, the only one within fifty Miles, is* not only at *Amity, but desirous to be Subjects to the his Majesty King* George, *to have Lands given them among us, and to breed their Children at our Schools. Their Chief, and his Beloved Man, who is the Second Man in the Nation, desire to be instructed in the* Christian *Religion. I am,*

Gentlemen,

Your Most Obedient,
Humble Servant,

James Oglethorpe.

A Copy of the Governor and Council's Letter to Mr. *Oglethorpe.*

SIR,

We can't omit the first Opportunity of Congratulating you on your safe Arrival in this Province, wishing you all imaginable Success in your charitable and generous Undertaking, in which we beg Leave to assure you, any Assistance we can give shall not be wanting in promoting the same.

The General Assembly having come to the Resolutions inclosed, we hope you will accept it as an Instance of our sincere Intentions to forward so good a Work, and of our Attachment to a Person, who has at all Times so generously used his Endeavours to relieve the Poor, and deliver them out of their Distress, in which you have hitherto been so successful, that we are persuaded, this Undertaking can't fail under your prudent Conduct, which we most heartily wish for. The Rangers and Scout-Boats are order'd to attend you as soon as possible.

Col. Bull, *a Gentleman of this Board, and who we esteem most capable to assist you in the Settling your new Colony, is desired to deliver you this, and to accompany you, and render you the best Services he is capable of, and is one whose Integrity you may very much depend on.*

We are with the greatest Regard and Esteem,

SIR,

Your Most Obedient,
Humble Servants.

Council-Chamber,	Robert Johnson.
26th *of* Jan. 1732.	Thomas Broughton.
John Penwicke.	Al. Middleton.
Thomas Waring.	A. Skeene.
J. Hammerton.	Fra. Yonge.
	James Kinlock.

[192]

A Copy of the Assembly's Resolution.

The Committee of his Majesty's Honourable Council appointed to confer with a Committee of the Lower House, on his Excellency's Message relating to the Arrival of the Honourable *James Oglethorpe*, Esq; *Report*,

That agreeable to his Majesty's Instructions to his Excellency, sent down together with the said Message, we are unanimously of Opinion, that all due Countenance and Encouragement ought to be given to the Settling of the Colony of *Georgia*.

And for that End your Committee apprehend it necessary, that his Excellency be desired to give Orders and Directions, that Capt. *Mac Pherson*, together with fifteen of the Rangers do forthwith repair to the new Settlement of *Georgia*, to cover and protect Mr. *Oglethorpe*, and those under his Care, from any Insults that may be offer'd them by the *Indians*, and that they continue, and abide there 'till the new Settlers have enforted themselves, and for such further Time as his Excellency may think necessary.

That the Lieutenant and four Men of the *Apalachucola* Garrison be order'd to march to the Fort on *Cambahee*, to join those of the Rangers that remain; that the Commissary be order'd to find them with Provisions as usual.

That his Excellency will please to give Directions that the Scout-Boat at *Port-Royal*, do attend the new Settlers as often as his Excellency shall see Occasion.

That a Present be given to Mr. *Oglethorpe* for the new Settlers of *Georgia* forthwith, of an hundred Head of breeding Cattle, and five Bulls, as also twenty breeding Sows, and four Boars, with twenty Barrels of good and merchantable Rice: The Whole to be deliver'd at the Charge of the Publick, at such Place in *Georgia* as Mr. *Oglethorpe* shall appoint.

That *Parriauguas* be provided at the Charge of the Publick to attend Mr. *Oglethorpe* at *Port-Royal*, in order to carry the new Settlers, arrived in the Ship *Anne*, to *Georgia*, with their Effects, and the Artillery and Ammunition now on Board.

That Col. *Bull* be desired to go to *Georgia* with the Hon. *James Oglethorpe* Esq; to aid him with his best Advice and Assistance, in the Settling of that Place.

Extract of a Letter from his Excellency *Robert Johnson*, Esq; Governor of *South-Carolina*, to *Benjamin Martyn*, Esq; Secretary to the Trustees.

Charles-Town, Feb. 12, 173$\frac{2}{3}$.

SIR,

I have received the Favour of yours, Dated the 20th *of* October, *and the Duplicate of the* 24th. *I beg you will assure the Hon. Trustees of my most humble Respects, and that I will attach myself to render them, and their laudable Undertaking, all the Service in my Power.*

Mr. Oglethorpe *arrived here with his People in good Health, the* 13th *of* January; *I order'd him a Pilot, and in ten Hours he proceeded to* Port-Royal, *where he arrived safe the* 19th; *and I understand from thence, that after refreshing his People a little in our Barracks, he with all Expedition proceeded to* Yamacra *upon* Savanah *River, about twelve Miles from the Sea, where he designs to fix those he has brought with him.*

I do assure you, that upon the first News I had of this Embarkation, I was not wanting in giving the necessary Orders for their Reception, and being assisted at Port-Royal; *altho' they were here, almost as soon as we heard of their Design of coming. I am inform'd Mr.* Oglethorpe *is mighty well satisfied with* Georgia, *and that he says, Things succeed beyond his Expectation.*

Our General Assembly meeting three Days after Mr. Oglethorpe's *Departure from hence, I moved to them, their Assisting this generous Undertaking: Both Houses immediately came to the following Resolution, that Mr.* Oglethorpe *should be furnish'd at the Publick Expence, with one hundred and four Heads of breeding Cattle, twenty five Hogs, and twenty Barrels of good Rice; that Boats should be provided also at the publick Charge to transport the People, Provisions, and Goods from* Port-Royal *to the Place where he design'd to settle; that the Scout-Boats, and fifteen of our Rangers, who are Horsemen, and always kept in Pay, to discover the Motions of the* Indians, *should attend Mr.* Oglethorpe, *and obey his Command, in order to protect the new Settlers from any Insults, which I think there is no Danger of; and I have given the necessary Advice and Instructions to our Garrisons, and the* Indians *in Friendship with us, that they may befriend and assist them.*

I have desired Col. Bull, *a Member of the Council, and a Gentleman of great Probity, and Experience in the Affairs of this Province, the Nature of Land, and the Method of Settling, and who is well acquainted with the Man-*

ner of the Indians, *to attend Mr.* Oglethorpe *at* Georgia *with our Compli-*
ments, and to offer him his Advice and Assistance. Had not our Assembly
been Sitting I would have gone myself.

   I have received the Trustees Commission, for the Honour of which, I beg
you will thank them, I heartily wish all imaginable Success to this good
Work, and am,

Sir,

Your Most Humble Servant,

Robert Johnson.

   P. S.   Since the Above, I have had the Pleasure of hearing from Mr.
Oglethorpe, who gives me an Account, that his Undertaking goes on very
successfully.

A Sermon Preached
at St. George's Church

A

SERMON

PREACHED AT

St. *GEORGE's* CHURCH

HANOVER SQUARE,

On Sunday February 17, 173¾.

To recommend the Charity for eſtabliſhing the
New Colony of *GEORGIA.*

By *T. RUNDLE*, LL. D. Prebendary of
Durham.

Publiſhed at the Requeſt of the Right Honourable the
Lord Viſcount TYRCONNEL, the Honourable
Colonel WHITWORTH, Churchwardens,
and Several of the Pariſhioners.

L O N D O N:

Printed for T. WOODWARD, at the *Half-Moon* between
the two *Temple Gates, Fleet-ſtreet ;* and J. BRINDLEY,
in *New Bond-ſtreet.* MDCCXXXIV.

A Sermon Preached
at St. George's Church

*The Poor shall never cease out of the Land, therefore I command thee saying, Thou shalt open thy hand wide unto thy Brother, to thy poor, and to thy needy in the Land.**

N O Motive can influence a grateful mind to a generous compassion for the poor more than the words of my text. The Nature of Society is such that it could not flourish or be preserved, unless God had appointed various conditions among men, and united them together by an exchange of advantages. Habits of labour give ease and chearfulness to the severest employments, which none could perform, unless inured to them by early and constant practice. Some again improve their abilities, and call forth those Inventions which add the comforts and conveniencies to the necessaries of life. The Creator *hath opened his hand and filled all things living with plenteousness,*† if men will, by proper industry, gather the harvest which he hath sown. A few are placed in leisure from such low diligence, to cultivate their minds, to be enabled to see wherein the common good consists, to make right laws, and protect all, by a due execution of them, in the enjoyment of the fruits of their patience; to instruct and educate and guide men to

* Deut. 15:2.
† Ps. 145:16.

happiness in the paths of virtue and religion. Honour and respect will be given to each of these orders in a people, as it most contributes to the general prosperity and welfare. *Plato* and *Tully* and St. *Paul* have reasoned on society, after the same manner and almost in the same words, from the similitude of a body and its members, all mutually necessary and contributing to the Happiness of the whole. Labour and different abilities are the portion which God hath bestowed on all men, various indeed not only in their kind, but in degrees. Yet that which separates society into its numerous conditions, is not so much the talents themselves, as the discreet improvement of them, and then enjoying the encrease by discreet frugality. Though some squander it immediately in self-gratifications, yet others treasure *it up with a* self-denying *fondness for their offspring.*

Poverty and the recompence of reward placed before it, are the parents of every invention, awaken the ingenuities of the mind, and the dexterities of our strength. Without this all the elegances and enjoyments of the rich; all that pleases the natural taste for harmony, decency and order; all the assisting arts of wisdom and knowledge; all that raises the best governments into a more rational condition than a clan of Indians, would be unknown. 'Tis therefore wise and benevolently ordained that the *poor should never cease out of the land.* But God desires the happiness of all his creatures, tho' not equal happiness to all; as Elihu speaketh to *Job, He accepteth not the persons of Princes, nor regardeth the rich more than the poor; for they all are the work of his hands.** Since Poverty therefore is for the general advantage, God hath justly enjoin'd those in affluent circumstances to watch over the industrious, to return, in real Gratitude to those below them, all the offices of kindness and tenderness, to guide and encourage their labour, compassionate them in distress, relieve them in sickness, and guard them from injury and insult. *That your abundance,* in the words of St. Paul, *may be a supply for their wants, that* in some sort *there may be an equality.*† Let us therefore as we have opportunities do good unto

* Job 24:19.
† 2 Cor. 8:14.

all men. An opportunity is now offered to you of doing good in a way as truly useful, as uncommon. And that you may not neglect it; I design to mention some of those inducements which should incline us to be merciful to the poor in general.

And secondly shew, That the method now proposed to you should in a very particular manner affect our hearts, as we are men and Englishmen, as we are protestants and Christians.

The first consideration which I shall mention is that we are form'd with natures to delight in doing good, and love each other.

God made man a social creature, and actuated his heart with various affections; Some tending to preserve himself; some those most nearly intrusted to his care; and some regarding the prosperity of the whole. Having these duly balanced is the perfection of our natures; loving this moral harmony and enjoying it is the perfection of our hearts. To preserve the first is the duty and authority of Reason and Conscience; the other its end, and an immediate reward. There is a resemblance between the constitution of the intellectual and material world. In the heavens every habitable Globe hath a motion imprest on itself strongly urging it to pursue its own direct path for ever, but is for ever bended towards the sun by their mutual tendency. From the union of these differing forces each body enjoys light and warmth to unfold and ripen all the variety of bounties with which it is enriched. But if they separate, the sun would be only a barren fire, the others filled with darkness and desolation.

Cicero observes that the reason why we were formed pleased and able to admire the beauty and regularity in the heavenly bodies, was to admonish us to imitate their constancy and order in the nobler beauty of a worthy behaviour. There is a philter, says one of the *Fathers*, placed in the human breast which makes men love each other. The gratifying an affection is happiness: the stronger it is, the more delightful the indulgence. The warmest which God hath kindled in our bosoms, is the inclination of doing good, and reverencing our species; and whilst we are aiming at the felicity of others, we enjoy not only the most worthy, but most exquisite satisfaction. All who have experienced it, confess they feel the truth

[201]

of that saying of our Lord, that *it is more blessed to give than to receive*. Those mistake their own views in life who squander away their fortune to purchase a vain shadow of respect from a false magnificence and the flutter of fashion and shew. There is no true magnificence but in a generous character; and there is nothing beloved but goodness, or what resembles and seems to flow from it. Parents feel this joy in the most disagreeable and painful circumstances. Friends run with ardour into dangers for their friends, and all applaud the behaviour. Be thou the friend of man (and who deserves the name that is not so?) and thou wilt own the transport of serving him. Doing good employs infinite Wisdom and Omnipotence through Eternity; Cannot that which gives happiness to the Almighty give it us also? Nothing but a long indulgence of the private affections could weaken this natural inclination, as contrary forces destroy each other. The propensions of our hearts as well as the activities of our bodies may by early practice, or disuse, be so strengthened or diminished, that either may almost seem the only affection belonging to it, or not belonging to it at all. And thus a cherished attention to a little selfishness, be it of pleasure or of gain, and false education from the beginning, can quench the light of goodness kindled in our natures, as his image, by the Infinite Goodness that formed them. He that hath early practised beneficence will acknowledge that the giver is at least equally the gainer. When hearts are in unison of kindness, the joy that vibrates in one communicates to the other also. But the longer men defer their acquaintance with the transports of doing good, they will the less desire them. Age, which weakens every other passion, encreases that for an useless love of money. Men become fondest of an abundance of the good things of this life, when they are least able, have least time, and it is least becoming to enjoy them. Such love of money is a superstition separated from religion. 'Tis a resting in the means without regarding or valuing the end. He who puts off his alms and his repentance till his death-bed, will find his inclination faint and turned from performing either. If he does, they rather oftner flow from fear than a right mind, and give as little comfort as they shew worthiness. It declares indeed that they always knew their duty; atones not for their fault, but proves they were self-condemned. The best affections of our temper must be nourished by right education, as well as our understandings. He that neglects both, will lose both. 'Tis exercise gives strength and health. He that reasons most frequently becomes the wisest, and most enjoys the pleasures of wisdom. He who is most often affected by objects of compassion in poetry, history, or real life, will have his soul most open to pity and its delightful pain and duties. So he also who practices most diligently the offices of kindness and charity, will by it cultivate that disposition from whence all his pretence to personal merit must arise; his happiness in this life and thro' eternity.

Let us now see how this command, written on our hearts by the Author of our natures, is enforc'd by revelation. When the whole of religion is summ'd up in a few words, this is always a chief branch of it. *What doth the Lord require of thee, but to do justly, and to love mercy, and to walk humbly with thy God?** says a prophet. It consists in a *faith which worketh by love.*† *The end of the commandment is Charity*, says St. Paul.‡ *Pure Religion and undefiled before God and the Father, is this, to visit the fatherless and widows in their affliction*, says St. *James*.§

This temper and behaviour enters into the scripture characters of every righteous man; 'tis that for which they are beloved whilst living, lamented and remember'd when dead. 'Tis the expected fruit and proof of our love, our faith, our obedience to God. Our Lord who came to restore our natures to their original perfection, gave this as his new commandment, appointed this as the mark by which men should know his disciples, *if they have love one for another*. If alas we are to examine by this rule who are real Christians, amidst the mutual misrepresentations and calumnies, envyings and revilings of men in different, sometimes in the same communion; if we view the injustice and oppression, the secret arts of avarice, or

* Mic. 6:8.
† Gal. 5:6.
‡ 1 Tim. 1:5.
§ Jam. 1:27.

undisguised rapine, the extravagance of selfishness, and the insensibility to the wretchedness of others in common life, where would his true disciples be found?

No duty hath higher rewards promised to it; the favour, the mercy, the blessing of God attends the merciful to the poor, say the Prophets, Apostles and our Lord. Success in all their undertakings, length of tranquillity, protection from danger, deliverance from evil; strengthening in the bed of languishing, and comfort on the bed of sickness; compassion in their distress, a blessing on their posterity, a treasure that shall not fail, every valued possession here, and everlasting felicity hereafter, are represented as belonging to them in the affecting eloquence of Scripture. Such various force of phrase is there used as must subdue the heart, or prove it lost to all sense of humanity as well as Religion. Every threatning of the Gospel also is denounced against those, who by the voice of nature are declared the most odious, the unmerciful. *He shall have judgment without mercy who hath shewed no mercy.* The mercy of God is the only confidence and hope of the most upright among men. Who dares then omit any opportunity of shewing his sense that he wants, and his desire to deserve it? What variety of wretchedness doth *Job* denounce against those who have not only oppressed, but forsaken the poor? How miserable are the consolations that the splendour of unbenevolent riches can bestow! the possessors enjoy not the only true enjoyment of this life, and are often seduced by their flattery to lose all hopes in any other; tho', when distributed by charity, they would become a means to encrease their felicity in both. How upbraiding is the sarcasm mentioned in the parable of the rich man and *Lazarus? Son, remember that thou in thy life time receivedst thy good things.* Despicable good things indeed! the squandring his fortune in the pomp and vanity and vexation of luxury, which is never praised and esteemed even by those who surfeit with his unreligious generosity. But with what pious boasting doth *Job* draw consolation in his misfortunes from the consciousness that he deserved well of the unhappy during his own prosperity? *When the ear heard me it blessed me—because I delivered the poor—the fatherless and him that had none to help him. The bless-*

ing of him that was ready to perish came upon me, and I caused the widow's heart to sing for Joy.

Bounty to the poor is represented as the most acceptable gratitude to God, *for with such sacrifices he is* always *pleased. What reward can we render unto the Lord for all his benefits?* A sense of them. If bounty deserves our praise and thanksgiving, can we be mean enough not to desire to merit them ourselves? and be as *Nazianzen* says Θεος ατυχοντι a God to the unfortunate? A strong expression indeed, but tho' hard in our language was inoffensive in his own. This the Scripture assures us must make our most sacred performances accepted. Devotion is designed to implant in us a resemblance of the goodness we adore, and we must worship by imitating him: By deeds as well as sounds. Prayers like faith without works are dead. Alms are represented as a sacrifice that purifies men from iniquity, and atones for offences. *Daniel* advises the King he had sentenc'd, to endeavour to soften the Divine Judgments by works of mercy. But we must remember, that they can never be effectual, till by repetition they create within the habit and temper of Charity; and thus become real means to purify the heart. No sacrifice can avail for those that continue in transgressions, nor can the most extensive and best placed generosity. Charity will cover a multitude of sins that are past, none that are retained. But a constant practice of this duty will extinguish the narrow spirit which ever accompanies and occasions vice. For vice generally is selfishness; and a disregard to what others feel, if themselves are but amused for a cruel moment. 'Tis pursuing unexamined indulgences, recommended by fashion and fancy, tho' the consequences are ruin and infamy, tho' they scatter firebrands and death around them. But *love is the fulfilling of the law.* As from light every colour is separated by the different surfaces of bodies, which reunited compose whiteness again; so from benevolence by the different relations in life every duty is separated and deduced; which reunited compose again the Grace of Christian Charity. Without this therefore nothing can make us acceptable in the sight of God. 'Tis his infinite Goodness that consecrates his other attributes, and makes those, which without it would have been dreadful, adorable. This in him demands our love and thanksgiving. This he requires in us, as our love and gratitude and service. Endeavouring to imitate him is the sincerest praise. God would not love himself, if he did not love those that resemble him in his imitable perfections.

Penitential devotions also are only valuable when accompanied with bounty; and a prophet assures us, that the fast which God hath chosen consists in kindness to the poor. The first Christians observed a weekly religious frugality, that by saving from their own gratifications, they might be enabled to give more largely to the needy. Seasons appointed for retirement from the expensive pleasures and hurry of the world give calmness and leisure for consideration. *'Tis better sometimes to go to the house of mourning than the house of feasting.* Recollecting the distress of others, and feeling by a voluntary self-denial what many constantly feel, tho' they labour honestly and diligently; to place ourselves by serious reflections in their circumstances, and ask how we should then think it right that the rich should dispose of their superfluities, may make even pride and vanity blush at their unnecessary indulgences. Thoughtlesness is the blindness of the heart, which prevents men from seeing their neglect of many duties of humanity, which would be insupportable carelessness if beheld. The sobriety and withdrawing from costly amusements may contribute at least to enlarge if not make up their Charity. For the greatest fortunes have sometimes proportionable demands. *When goods encrease, they are encreased that eat them; and what good is there to the owners thereof, saving the beholding them with their eyes?* Such therefore may not have at command so much perhaps as those who are less envied, but have more real affluence; and may without this art to assist them in doing good, lose that joy for which alone life is worth accepting.

Lastly to learn in the strongest manner the value our Lord places on bounty to the wretched, read the description of the last great day. What is his inquiry into our conduct then? is it not wholly concerning our kindness and diligence in relieving the various distresses of human nature? By the fruits every principle of action alone is known; and if the behaviour is right the Christian Graces actuate the heart. The end of our faith is love. If we represented to our selves by the eye of faith our Lord coming in the Majesty of Judgment and Mercy; Heaven and earth assembled around him; all in awful silence waiting till he pronounces the just and impartial sentence on every man that ever lived; and ask our selves what thought and wish must agitate our minds in that solemn moment, when the very best must rejoice with fear; we shall confess that, in the silence and bitterness and confusion of an ill timed repentance, we should lament the ever having omitted one opportunity of doing good. Remember, that 'twill then be some aggravation of thy uncharitableness that thou wast this day reminded, of what thou wouldst in that important crisis uselessly desire. How terrible is the thought that Goodness itself is obliged to condemn thee! Thus our Natures and the Gospel (both of them the voice of God) injoin the duties of benevolence in general.

I come now to propose to your consideration some peculiar motives to induce you to perform the duty on the present occasion, as you are Men and Englishmen, Protestants and Christians.

No beneficence can be more lasting in its nature, or more serviceable to the poor themselves, and therefore none can be more agreeable to a generous mind. Relieving present hunger indeed is necessary, but in a few hours the want returns and the duty is to be repeated. Employing the poor in some industry which cannot but be successful, is securing them happiness, and enabling them to hand it down to their posterity; as a Magnet communicates its force to a ring of iron, which is enabled to sustain a second, and that another thro' a long descending series. The peopling new Colonies with the industrious, who, tho' desirous of work, are unemployed, was always esteemed humanity to the necessitous, and new strength to the Parent nation. 'Tis removing out of temptation those who might probably have had no means for a livelihood but rapine, violence and disorder. 'Tis making those useful to the whole, who by idleness might have been debauched, and by want embolden'd to injure, perhaps our selves, or those we love better, our dearest friends and relations. 'Tis cultivating a country by them, whose soil and climate produce the greatest abundance, and yet where the fewest necessaries of life are wanting. No settlement was ever before established on so humane a plan. Slavery is absolutely proscribed from this Colony; the misfortune, if not the dishonour of other plantations. Let avarice defend it as it will, there is an honest reluctance in humanity against buying and selling and regarding those of our own species as our wealth and possessions. Those who direct this Charity have, by their own choice in the most open and disinterested manner, made it impossible for any one among them to receive any advantage from it; besides the consciousness of making others happy. Voluntary and unpaid directors (as is seen in our hospitals) carry on their designs with honour and success. Such associations of men of leisure and fortune to do good, is the glory and praise of our Country. We read that some of old left their families to plant new nations, but they were driven from their homes by oppression and distress; or made themselves Princes of the cities they founded. But to lead the unhappy into a land flowing with all the comforts of life, without a possibility of outward reward; to run the greatest danger, and despise every expence, is a virtue as little to be expected in an age so often named degenerate, as unexampled in those as often and as reasonably called heroick. Who that considers the humanity of this undertaking, can refuse to applaud their labour, by assisting them?

As *Englishmen* we must recollect that 'tis our trade and our free constitution that makes us so powerful, so admired, and envied in *Europe*. With us there can be no oppression, *no leading into captivity*; would to God therefore there was *no complaining in our streets*. By observing what blessings traffick hath bestowed on this Island, other nations have been excited to try the same method of becoming great. But we need not fear their rivalry. Trade is a plant which will not thrive but in places warmed and cherished by civil and religious liberty. It may flourish for a time, under the influence of a wise and well disposed Prince in absolute governments, but like southern trees transplanted from their natural climate, it will be ever subject and exposed to such blasts and tempests as may in a moment destroy it. 'Tis the security of possessions by voted laws, that can alone ripen its fruits, or extend its branches. 'Tis the consolation of being permitted to follow undisturb'd the dictates of conscience, which can incite the distress'd to fly to any country as to their haven, from storms of persecution at home. If our neighbours would rob us of the nourishment of trade, from whence alone there is health and strength to our invaluable constitution, we ought to be as vigilant to enlarge and secure it. This is the intention, and must be the consequence of this Colony. There those materials for our manufactures, that are now annually purchased at a great expence, will be cultivated. The climate can produce them in perfection, if we encourage and assist, by our Charity, those to settle there who understand their management. Every branch of manufactures from whence the wealth and power of this nation have arisen, is the reward of its hospitality in receiving strangers among us. From the like ingenuity of foreigners, who now desire to be established in the new Colony, silk and cotton, flax and naval stores, dying-drugs and medicine, wine and oil, and all the fruits that require warmer suns and more constant skies, may there be manured with ease, and reaped in plenty. Our people will be maintained in honest industry at home, by their purchasing the conveniencies of life from hence with their unwrought products; which here will be fashioned thro' numerous arts into use. The prosperity and dignity of *England* are concerned in giving success to such undertakings. *Cast thy bread on the waters, for thou shalt find it after many days.* The expence contributed in this case, is like the disbursements for tilling the land, and buying seed; and we shall be repaid if we will wait for harvest, In every *English* Plantation the same love for liberty that is our distinguishing spirit is infused; and the same plan of constitution transcribed which is our happiness and our boasting. But it is in none so amiably copied as in this. The name of slavery is here unheard, and every inhabitant is free from unchosen masters, and oppression. In future Ages when these climates shall be fully peopled, and thro' the revolutions of time become considerable in power and riches, these children of *England* will bless their mother-country who educated them under the government of *Laws*; and made the united reason and common good, not caprice and false grandeur, the rule of their obedience. Who that loves and feels the honour and privilege of being an *English-*

man, but must have his heart touched with these considerations?

This Charity is recommended to us as protestants, because it is peculiarly design'd to relieve and refresh the persecuted; and settle in this Colony those who are forced to leave their native country, for the sake of their *Religion* and *Virtue*; the last of which will soon be given up by all who give up its best support, and noblest branch, the former. This is giving to *a disciple in the name of a disciple*; and our blessed Saviour and Judge says that what is done to the *least of his brethren*, he will esteem as done unto himself. Shall not a pure and undefiled Religion, undefiled by oppressing men's Consciences and by persecution, be as zealous to support, as Idolatry and Superstition to destroy those who desire to obey God rather than man? The Parliament hath given us an approbation of this design by their bounty to it; an example that all who value the blessing of religious liberty should rejoice to follow. Let us gladly shew a regard to our Brethren driven from their homes by the tyranny of their Princes; Princes themselves slaves to popish bigottry; who are weak enough, and wicked enough to dispeople their countries at its command: but we may gain by our Virtue what they lose by their Cruelty, which they blasphemously call, piety and religion. God hath, to reward hospitable nations, hid from the eyes of the oppressor this truth, that the numbers of subjects happy by their ingenuity, labour and honesty, is the only Wealth and only Glory of every Government. *England* is at the head, and therefore should be the defender of the whole Reformation. Its love for it, can be proved by no nobler instance than protecting and rewarding all who suffer for it. And no reward so valuable as transplanting them into possessions, and giving them a property in one of the finest parts of the world, where they may enjoy their labour, their families, their consciences. Such a supply of their necessities would shew a zeal consecrated by Charity and Knowledge. The church of *England* is there established in the same purity as at home; and care will be taken that every person belonging to it shall be brought up in *the nurture and admonition* of our Lord. But there also a full and free toleration will be inviolably secured for those whose education, prejudices and scruples incline them to worship God in a way they think more agreeable to his will. The most applauded scheme of Government,* is that which not only punishes men when guilty, but is diligent so to form and educate and watch over the people, that none shall be guilty. This great end was no where ever accomplished (which seems a theory and wish of a Philosopher and not a reality) till Christianity was interwoven into civil government; and its religion taught, and the practice of holiness and righteousness supported and encouraged by the authority of Laws. And this is the view which will be ever regarded, and pursued in this new settlement. Publick and constant instruction in the knowledge and love of God, in the necessity and value of a redemption from impiety and wickedness, in the duty of doing good not only to the family of faith, but to all men, under the expectation of everlasting life, was a blessing unknown to the world till commanded and instituted by our Lord Jesus Christ; tho' most worthy of God and most necessary to man. So necessary for the righteousness, and consequently the happiness of mankind, that there can be no truer charity than endeavouring and praying that this his Kingdom of discipline to holiness and piety may come, and be extended through all the earth, to prepare and conduct them to his Kingdom of Glory. And to encourage our pious labour, we have the sure word of prophecy that one day the Kingdoms of the earth shall submit to his religion and become his real subjects. Let us in the last place see

How this method of doing good now proposed unto you, will contribute to it.

This Colony is placed near many Indian Nations which are still plunged into the meanest Idolatries, busied in dishonest Superstitions, and deprived by ignorance and fears of the comforts of a life civilized by instruction and laws. The trustees of this Charity resolve to watch over the Virtue and Religion of the people committed to them. All will be there permitted to worship God according to their conscience, but none to live without a regard to God and Conscience. They hope to *make the light* of this settlement *shine before*

* Xen. Cyr.

their neighbours, *that they may glorify their Father which is in Heaven*. The force and eloquence of this silent argument for Christianity will convert those who cannot so well feel the force of other reasonings; tho' no other will be omitted, as opportunities to enlighten their minds, and friendly meetings shall offer. 'Tis a prophane observation often repeated in conversation, that introducing our Religion among Indians will disturb these well meaning people, and destroy their simplicity of manners and their innocence. What dishonour to our Lord and his holy Religion! *but we have not so learnt Christ*. What St. *Peter* observes is undoubtedly true, that the Father of mercies is no respecter of persons, but in every nation *he that feareth God, and worketh righteousness, is accepted of him*. But alas, if we read the Histories of the world before the coming of our Saviour, or behold at present those Countries where *the sun of righteousness* hath not *yet risen with healing in its wings*, we shall confess that amidst Idolatry and Superstition, both which united to encourage cruelty and debauchery, scarcely any but in *Judea* had knowledge or inducements to fear God and work righteousness; and that no other name hath been given among men, but that of our Lord Jesus Christ, whereby they can be saved; none but his Religion, plainly teaching us the nature of the Governor of the world, that he can alone be served by imitating his goodness, and supporting men during their growth in grace against the temptations of the world, by the noblest of all motives his favour through eternity. So far will Christianity be from corrupting them, that corruption here at home arises from nothing but a secret disbelief, or doubt at least of Christianity, and then we must not wonder it hath no real or so little influence. Those who bear and boast of the name, are not always the disciples of our Lord. *By their fruits only you can know them*. Custom and education, fashion and interest make such sometimes appear in publick assemblies, and call our Saviour Lord, Lord, but he will disown them before his Father which is in Heaven. The establishment of meer nominal Christianity in this Colony can do them no good, nor us. Making them assume the name to imitate the manners of those that in vulgar phrase are called by that sacred abused appellation, is doing dishonour to our Lord, and no good to them. But if true Christianity be there practised as well as taught, if men be constantly exhorted to live in holiness and righteousness, if they really become more humane, more benevolent, more neighbourly; if they are more chaste, sober, honest and diligent, if they appear with a Piety adorned by cheerfulness and good nature, and in every respect better than they would have been without its instruction and discipline, converting the *Indians* thus to the Religion of our Lord, will not only be the best charity, but the sincerest piety in all that contribute to it. No care will be there wanting effectually to make all shew by its fruits the goodness of the tree that produces them, and invite all to love and value the faith which they see renders its true believers not only happy, but, as much as human nature can be, worthy to be so: and by removing all offences prepare their hearts to receive an instruction in that religion, which alone is agreeable to God, and a service fit for reasonable creatures. This sure is unable to corrupt, but must perfect their innocence by the knowledge of the only object of a rational worship, and the only motive to support virtue in its struggles here, that is worthy its regard. May God give his success to this infant people in proportion as they deserve it by holiness and virtue. Nothing promises fairer to make Christianity extend its light and warmth, to dissipate the ignorance, and cherish among them the charities and civilities, as well as righteousness, that accompany true religion and knowledge. And who will be disinclined to contribute and try at least what service it will be for this best purpose, that remembers these affecting words,

They that turn many to righteousness shall shine like the stars for ever and ever.

Finis.

Select Bibliography

Anderson, Jefferson R., "The Genesis of Georgia," *Georgia Historical Quarterly*, 13 (Sept. 1929), 229–84.

Archdale, John, *A New Description of that Fertile and Pleasant Province of Carolina* (London, 1707).

Callaway, James E., *Early Settlement of Georgia* (Athens, 1948).

Carroll, Bartholomew R., *Historical Collections of South Carolina; embracing many rare and valuable pamphlets, and other documents, relating to the history of that State, from its first discovery to its independence, in the year 1776* (2 vols., New York, 1836).

Chatelain, Verne E., *The Defenses of Spanish Florida, 1565–1763* (Washington, 1941).

Chubb, T., *Some Observations . . . occasioned by the opposition made to Dr. Rundle's election to the See of Gloucester* (1735).

Cohen, Hennig, "Two Colonial Poems on the Settling of Georgia," *Georgia Historical Quarterly*, 37 (June 1953), 129–36.

Coleman, Kenneth, "Colonial Georgia: Needs and Opportunities," *Georgia Historical Quarterly*, 53 (June 1969), 184–91.

———, "A Rebuttal to 'The Georgia Concept,'" *Georgia Historical Quarterly*, 55 (Summer 1971), 172–6.

Coulter, E. Merton, *A Short History of Georgia* (Chapel Hill, N.C., 1933).

Crane, Verner W., *The Promotion Literature of Georgia* (Cambridge, 1925).

———, *The Southern Frontier, 1670–1732* (Durham, N.C., 1928).

———, "The Origin of Georgia," *Georgia Historical Quarterly*, 14 (June 1930), 93–110.

———, "Dr. Thomas Bray and the Charitable Colony Project, 1730," *William and Mary Quarterly*, 19 (Jan. 1962), 49–63.

Egmont. *The Diary of Lord John Percival, First Earl of Egmont, 1730–47* (3 vols., Historical Manuscripts Commission, London, 1920–3).

———. *The Journal of the Earl of Egmont. Abstract of the Trustees Proceedings for Establishing the Colony of Georgia, 1732–1738.* Edited by Robert G. McPherson (Wormsloe Foundation Publication, No. 5, Athens, 1962).

Ettinger, Amos A., *James Edward Oglethorpe, Imperial Idealist* (Oxford, 1936).

Fant, H. B., "Picturesque Thomas Coram, Projector of Two Georgias and Father of the London Foundling Hospital," *Georgia Historical Quarterly*, 32 (June 1948), 77–104.

Force, Peter, comp., *Tracts and other Papers relating principally to the origin, settlement and progress of the colonies in North America from the discovery of the country to the year 1776* (4 vols., Washington, 1836–46).

Gee, Joshua, *The Trade and Navigation of Great Britain Considered* (London, 1729).

Hubbell, Jay B., *The South in American Literature, 1607–1900* (Durham, N.C., 1954).

King, Spencer B., *Georgia Voices: A Documentary History to 1872* (Athens, 1966).

Knorr, Klaus E., *British Colonial Theories, 1570–1850* (Toronto, 1944).

Lanning, John T., *The Spanish Missions of Georgia* (Chapel Hill, N.C., 1935).

McCrady, Edward, *The History of South Carolina under the Royal Government, 1719–76* (New York, 1899).

Martyn, Benjamin, *Timoleon: A Tragedy* (London, 1730).

——, and A. Kippis, *The Life of A. A. Cooper, First Earl of Shaftesbury*, edited by G. W. Cooke (2 vols., London, 1836).

Meriwether, Robert L., *Expansion of South Carolina, 1729–65* (Kingsport, Tenn., 1940).

Miller, Randall M., "The Failure of the Colony of Georgia under the Trustees," *Georgia Historical Quarterly*, 53 (March 1969), 1–17.

Montgomery, Sir Robert, and Colonel John Barnwell, *The Most Delightful Golden Isle: Being a proposal for the establishment of a colony in the Country to the south of Carolina*. With an introduction by Kenneth Coleman (Atlanta, 1969).

Patrick, J. Max, ed., *Azilia: a discourse by Sir Robert Montgomery projecting a settlement in the colony later known as Georgia* (Emory University Publications, Sources and Reprints, Series 4, No. 3, Atlanta, 1948).

Philomusas, pseud., *Remarks on the Tragedy of Timoleon* (1730).

Purry, Jean Pierre, *Mémoire sur le Pais des Cafres, et la Terre de Nuyts; par raport a l'utilité que la Compagnie des Indes Orientales en pourrait retirer pour son commerce* (Amsterdam, 1718).

——, *A Method for Determining the Best Climate of the Earth, on a principle to which all geographers, etc., have been hitherto strangers*. Translated from the French (London, 1744).

Ready, Milton, "The Georgia Concept: An Eighteenth Century Experiment in Colonization," *Georgia Historical Quarterly*, 55 (Summer 1971), 157–72.

Reese, Trevor R., "Benjamin Martyn, Secretary to the Georgia Trustees," *Georgia Historical Quarterly*, 38 (June 1954), 142–7.

———, *Colonial Georgia: A Study in British Imperial Policy in the Eighteenth Century* (Athens, 1963).

Rundle, Thomas, *Letters . . . to Mrs. B. Sandys . . . with introductory memoirs by* J. Dalloway (2 vols., Gloucester, 1789).

Saye, Albert B., "The Genesis of Georgia: Merchants as well as Ministers," *Georgia Historical Quarterly*, 24 (Sept. 1940), 191–206.

———, "The Genesis of Georgia Reviewed," *Georgia Historical Quarterly*, 50 (June 1966), 153–61.

Sherman, Richard P., *Robert Johnson: Proprietary and Royal Governor of South Carolina* (Columbia, S.C., 1966).

Smith, Henry A. M., "Purrysburgh," *South Carolina Historical and Genealogical Magazine*, 10 (Oct. 1909), 187–219.

Vanstory, Burnette, *Georgia's Land of the Golden Isles* (Athens, 1956).

Trevor R. Reese teaches at the University of London Institute of Commonwealth Studies. He is author of *Colonial Georgia: A Study in British Imperial Policy in the Eighteenth Century* (Athens, 1963). All of the original documents for this new edition of colonial Georgia propaganda pamphlets have come from the collection of the University of Georgia Library at Athens. § This book was planned and edited at Savannah, Georgia, by The Beehive Press, which publishes sources and studies of Georgia history and literature. Its pressmark, which appears above and pictures bees busy at their hive, expresses the enthusiasm of this work; the source of the pressmark—an early Georgia colonial pamphlet entitled *An Impartial Enquiry into the State and Utility of the Province of Georgia*, London, 1741—suggests a spirit of free intellectual endeavor. § This book was printed at The Stinehour Press in Lunenburg, Vermont.